History of the World
From the Back of a Boat
Volume 2

Rob Peterswald

TABLE OF CONTENTS

~ DEDICATION ~

To my family.

~ INTRODUCTION ~

Sea Dreams leaves a small port in southern Turkey and sails north along the coast that has been the fault line between East and West for all of history. Some of the great men and women whose paths we have already crossed in Volume One appear again in Volume Two. Julius Caesar, in some small islands in the Mediterranean, and later on beside a couple of riverbanks in France and Belgium. Odysseus, who we last saw on a luxuriant island in the Adriatic Sea, is now hanging out with some other Greek thugs on a beach at the top of the Aegean. Winston Churchill is orchestrating more disasters in the Greek Islands and at Gallipoli. The rapacious pirate admirals, the Barbarossas, are still creating mayhem. Crusaders of the Fourth Crusade, who we met leaving Venice and indulging in a bit of rape and pillage in the Adriatic, are now before the walls of the great Christian city of Constantinople, and about to commit one of history's foulest betrayals. We again come across the intrepid Dutch explorer, Abel Tasman, in a small village near the North Sea.

But there are many new faces. While we are still in the sparkling blue waters of the Mediterranean, we find Alexander the Great crossing into Asia. The Emperors Constantine and Theodosius who founded great cities and a ruthless religion. Sultans, Mehmet the Conqueror who stormed the walls of the city that was the world's greatest for fifteen hundred years, and Sulieman the Magnificent who nearly conquered Europe. The Greek scientists, Posidonius, who calculated the circumference of the world in c100 BCE, and Archimedes, who built an analogue astrological computer c250 BCE. And the Empress Theodora and the Hurum Sultan Roxelana, two women who came from nowhere to become amongst the most powerful the world has known.

And many, many others before we return to Papua New Guinea and the great massifs on the border with Indonesia and, then start winding our way through the waterways of Europe from the North Sea to central France. Here our path led us to the men who made a small fenland into a nation, that for a while was the most powerful on earth, before it was betrayed by its prince. Our path took us to where the world's greatest ever business was founded by a group of sailors, to the monarchs and dynasties who created Europe, and others who are amongst the most evil the world has seen. To the scenes of some of the world's epic battles and the men who fought them and to some of the philosophers, scientists and artists who began to rediscover what the ancient Greeks had known fifteen hundred years before and, had been destroyed on the orders of a god.

I hope you enjoy meeting them and sharing the great beauty of the Aegean Sea, Papua New Guinea, the inland waterways of Europe and the wonderful island of Tasmania, which are the settings of this volume.

This book is primarily designed to be read on a computer or tablet. Clicking on a blue link will open up dozens of interesting photographs. On a computer clicking out of the photo will take you back to the book. On a tablet press *kindle* in the top left corner to return to the book.

~ THE ANCIENT COAST ~

Unable to sleep I crept from our bed in the forward cabin and went on deck, leaving Rosemary (Ro) with her dreams, her beautiful face lit by gentle moonlight flooding through an open hatch. The earlier clouds had drifted off to the south. The light of a full moon shimmered on the silvery water and cast a pale glow over the mountains above our anchorage, a remote bay in Turkey. There were no riding lights, nor sign of man on shore.

We had wintered *Sea Dreams* at the small port of Finike, a day south on the Turquoise Coast of Turkey and had returned with the first hints of summer. Our plan for the sailing season was to head north along the coast to the top of the Aegean Sea, then begin to thread our way back south through the Greek islands. On a yacht the Turquoise Coast is one of the most wonderful places in the world. Hot in summer but being on the fringe of the *meltemi* there is generally enough breeze to cool things down. Clean sparkling water, an abundance of fresh seafood, a mostly jovial people and a rich cultural heritage going back to the dawn of civilisation. Further north the land is harsher, but the richness of the history is spellbinding. We planned to take our time, ambling along, avoiding the worst of the *meltemi* in the central Aegean Sea.

Finike was founded by the Phoenicians around the 5th century BCE and, became an important trading port of the ancient Kingdom of Lycia which covered much of the southern Turkish coast. Lycia is first mentioned in Western literature in Homer's Iliad as an ally of Troy in the Trojan Wars. Its warrior king died there, fighting the Greeks. Around a thousand years later Alexander the Great conquered this area on his march to Egypt and in time the area became totally Hellenised. It was later conquered by the Romans, then became part of the Byzantine Empire before being taken over by the Seljuk Turks and in 1426 by the Ottoman Turks.

The region had predominantly remained Greek, as was much of the eastern Aegean until the early 1900s. Turkish pogroms then forced many Greeks to flee, and finally in the 1920s led to the expulsion of all those remaining as part of a forced population exchange between Greece and Turkey. This was an horrific event for the nearly two million people involved: the Christian Greeks of Turkey and the Muslims of Greece. Most were expelled with only what they could carry, and for the Greeks it meant ejection from what had been their homeland for over two thousand years. Though there was certainly a racial element it was based mainly on religious identity. It was justified as avoiding more of the atrocities such as the genocide of Greeks in Anatolia in the previous decade.

These days the town is a quiet rural backwater, and there is still a hint of Greek architecture about the old town, although the fringes are spoiled by some modern cement boxes. There are a few restaurants with local menus, some excellent fish restaurants near the marina and a pleasant landscaped park beside the water. The surrounding coastal plain is fecund and is one of the largest citrus-growing areas in Turkey. In spring it is a living canvas of waiving blossoms, the air succulent with their fragrance and full of promise of rich harvests. Unfortunately, the old recipes for Limoncello, Cointreau, mandarin vodka and the like, which were such great by-products in earlier times, all but disappeared with the last Greeks sometime around 1922.

The marina was a friendly place, with a management and technical staff that do their utmost to keep everyone happy—social get togethers, expeditions to historic sites, free Wi-Fi and special rates. The only negative, at least for unbelievers, was the cacophony from a nearby mosque. I must confess again, that from a fairly young age I have been drawn to the religious ideas of the ancient Greeks and Romans. If you want supernatural explanations for things, they had a multitude of gods and semi-gods who were arrogant, spiteful, manipulative, incestuous, rapacious, conceited, interfering and jealous on whom you could blame the confusions, tragedies and vagaries of mortal life.

Over time the once melodious 'calls to prayer' that wafted with a certain mystic and romance over the countryside, have changed. Most mosques in Turkey have enthusiastically embraced electronic amplification while neglecting the voice training of the imams. Now the so called 'singing' is loudly amplified over cheap music boxes and makes 'punk rock' sound really good. Very jarring in an otherwise peaceful night, while you are enjoying the slowly revolving heavens, or in the quiet before sunrise when the flush of the eastern sky hints at what the day has in store.

But still, it was hard not to fall in love with the town and the marina which had done a great job over winter. There are many fine things about sailing in Turkey. The clear warm water, numerous beautiful bays and anchorages away from the worst of the *meltemi*, fine food and wine, friendly people, an ancient country with so much of the past still there to explore. But one of the very best things is the mechanical and engineering support that is available, and its cost. In the first few years we had added some 'extras' to our fine yacht. We had had a small solar panel on our previous yacht, *Oceania*, mainly to just keep the engine starting battery topped up. While wandering around Formentera in the Balearics, after we had been afloat in *Sea Dreams* for a month or so, I had come across a wind generator in a chandlery. It looked easy enough to install, and as I always have plenty of good advice available onboard, I decided to put it in. That was good, but we found we still needed more power. It is amazing how much you use running refrigerators, freezers, computers, fans etc and we never had enough. And, as on most yachts there were frequent discussions, some a bit acrimonious, between the one creating the electricity—me, of course—and the one using most of it—you know who!

So, while in Split we got Igor Gazin to put in a second wind generator and two large solar panels—all mounted on some fine stainless-steel work above the cockpit canopy. Arriving in Turkey we had been seduced by the prices and added stainless steel davits and nice hull covers for the dinghy, and shade canvases to mitigate the mid-summer heat. I do not wish to boast, but now there were not many cruising yachts which did not look at us with unconcealed envy, when our paths crossed. Now we only had to run the diesel generator for one hour a day to make our own water, the rest of the time we were at one with nature. We felt very self-sufficient and comfortable, and able to boast to all and sundry about the miniscule size of our carbon footprint. Of course, taking our cue from Al Gore and many other self-righteous preachers, we do not mention about flying business class—it is in Ro's contract—around the world each year.

Before long we were on our way, the summer stretching ahead full of promise. We edged *Sea Dreams* out of the marina and filled our sails with a gentle land breeze as the sun climbed over the eastern mountains. As with all oceans the world over, there was not a sign in the glittering water of the secrets that lay below. Back in 654 CE, at this very spot in the waters off this now sleepy township, the first naval battle was fought between the forces of Christianity and the armies of the Prophet Mohammed. The beginning of a conflict that changed the face of the world. Only a few decades before the battle, the Muslim storm began to sweep westward along the north African coast, eventually, almost to the gates of Paris. The two superpowers of the era, the Byzantine and Persian Empires, had been locked in a titanic struggle. Finally, in 627 CE the Emperor Heraclius had defeated the Persians and, the threat they had posed to the West for nearly a millennium was over. The Byzantine Empire was exhausted by the effort, and the schism between the Roman Catholics and the Eastern Orthodox Christians made it impossible to present a united front.

By 647 the Muslims controlled nearly the whole of the north African coast and had captured many of the Mediterranean islands. At this stage the Emperor Constans, realised he must take action against this emerging holocaust and sailed south with the Imperial Fleet. The first sea battle, of the countless clashes over the next millennium, was a disaster for the Christians. Off Finike, the fleet was shattered, and the Emperor only escaped by changing clothes with a common sailor and fleeing. Two years later the Caliph Othman, and his successor, the Prophet's son-in-law, Ali, were assassinated and, the ensuing turmoil gave the Byzantines a chance to regroup. It was not until three decades later that the Muslims arrived before the great walls of Constantinople but, were thrown back by the use of the nuclear weapon of the era, the newly discovered 'Greek Fire'. It would be many centuries before they would get their next chance.

A few miles north of Finike the rich coastal plain gives way to high rocky mountains crowding onto the shore. At Kekova Roads they spill out into the ocean, creating a dramatic archipelago enclosing a number of beautiful bays and dozens of anchorages with wonderful ambience and protection from the boisterous winds. The largest of these is dominated by an old Crusader fortress overlooking the entrance to a smaller bay where there is all around protection. The castle stands on a craggy hilltop, where strongholds have stood since man first realised that a fortress on the top of a hill could lead to a longer happier life. Even today it still radiates a sense of power and has a presence that evokes a majestic past. With the last rays of the sun shimmering over the turquoise water the burnished sandstone ramparts were glowing, illuminated in a golden aura.

From the top of the walls there are great views up and down the coast. It is easy to imagine armoured lookouts watching great beak-nosed galleys sweeping in through the northern entrance with the winds behind them or, battling their way north from the Levant carrying the riches of Egypt and the Orient to Constantinople. Below the walls of the fortress there is a small village where a cluster of tavernas almost smothered in riotous displays of flowers, serve seafood pulled from the surrounding waters and grilled over smoky fires, with vegetables from gardens in a narrow valley not far away.

... easy to imagine armoured lookouts watching great beak-nosed galleys sweeping in through the northern entrance with the winds behind them or, battling their way north from the Levant carrying the riches of Egypt and the Orient to Constantinople...

We spent a few days in the outlying bays, forty metres of chain out and our great anchor embedded in the clear sandy bottoms, before coming into the enclosed bay and anchoring behind a spit near the entrance. Here we had a panoramic view and could dinghy to the castle restaurants or to the small town on the mainland shore. We had a few memorable meals; a favourite was slow-roasted lamb ribs at the Hassan Denic Restaurant on the waterfront below the castle. The ribs had been marinated in olive oil, chilli and rosemary overnight, before being singed over an open fire and slow cooked in a clay (guvec) pot for a few hours. Then served, sprinkled with lemon juice and zest, rosemary and parsley, along with pita bread and heaps of salad. Mostly however, we could not go past freshly caught sea bream or bass grilled over the coals and drizzled with lemon.

By day we snorkelled among the submerged Lycian tombs and ruins and sauntered around the ancient sarcophagi still giving imperium to the rocky shoreline. It is amazing to think that buried in these ancient tombs, could be the dust of warriors who stood on the walls of Troy, perhaps ogled Helen, fought Achilles and Odysseus and according to the legend, helped drag the great wooden horse that was their doom inside the walls of the city.

We would like to have stayed here longer; it is a wonderful, wonderful place. However, as this was to be our last summer on this part of the Turkish coast, and there were many other places we had fallen in love with, and we needed to say farewell to, we pushed on. To Kastellorizo the small and lonely, but hauntingly beautiful Greek island lying only a mile or so off the Turkish coast. A hundred years ago it had a population of twenty thousand but today there are only a hundred or so residents. It turns out that the family of one of our 'in laws' came from here and she guesses that there are at least twenty thousand Australians who claim to own land there, and that the island would have to be the size of France if they were all telling the truth.

Then on to the nearby town of Kas on the Turkish coast. On the way south the previous year, I had broken a promise to Ro that we would spend some time there.

'Is he mad?' I can hear you ask. It is an attractive and vibrant village that has retained a very Greek air and offers much: kayaking in lovely bays, scuba diving on ancient ruins, Greek theatres where Alexander the Great could well have sat, plentiful seafood, good shopping. Unfortunately, our arrival had been late in the day and the tiny harbour was crowded. The *meltemi* was strong and I could see disaster waiting for us if we tried to dock. There was a sullen air on board as we anchored in a bay a mile or so away, and where I did not feel happy about leaving *Sea Dreams* unattended. So, we stayed onboard, and had to keep heading south the next day.

Sometimes we find that bringing the fifty foot *Sea Dreams* into a small Mediterranean port can be a difficult proposition for the two of us, particularly if it is windy and crowded. It sounds simple. You drop your anchor about forty metres from the quay, reverse in and tie-up stern in. However… first you need to locate a spot that is not 'owned' by a local, and while manoeuvring make sure you are not blown down-wind onto another boat or the rocky quay or have a French yacht dive into the spot you have your eye on.

Then you need to drop your anchor while making sure it is not fouled on underwater debris, particularly in Greek harbours which are the repositories of a couple of thousand years of undisturbed maritime history. Or on other anchors or chains laid haphazardly across the bottom by boats not terribly interested in how they may affect others, that is: most other boats and all charter yachts. Next, the anchor must be 'set', or pulled into the mud as you are reversing in. So, one person is required at the front of the boat to supervise the anchor. The helmsman must keep the yacht moving straight back while the wind, propeller and drag of the chain try to swing the boat off course. Here, the fifteen-knot wind was straight over the stern, and a moment's loss of way would see the yacht swept sideways.

Also, it is really very desirable to have another person or two, to fend off boats either side of the very narrow space you are trying to squeeze into, and it is handy to have another person to shout advice to the helmsman, although the 'fenderers' can generally handle this at a pinch. It would be nice to have another couple to throw the mooring lines ashore to be tied on by helpful bystanders. But if you are surrounded by French or Italian boats there will probably be no helpful bystanders and your crew will need to jump ashore with the ropes themselves. Generally, these two will also shout advice and swear volubly that you are too far away from the pier or that it is too high, slippery etc

So, you can see that you really need a crew of at least four, seven wouldn't be too many, even if they are multitasking and also doing the shouting and swearing. We have found 'shouters' need no experience or training—most only need five minutes on board to be able to do that job, as well as telling you how to do yours. There are generally plenty around from other yachts, even French and Italian ones will help with shouting and swearing. Most of this nastiness can be avoided by arriving at the right time. After the morning rush hour, before the sea breeze comes in and when the water could be translucent and the bottom visible and before the arrival of desperate late comers who will kill for a berth. It can be avoided altogether by anchoring in a quiet bay, where the swimming will be idyllic, and coming in by dinghy.

Alas, on arriving back at Kas a strong northerly was blowing again, the harbour was crowded and even smaller than I remembered. I could see disaster was still waiting among the idlers on the quay. However, this time we were not in a rush and, I was allowed to anchor in the same bay as the previous year and come in the next morning in the dinghy when the weather was placid. In appreciation of her consideration, after drinks on the rear deck while the setting sun was lighting up the golden hills behind the town and the last of the wind was dropping out, I cooked a very tasty mussel stew. The moon rose in the cloudless sky and we were perfectly content.

The next morning, we motored into the quay in the dinghy and had a delightful time rambling around the town, inspecting the Greek theatre which is in good condition with seating for four thousand, the 'King's Tomb' which is a 4th century BCE Lycian sarcophagus and rock tombs from the same era. This turned out to be quite hot work and by noon we were ready for lunch in a shaded backstreet restaurant where we dined on fresh sea bass, a bounteous fresh local salad and fruit. All delicious. Afterwards the shops were inspected while I kept an eye on the dinghy from a shady spot.

The brisk northerly was still blowing the next day and as it was forecast to strengthen, we thought it best to get up the coast a bit while we were able to. A morning's run took us to the bay just north of the village of Kalkan where we found ourselves a nicely protected spot with plenty of room to let out sixty metres of chain and with no dangers to leeward if we dragged. By nightfall our mighty 'spade' anchor was deeply buried in the sand, had been inspected by snorkel and, although the wind was now moaning in the rigging there was no chance of us moving. Another of life's great joys. Secure at sunset in a deserted windswept bay. The only sounds are the wind, the wash against the hull and raucous birds preparing to nest.

In recent years technology has thrown up some devices that are godsends for sailors—no, not a third hand. An offshoot from electronic charts and position fixing are a number of apps called 'anchor watch' or similar. If you have a decent GPS signal you will be warned if your anchor is dragging. So, in our present situation, we simply marked on the electronic chart the spot where we dropped our anchor, then drew a circle around it with a radius equal to the length of chain laid plus the length of the boat, and an alarm is activated if we drift outside the circle. Now, this may not be foolproof, but with a crew of two it is a very nice back up in a roomy anchorage. Not so good if the anchorage is crowded and you have to worry about other boats dragging onto you, or if you have a rocky shore or another boat close astern where the warning may come too late.

Our anchorage was before one of the more notorious stretches of the Turkish coast, known as the 'Five Capes'. Here the steep waves, driven south for many miles by the northerlies, batter against rocky headlands that thrust out from the high mountains into the turbulent sea. Often, particularly later in the year when the *meltemi* is over forty knots and the sea is short and steep it is very difficult for a yacht to make ground against. Even the large gullets weighing lots of tons with very powerful engines find the conditions difficult to dangerous. The 'pilot' recommends doing as much of the passage as possible before dawn when perhaps the winds will be less severe.

So, we settled down to wait for the strong winds to abate. On a yacht a lot of time is spent waiting for the wind to come or go, to back or veer, peering at wind charts and forecasts and watching the clouds. Fortunately, my previous life as a soldier has made me good at waiting.

Not having electronic charts or radios, the ancient Greeks had to rely on the confusing advice given by the large number of gods who looked after the winds. As we already know, the god Aeolus was in overall charge of the winds, but he was assisted by and argued with Boreas, god of the north wind and winter, Eurus, god of the east wind, Notus, god of the south wind, and Zephyrus god of the west wind. Moreover, there were also a dozen or so other gods in the mix: of the north east winds, south west etc. As well as a number of nymphs, as well as Zeus the king of the gods himself and Poseidon, god of the oceans and brother of Zeus. And on top of all that, the gods often had their own agendas, in which you were not necessarily very important, even if you had sacrificed a sheep to the right one! No wonder there were so many shipwrecks!

These days we more or less understand the basic dynamics, but the winds themselves still remain temperamental divas. The wind channels right around islands, turning at right angles or more. In some places, such as the gulfs of the Greek Peloponnese, it turns nearly completely back on itself. In some islands, Crete is a good example, the winds on the leeside are stronger than the windward as they howl down from the high mountain ranges, accelerated by the katabatic effect. Here forty knots of wind on the north coast can be fifty or sixty on the south, with very few refuges. Our 'pilot' gives the sage advice that it is crazy to take a yacht near Crete before mid-September.

Anyway, in due course the wind abated, we thanked the gods and made a very early start. We were past the difficult bit well before noon and not long afterwards in a snug anchorage that was protected from the northerlies. There was an isolated restaurant ashore and we dinghied in. We found ourselves dining in a deserted hall surrounded by fading photographs of the rich and famous who had passed by this remote spot over many years – the Agha Khan, Omar Sharif, a number of dukes and duchesses, various Greek tycoons.

The next day we got as far as a small semi-enclosed anchorage under the southern headland of the Gulf of Gocek. As we had enjoyed a very convivial night here at the isolated taverna Karacaroen on the way south, we picked up a mooring and booked a table and a ride in with the ferryman and his girlfriend. The proprietors are so confident of their hospitality that they do not trust patrons to safely return themselves to their yachts. This will probably change once the imams are running things, and people are not allowed to enjoy themselves so much. The taverna is supported over the water by long poles and has a great view to the harsh rocky coastal mountains. As twilight turned to darkness their colours muted from glimmering golds and reds, to greys and rich blues, before being lost in the shadows.

Taverna Karacaroen is an extended Turkish family affair where the sons and girlfriends—plenty of vivacious girls from everywhere—are front and centre. It has a set menu of fish caught out the front, lamb or goat stews, a smorgasbord of fresh vegetables from their prolific garden, yoghurts, and freshly baked breads topped with vegetables, cheeses and finely chopped and seasoned goat. The road-head is some miles away around the coast, so everything not produced on the spot has a difficult journey by truck over mountain tracks, then a launch trip over a rough bay. Despite this the wine was plentiful, rich and aromatic.

There was still much music and singing as we were ferried home, leaving the younger revellers—everyone—to it. The previous year we had picked up a mooring that was not far from the rocky foreshore and we had a very worrying couple of hours when a squall came through. It is amazing how quickly you can start to lose faith in restaurant moorings in the dark, with a bit of wind and, only a few metres between your stern and the rocks – and how quickly you forget about it for that matter. We were moored in much the same spot. However, this night Aeolus treated us kindly and we drifted off to peaceful sleep despite the loud merriment from shore.

We were looking forward to coming back to the Gulf of Gocek. The Mediterranean has so many great places to visit in a yacht that it is very hard to pick a favourite - but the Gulf of Gocek would have to be on any short list. As with most places in the Aegean the gulf has a link with Greek mythology, and lays claim to a connection with one of the most famous of all fables —Icarus, the boy who flew too close to the sun. We find it wonderful to be on the stage that is the setting for tales that are over three thousand years old — sailing over the same water, climbing the same hills, smelling the smells, breathing the air. Remarkable.

Icarus and his father Daedalus were talented Athenian craftsmen who were hired by King Minos of Crete to build the 'Labyrinth' in which to imprison the Minotaur, a creature half-man and half-bull. Very unfortunately the creature was the product of a liaison between his wife the queen and, a bull. When Minos discovered Daedalus conspiring with his enemy Theseus, he was imprisoned in a tower. To escape, Daedalus made two pairs of wings of wax and feathers and Daedalus and Icarus took flight. He warned his son that he must be careful and fly neither too low where the feathers would become wet or, too high where the wax would melt. In his exuberance, and disregarding his father's advice, Icarus flew too close to the sun, his wax melted, his feathers came off and he fell to the sea. In the Greek tradition he fell near the island of Icaria west of Samos, however the Turkish tradition claims Gocek and they are not that far apart, although both are well to the east of the flight path to Athens.

The intent of the fable was to encourage youths to listen to their elders and not be 'know all's—Icarus is the first recorded teenage 'know-all'. It was the first exploration of a theme that has been the inspiration of many, many tales, plays, books and movies. And reminds me of Mark Twain's famous aside: *'When I was a young teenager, I was ashamed of how little my father knew. However, several years later I was astounded how much the old man had learned'.*

***

There were a number of reefs to avoid the next morning, and a brutal headland to round with a strong on shore wind, as we turned into the gulf. Giving lee shores a wide berth is one of the first and most important rules of sailing, up there with keeping water under the keel. However, when rounding windy rocky headlands, no matter how far off we stay, in the end it never seems quite far enough. The rocks always begin to creep dangerously close, and closer, and closer, and closer.

...close under a steep cliff face that glows golden in the morning sun and, gives us a deliciously cool shadow in the late afternoon...

If we are relying on the motor to keep us safe, I find myself wishing the Greeks had had a god of diesel engines, but they didn't! And I have to satisfy myself with patting *Sea Dream's* stern rail and telling her what a reliable, beautiful girl she is. Once we were into the <u>Gulf of Gocek</u> we had a very pleasant reach across to the islands on the northern shore, behind which lies another enchanted waterway. Apart from a few narrow entrances, it is surrounded by islands and pine-covered mountains. At one end is the township of Gocek and some half dozen miles to the north west is Seagull Bay, linked by the sparkling, winding waters of the gulf. Along the miles and miles of shoreline are innumerable protected bays with water of the clearest blue, beautiful surrounds and with a nice sea breeze in the afternoon - the remnants of the near constant gale blowing outside - to tame the temperatures ashore, which are often over 40C. On our first visit here, we discovered Seagull Bay decorated with a large white seagull, made from white rocks and it is to here we always come back to first. The water in this bay is too deep to anchor, but there are three widely spaced mooring buoys. One of these, which is our favourite and was generally available and waiting for us, is close under a steep cliff face that glows golden in the morning sun and, gives us a deliciously cool shadow in the late afternoon. This is important when it is time for a cool wine or two before dinner. Having a fierce late afternoon sun bouncing off the water into your face, while it is still close to forty degrees doesn't do much for the wine.

It is a short swim to a pebbly beach at the very head of the bay, where there is a small spring that attracted a flock of goats each evening—they relished their drinks as much as we did. Anchored here, apart from the other two buoys if they had been taken, there were few other boats to be seen. Only the occasional wandering yacht or passing fisherman. But a mother and her young son, with a wood-fired oven on their small launch, brought hot bread and crepes for breakfast. A market boat visited each afternoon, bringing the necessities of life: fresh fish, salads, local wine and beer. Not too far away there were other bays, obscured by our golden bluff, where boats could anchor with their sterns tied to the shore and in two of the bays there were summer restaurants. One was on an old barge with tables set up on shore and the other was under a shady tree beside a crumbling old stone cottage. The former had the more extensive menu: fish, goat or wild boar, and we had actually seen them carrying pigs out of the mountains after hearing the fatal shots, so it was definitely the real thing. The second, which was run by a lone elderly man, was famous for only its fish.

There were no roads in the area, only a track that wandered through the hills and eventually ended up in Gocek village in one direction and, in the other came to a restaurant on the coast of the open gulf. This was operated by a man and his hardworking wife. Every couple of days she would come to the beach with a donkey and meet a launch carrying supplies from Gocek, load her donkey and toil back up the steep slopes in the baking sun to her restaurant. One day she came with two donkeys and we expected a large cargo to be delivered. Alas, no. It was the husband returning from men's business in town. He sat in the shade as she unloaded the launch, carried everything ashore and strapped the load onto one of the donkeys. When this was done, he bestirred himself and mounted the second donkey and rode off, leaving the poor, black-robed wife to struggle up the hills, leading the heavily-laden donkey. That gives you a general idea of a woman's role in some traditional Muslim households. Which it must be said, is still much better than being a jihad bride.

It is only a couple of hours to Gocek village by the most direct route down the centre of the gulf. But it could take the whole summer if you felt inclined to tarry in the many delightful anchorages on the way. Each day here has a delicious sameness. As dawn approaches the eastern sky begins to flush, then fades to a pale blue as the sun rises above the inland mountains. The water is placid and, as the sun rises, takes on the green of the surrounding forests, then the blues of the ripening sky. The water is irresistible, wood-smoked bread is delivered, the paths through the forests to the ancient tombs of the Lycians call, or otherwise a kayak inspection of the submerged stone jetties that have been in place for three thousand years.

As the midday heat builds, the shaded cockpit and good books beckon. In the early afternoon the tail end of the *meltemi* forces its way over the hills, the water ruffles, sleepers bestir, the wind generators whirl, the water calls again, there are photos to edit, words to write, circuits of the boat to swim. As the sun begins to slide towards the shadowed ridges thoughts turn to dinner—dining onboard or stimulating the local economy. Decisions best made over drinks, problems of the world solved, plans made. Dinner under the trees near a smoky wood oven, a row back to the boat over the once again placid water. Overhead the constellations blaze the moon rises and sets, the eastern sky begins to flush...

23

In fact, it is a rare place where such a harmonious and enjoyable routine is possible. In most places one of the old Greek gods will bring some unpleasantness; storms, thunder, strong winds from the wrong direction or the local bureaucracy will interrupt you, or some fool in a French yacht will anchor too close, or over your anchor.

Anyway, after either a few hours or a few weeks, depending on how long you have tarried you will hove in sight of the waterfront at Gocek, tucked into the very top of the gulf. Not that much of the small village is visible, no multi-story development is allowed. The waterfront is lined with marinas, and there are yachts of all shapes and sizes anchored off. It is a place for sailors; the harbour is too small for cruise liners and there are no beaches to attract hordes of sunseekers. So, while it has a bit of a vibe after dark it is not overrun, and the waterfront is a nice place to stroll without feeling as if you are in the midst of a drunken soccer crowd on the fringe of a heavily amplified rock concert—which unfortunately can be the case in some Mediterranean destinations where there are cheap direct flights from large European cities to a crowded beach.

For Turkey, Gocek is a very well-to-do town, prosperous because of the beauty of the bay and the sailing industry they have developed. They have gone to extreme lengths to preserve the purity of the water and the ecology of the surrounding mountains, and free buoys have both made it easier to visit as well as controlling the numbers. Anything you need for a yacht can be provided at a reasonable cost. In small shops behind the village they fabricate stainless steel for anchors, chains, rollers, rigging and anything else you can think of. Sails, shade cloths, dinghy covers—this is the place to come to. Mechanical repairs—no problems. It is busy, cheerful and a contrast to so many rural Turkish towns, particularly in the east of the country where Muslim attitudes imprison the communities in orthodoxy and stifle most economic activity.

As with all the Mediterranean, there are reminders of the past, and the more you see of history the more you realise that there are few happy endings. Everything that man creates is eventually destroyed, by the gods, if not his enemies. Not far off is the ghost village of Kayakoy with a history going back some three thousand years and through a number of re-creations. In ancient times as part of the Lycian Empire it was known as Lebessos and later as Livissi. It became a Greek settlement as part of the great Greek colonisation of the Mediterranean. For a while it was a Catholic bishopric and had a population of around six thousand Greeks in the mid-nineteenth century, with more than twenty churches and chapels.

In the early twentieth century the widespread persecution of the Greek population in Turkey resulted in the ethnic cleansing of Kayakoy and nearby villages, just as it did in Finike and Kas. Over a period of four years, groups of villagers were force marched to Denizli over two hundred kilometres away where they were brutalised, some murdered, and the survivors shipped to Greece with virtually nothing. The march took up to fifteen days, and as many were women, children and the elderly—these were literally death marches with many dying on the road, their bodies left to rot in ditches. In 1922 the few Greeks who had so far escaped the pogroms, abandoned their homes and left.

Today, a hundred years later, the tragic village remains a ghost town and a reminder of a brutal past and a harsh warning for the future. It serves as a grim museum with the ruins of around five hundred houses and a few churches still evident. The excellent book *'Birds Without Wings'* by Louis de Bernieres tells the heart wrenching story.

Onwards to Marmaris where our friends, Megan and Vince Thompson were joining us. This is also an ancient place, part of the Carian Kingdom late in the second millennium BCE. It was colonised by the Greeks in the 6th century BCE and, Herodotus who was born not far away, mentions there had been a castle here since the 4th century BCE. In 333 BCE it was captured by Alexander the Great as his army marched down the Aegean coast before heading to Egypt, Persia and far off India. It was incorporated into the Ottoman Empire by Sultan Mehmed the Conqueror and, later Lord Nelson anchored here on his way to destroying Napoleon's fleet at the Battle of the Nile in 1798. Aficionados of Patrick O'Brian will recall that the inimitable Captain Jack Aubrey outwitted a Turkish battleship in this very bay and, may remember Jack's often repeated words of Nelson. *'Never mind manoeuvres, always go at them'*, or his own reflections that *'trollops are capital in port but will not do at sea'*. Not too many modern yacht skippers seem to agree with Jack on this one, particularly Russians on large motor yachts.

Not so long ago it was primarily a fishing village, but these days it is a tourist mecca. In the height of summer, the population can swell from around thirty thousand to over two hundred thousand, unfortunately many of whom are oversized, sunburnt, loud, inappropriately dressed British and Russian soccer fans. Nevertheless, it is fun, the waterfront is a lively and noisy place lined with bars, plenty of fine restaurants and really great shopping, where even a skinflint like myself can be tempted by a Gucci leather coat or a Rolex. But anchoring in the harbour does not make for a quiet and peaceful night.

Our plan for the summer had us well on our way before any soccer fans showed up, and to revisit many of our favourite places along Turkey's coast. We would continue to take it slowly, enjoying its many enchanting anchorages and fossicking in the rich history. But it's very hard not to be seduced by the Marmaris bazaar, and there was a bit of frenetic shopping, some lovely meals and much laughter with Vince and Megan before we headed off. Out of the narrow entrance of the bay heading for the quiet and charm of Bozukkale, another of our favourite havens.

By now the *meltemi*, the strong northerly wind that howls down the central Aegean in summer, was beginning to make its presence felt. The further you go along the Orhaniye Peninsula the rockier and more windswept it becomes. The *meltemi* swings around the southern tip of the Greek Island of Symi and sweeps up the south-eastern side of the barren coastline of the peninsula. By the time we were nearing the entrance to Bozukkale there was a considerable sea running and *Sea Dreams* was digging her bow into the waves, sending spray flying over the cockpit and foam-flecked water gushing down the leeward deck. We had to tack repeatedly to get to windward of a number of small hard islands, with the sea smashing into the hungry-looking rocks. It was a relief to get into the calmer waters of Bozukkale, furl our sails, thank Zeus and pick up a mooring close to another one of our favourite eateries, the Alibaba Restaurant. We had had a couple of very happy nights here with our daughter, Georgie, and her husband, Simon, and their children. Joseph and Eleanor. after our first crossing of the Aegean.

There are the remains of a mighty fortress guarding the entrance to the bay. It is a wonderous thing and I have not really been able to uncover an explanation of how it was built. The sides of the eminence on which it sits are covered with large boulders and crevices. There is no sign that there was ever any sort of road, or even a footpath from the shore to the fortress, some six or seven hundred metres. These days it is an uncomfortable scramble for an unladen person. The walls of the fortress are constructed of large rectangular, carefully chiselled sandstone blocks, each many tons in weight and fitted together as perfectly as laid brickwork.

How did they get here? Were they quarried on site and the works now hidden by rubble? Were they quarried elsewhere, brought by ship and pulled to the top by some mighty 'flying-fox', was there once a road that has been obliterated by an earthquake?

And this is certainly not the only great engineering feat of ancient times in the area. On the nearby island of Rhodes, a thirty-metre-high statue of the sun god Helios was built in 280 BCE. It became known as the Colossus of Rhodes and was one of the wonders of the ancient world. And there is a connection to this wonderful bay at Bozukkale. In 305 BCE the king of Cyprus decided to conquer Rhodes. An invasion force was assembled where we were now anchored and, some mighty siege equipment was built to breach the strong walls of the city. Included amongst the equipment was an eight-storey high siege tower. But Rhodes was saved when a fleet sent by Ptolemy I of Egypt, formerly one of Alexander the Great's Greek generals, arrived. The invaders were routed and forced to flee, leaving behind their siege equipment and many valuables. The lot was sold for a fortune and used to finance the statue.

So, there is plenty to ponder while standing on the walls of the mighty fortress or relaxing on the shaky piles of the Alibaba. However, I do not think that the builder of the Colossus, Chares of Lindos, would have been very impressed by the architecture of the anchorage's rustic restaurant, the Alibaba. Nor would the Greek architects, Satyros and Pytheos who designed the Mausoleum of Halicarnassus, another of the wonders of the ancient world at nearby Bodrum.

The Alibaba, sitting precariously on its motley collection of poles has a verandah that hangs over the water, which was obviously built to philosophise on and has a large outside woodfired oven.

There is only a blackboard menu, and everything must be brought in by water as the surrounding terrain is too hard for a productive garden. However, it is always a happy place. I think its remoteness and the sometimes difficult passage to get to it, promotes a sense of camaraderie amongst the patrons.

...Sea Dreams at Bozzukale ... the remains of a mighty fortress guarding the entrance to the bay... walls of large rectangular, carefully chiselled sandstone blocks, each many tons in weight and fitted together as perfectly as laid brickwork...

However, it is always a happy place. I think its remoteness and the sometimes difficult passage to get to it, promotes a sense of camaraderie amongst the patrons. There is a small rickety jetty long enough to take half a dozen yachts and three moorings.

We had a couple of nights here before pushing on northward. The sun glinted on the empty sea, a gentle shore breeze ruffled the water, the hard coast slipped by. Rocky crags, ravines, stunted wind-blasted trees clinging tenaciously to the sun-bleached soil. By late morning the wind had died out completely and we motored into the large bay with Bozburun harbour, enclosed by a rock wall, on the northern shore. We dropped the anchor a couple of hundred metres out and slid into the cool water to swim and check the set of the anchor, before retiring to the shaded cockpit to survey our world. Later we visited the large boatyard close by, where beautiful traditional gullets are built, inspected the rug traders in the dirt streets behind the esplanade and selected a restaurant with a fine view over the harbour to *Sea Dreams*, lying in the golden water of sunset.

The next morning the gentle land breeze was with us again and, we idled around to the almost enclosed bay at Agil Koyu on the northern tip of the Bozburun Peninsula. Much of the bay was well over twenty metres and too deep for us to anchor. But with a bit of hunting around we were lucky enough to find a spot close to the summer restaurant in the north-west corner, where we could take a stern line ashore. We were comfortably ensconced and thinking about a stroll when a harbinger of the dreaded *meltemi* blew in, but thankfully offshore and over our stern, for once. Thank you, Aeolus. When we were happy everything was secure and as it should be, we set off to check out the menu. No surprises, happy courteous staff serving the staples of the coast: fish, octopus or squid grilled over a smoky fire. Fine Turkish beer and reds. All good.

The wind had dropped out the next morning and we motored out while there was still a pink flush on the horizon, but not yet any sign of life on the other few yachts sharing the bay. We were heading for Datca a short hop on the other side of the Gulf of Hisaronu. Breakfast of freshly-baked bread we had brought back with us last night, as a gentle land breeze stirred the water. The sails filled enough to give *Sea Dreams* life and the details of the rocky coastline of the Datca Peninsula began to take shape. Before midday we had anchored in the northern bay.

The stopover gave us the chance of returning to the Culinarium Restaurant overlooking the harbour and run by a Turkish/German couple who have developed a Turkish 'fusion' menu which, from time to time we have enjoyed very much. It was still great and when we were finally back onboard, we were feeling a little maudlin wondering what the future held for the happy, hardworking and courteous couple. And for all the others who have made the coast such an unforgettable experience for cruising sailors. We also dined on the verandah of the Emek Restaurant with a lovely view over the bay and our beautiful boat, to the rocky mountains of the Greek island of Symi in the distance.

The next day took us westward in the lee of the rocky hills of the peninsula. A lively breeze was blowing, and we scooted along within a stone's throw of the shoreline. Here and there some beautiful traditional Turkish gulets were still sheltering in shallow coves, and some fishing boats were surrounded by wheeling clouds of seagulls demanding their share of the catch. We had stopped previously at Knidos which, from an historical point of view, is one of the most thought-provoking anchorages in the Mediterranean. We arrived early enough to give Vince and Megan plenty of time to clamber all over the ancient remains and sunset found us philosophising on the back deck before Vince rustled up a very tasty *Coban Kavurma*—a Turkish Casserole—which has gone on to become one of his most famous signature dishes. All was calm and peaceful as we turned in, although a Russian yacht had anchored a bit too close for comfort under our stern.

The wind during the day had been a northerly, but the noise of our anchor chain dragging over the bottom, heralding a wind shift, woke me around three a.m. Outside it was still pitch black, the darkness only broken by the half dozen riding lights of the other yachts in the ancient harbour. A light southerly, unusual this time of the year, had started to come in. Just enough to swing the yachts around and for them to start to pull back in the opposite direction on their anchor chains. Nothing to worry about at this stage. The old stone breakwater, built who knows how many centuries ago, gave some protection from the south and the wind would need to be much stronger to cause us concern—provided our Russian neighbour had not let out too much chain. If so, when we both had dragged back on our anchor chains, he would be over ours and perhaps on top of us.

I went below and checked the barometer, which had started to fall a bit, made myself a strong coffee and came back on deck. The wind seemed to have picked up a little but not enough to ruffle the water. I went forward and checked our anchor. The chain had stopped pulling across the bottom as we had swung around, and the anchor seemed to have reset. Before the wind had changed our bow had been about forty metres south of our anchor, now it was forty metres north of it. The Russian had dropped his anchor about ten metres behind us, and hopefully when he settled down, he would be ten metres in front of our anchor. But, if he had let out more chain then us, or dragged his anchor, he would be over our anchor and chain and, it would be difficult, perhaps impossible, for us to get our anchor up.

I stared through the darkness at the stern of the Russian. He certainly wasn't fifty metres in front, he was closer, perhaps he was over our anchor already. This is certainly not an uncommon thing to

30

happen in the Mediterranean, and it only becomes a problem if you need to get your anchor up. By four a.m. the wind had risen to around fifteen knots and things were not so comfortable. There was still no hint of dawn, *Sea Dreams* was bucking on the anchor chain and there was sound of breaking water where the wind was channelling into the gap in the breakwater. We now had to make a choice of trying to get our anchor up while manoeuvring in the dark, with every chance of colliding with the Russian, then getting out through the narrow entrance. Or doing nothing and keeping our fingers crossed. We were all feeling a bit apprehensive now. Although I consoled myself with the thought that some famous philosopher—whose name I could not recall—had once said that doing nothing was generally the best option.

With the first hint of a grey dawn we realised that the Russian was certainly over our anchor and still slowly dragging back. Unless they left or the wind changed again, we would not be able to get ours up. I went forward with a torch and urged him to get his anchor up and get out. By this stage we had our own motor going and had let out us much of our chain as we could without running aground. If he kept coming back on us, we might just have to jettison our chain and anchor and run for it. When he had come back so that he was only twenty metres in front of us, it finally seemed that his anchor had got a grip, and we were frozen in our dangerous dance. The outline of the rocky entrance was certainly now clear enough, and again, as politely as I could, I urged him to b **** off. He sulkily gestured to the greyness and shrugged. The wind came up a bit, gradually more light seeped into the greyness, the anchors continued to hold. I remained in the bow glaring at the Russian boat. Eventually a crewman went into their bow and the boat began to inch forward as their anchor chain came in. Then they were edging past the breakwater and we started to follow them out. Thankful to be away from the all too close rocky shore. By the time we had rounded the nearby headland and set a course for Bodrum it was fully light, the sun concealed behind grey clouds chased by a still freshening breeze. Soon we were comfortable with moderately reefed sails, enjoying a hearty breakfast and looking forward to the pleasures of our next port.

But Aeolos had not finished with us yet. Halfway across the intervening gulf the wind picked up again. We reefed the genoa some more and turned our attention to the mainsail. Alas, the reefing line snapped, and it unfurled, flapping madly. We had to drop it quickly, which first required removing the long vertical sail-battens —an awkward job in itself. Luckily Vince and I got plenty of shouted advice from the experts sheltered behind the dodger and we had it done in no time at all. Or at least before dark. The southerly was howling into the anchorage below Bodrum castle, so we tucked ourselves into a bay a little further north and set about getting things ship shape. Not the best day's sailing we had ever had!

... Knidos...a thriving city and centre of Hellenistic art... including Praxiteles's Aphrodite... for a thousand years from the 6th century BCE...Georgie, Ro, Simon, Joseph, Eleanor...

Here Vince and Megan left us as planned. Ro flew to the UK to meet Charlotte and attend a memorial service in honour of posthumous VC recipients, of which Ro's Uncles, Eugene Esmonde, VC. DSO and Thomas Esmonde, VC were two. There were a couple of small jobs to do on the boat: replace the mainsail furling line, the wind vane and recorder at the top of the mast and the usual housekeeping, that kept me occupied until she returned. We then headed north again, in company for a while with Robbie and Phil Hurst from Western Australia, exploring the anchorages and restaurants at Nimir, Gumusluk Limini, Torba, Port Iasos and Didim Beach.

***

In ancient times the coast northward from Didim to the island of Samos lying off the Yarimadasi Peninsula, provided a number of secure anchorages which had led to the establishment of thriving Greek cities—Miletus being the most famous. But as the centuries passed the ports were gradually buried in silt carried by the rivers flowing westward through the fertile plains to the sea, and the ancient cities fell into ruins. These days there is no anchorage for a yacht before the southern entrance of Mycale Strait. Here there is a shallow bay surrounding a small island with the entrance protected by another offshore island and a scattering of reefs. It had no name on our chart, but our 'pilot' informed us it was known as St. Paul's anchorage. It appears that a boat carrying St. Paul back from Ephesus to Jerusalem overnighted here, and he met with the Ephesian Elders, as described in *Acts 20:17-38*. It is now a remote spot surrounded by hard land. By the time we had the anchor down and buried in the sand the water was grey and the wind was chasing ominous clouds overhead. As darkness fell a small fishing boat anchored a couple of hundred yards away, but there was no other sign of life.

Sitting in the back of the boat and watching night fall, it was strange to think that two millennia ago one of the great apostles and founders of Christianity had once proselytised on this lonely shore. Stranger to think that six hundred years before St Paul, Thales of Miletus, perhaps the greatest intellect of the ancient world, had held court in the once great city of Miletus, now lying in ruins a short distance behind the dark hills lining the shore.

Now, here is a remarkable and not generally appreciated fact. The World's First Age of Enlightenment, the Hellenistic Era, started here over two thousand years before Europe threw off its own Dark Age and stumbled into the sunlit uplands of what the ancient Greeks had explored so many centuries before. The Hellenistic Era lasted for around a thousand years, until the burning of the Great Library in

Alexandria by a Christian mob, marked its demise. Although the old gods were still worshipped during the Hellenistic era, they co-existed with the development of science and philosophy. As well as religious temples there were schools of science, philosophy, politics, diplomacy, architecture and mathematics. There were libraries, theatres, museums, fabulous displays of art, not only in temples but also in public and private places.

Miletus was a thriving Greek city by the 6th century BCE and became home to a group of intellectuals who were the founders of Greek science and philosophy, and who became known as the Milesian School, or the Ionian Rationalists. The forefather was Thales, but it included a long list of immortal scholars whose names are still on our lips and remain in our thoughts. It is the legacy of these great men for which the city is mostly remembered. But, as with so many great ancient cities, not many years after Thales the city was reduced to rubble, the women and children sold into slavery and the men killed or castrated, as the Persian king Darius the Great, inflicted harsh retribution for rebellion. After this tragedy the city was gradually repopulated and twenty years later, after the Greeks defeated the Persians at the Battle of Plataea, it was freed from Persian rule. But a century later, it fell to the Persians again, before being liberated by Alexander the Great. Later it came under other masters; the Seleucids, Egyptians, Romans, Byzantines and the Turks. Today only ruins remain—but they are of considerable nobility. It is not possible to mistake them for the stones of some nondescript historical nonentity. At the height of its majesty it occupied a wonderful position, built around a defendable harbour within a large protected bay, all surrounded by rich farming land. But as the centuries passed the gulf has been silted up by soil carried downstream by the Meander River.

Thales is generally regarded as the Western world's first philosopher and mathematician, as well as being an astronomer and scientist. He may have also been the first articulated agnostic, perhaps the first atheist. To him the old Greek gods—whose stories seem to have been told from around 1700 BCE - had no role in explaining the mysteries of life. All things could be explained by rational thought.

For Thales there were practical, logical reasons why all things happen, and the gods had nothing to do with observable phenomena.

He was the first to ask what the building blocks of the universe were, and according to Aristotle, suggested it was water, because amongst its attributes water could change shape and move while remaining unchanged in substance. Among his other achievements were the study of electricity, the development of geometry, contributions to applied mathematics, the development of a crude telescope, the foundation of 'natural philosophy', the calculation of the seasons and the solstice. Various Roman writers credit him with the first 'globe' of the sky, which was the forerunner of the celestial analogue computer developed by Archimedes and of the 'Antikythera Mechanism'.

The following inscription was placed on his tomb:
'You see this tomb is small – but recollect,
The fame of Thales reaches to the sky.'

In his footsteps followed a host of intellectuals, the records of the works of many hundreds remain in the public domain. Far too many to even mention here, let alone try to do justice to. But here is a very inadequate sketch of a few.

Anaximander (610-545 BCE) who is credited with being the first known writer on philosophy, the first speculative astronomer and **created the first image of the universe.** He created **a map of the ancient world** that included an accurate depiction of the Mediterranean Sea, the Straits of Gibraltar and the major islands, the Black Sea, the Caspian Sea, the Red Sea. The great rivers; the Danube and Rhine in Europe, the Indus in India, the Tigris and Euphrates in Arabia and the Nile in Africa.

Parmenides (510-560 BCE) stated that everything 'that is' must have 'always been', nothing could come from 'nothing', and it was impossible to think of something that cannot be thought of.

Empedocles (490-430 BCE) the first to give **an evolutionary account of the development of the species.**

Zeno (490-430 BCE) the first to show that the concept of infinity exists for both time and distance.

Socrates (496-399 BCE) developed the application of philosophy in our daily lives, and an **ethical system based on human reason rather than theological doctrines**. He was executed for his beliefs.

Plato (427-347 BCE) was a student of Socrates. His most famous writing was *The Republic* which addressed **aspect of ethics, political philosophy and metaphysics into forming the best**

philosophical approach to life.

Aristotle of Stagira (384-322 BCE) a disciple of Plato whose interpretation of things was based on observable facts of daily lives. He broke the study of **knowledge into categories still used today, including; ethics, biology, mathematics and physics.** After Thales he was the most influential Greek philosopher.

Archimedes (c287-c212 BCE) the greatest scientist and inventor of antiquity and one of the greatest of all time. He is perhaps best known for his discovery that the weight of an irregular shape will displace an amount of water equal to its own weight. His designs included **an astrological analogue computer**, sophisticated war machines that became essential elements of the Roman arsenal, screw pumps and compound pulleys.

Posidonius (c135-51 BCE) left behind a vast compendium of work in many disciplines. He was the first Stoic to depart from the orthodox doctrine that passions were faulty judgements and subscribe to Plato's view that passions were inherent in human nature. That the human soul had elements that were spirited—anger, the desire for power, possessions—and considerate—sex, food, love—and ethics was the problem of dealing with these passions and restoring reason as the controlling faculty. **Most amazingly he calculated the circumference of the world, by measuring the distance above the horizon of the star Canopus when measured from Alexandria and Rhodes as 39,000 kilometres as opposed to the actual of 40,074 kilometres.** He linked the tides to the moon's orbit and cycles although he thought heat rather than gravitational pull was the cause.

Half a millennium after the flowering of the Miletian school a very different man stood on the shoreline adjacent to where *Sea Dreams* was anchored. Paul the Apostle certainly believed in the power of God. He was arguably the greatest apostle of the first great monotheist religion. Christianity was itself an offshoot of the preceding monotheist religion Judaism, whose doctrine is based on a belief in the supernatural and had begun being told along the western edge of the Arabic peninsula not long after that of the Greek gods, around 1500 BCE. Islam which was inspired by a dreamtime appearance by the archangel Gabriel was a late arrival, two thousand two hundred years after Moses and seven centuries after Jesus. Between the three, and to my mind perhaps the greatest tragedy of man's history, mysticism supplanted the age of reason for most of the next two millennia, after Paul had stood on this lonely spot.

Paul says he was born near Damascus in Syria (c5-66 CE) although Christian tradition says he was born in Tarsus in the south-eastern coastal region of Turkey, some six hundred and thirty kilometres by road from Damascus. By trade a tentmaker, he was on this road when he was famously struck blind by the resurrected Jesus appearing in *a great light*. He regained his sight after three days and 'having seen the light' began preaching that indeed Jesus was the Son of God. Prior to his conversion he belonged to a Judaist sect known as the Pharisee. Paul maintained that he had been personally anointed by Jesus to spread his message. The essence of which was that Jesus was the son of God, his crucifixion was a voluntary sacrifice, he lived in heaven and would soon return to usher in a new and fairer age, where all believers would be guaranteed eternal life in heaven. Which for the next two millennia was to prove a very attractive proposition to the masses facing only misery in their earthly life.

He was an influential teacher and missionary throughout much of Asia Minor and Greece and is considered one of the most important church figures in the middle of 1st century. In the New Testament there are seven letters from Paul and another seven which are believed to have been written by his disciples. They were not written as universal dictates of Christianity, as they addressed individual problems and circumstances, but over time their doctrinal importance grew. Paul undertook three missionary journeys, the third of which included nearby Ephesus, where there were certainly Jews following the dictates of Judaism at this time. But Paul's message was for all people, and indeed the city did become an important centre of early Christianity. He stayed there for three years and claimed to have performed many miracles, healing people and casting out demons.

He was forced to leave the city after an attack from a local silver smith resulted in a pro-Artemis riot involving most of the city. On returning to Jerusalem he was arrested for causing civil disturbances and imprisoned. As he was a Roman citizen, he had the right of appeal to the Emperor in Rome, which he exercised. Nevertheless, he was eventually convicted, beheaded and buried on the road to Ostia outside Rome, which eventually became the site of the basilica in Rome, St. Paul's.

So, our little anchorage had quite a history. First as a centre of the polytheistic belief in the old Greek gods. Then the emergence of belief in rational scientific thought. Then the three ancient faith based monotheistic religions. Today these still compete in communities all over the world, at times alongside a variety of 'isms'. But sadly, the old Greek gods have gone—except perhaps on the back decks of a yacht or two—leaving the world a much less colourful and dramatic place.

Just one more word on this subject before we leave St Paul's anchorage. Before long, and certainly once Christianity became the only legal religion of the Roman Empire, non-Christians were all classified as 'pagans'. The Christian Church still uses this derogative term to describe the pre-Christian world as barbarous, unenlightened, savage and ignorant. Certainly, in places it was. But it is unforgiveable to slander the enlightened scientists and philosophers, and the Hellenistic era itself, with this epitaph. And this, of course, includes all the great intellectuals and rulers of pre-Christian Rome.

It was a grey morning, the sun hidden by black clouds on the eastern horizon. A northerly, I could probably call it the *meltemi* by now, was already ruffling the water and *Sea Dreams* was laying back on her anchor, not looking all that anxious to go anywhere. But the motor started without complaint and Ro drove her slowly forward as I carefully layered the anchor chain in the well. As we edged out of the tight passage a small group of horses was standing on the water's edge below the scrubby hillside, looking thoroughly dejected and sorry for themselves. It did look hard pickings. We motored through the quite narrow channel between the Greek island of Samos and the Turkish mainland and before lunch took a berth at the large marina at the bustling village of Kusadasi. In the morning we hired a car to explore a bit of the hinterland and the old imperial capital of Ephesus, which in Roman times was, like Miletus, a port city. Here too, the ocean has been swallowed by silt and now a broad plain lies between the city and the sea, and all that remains are the noble ruins. But what still stands of the library, the huge amphitheatre with a capacity of twenty-five thousand, the Temple to Hadrian and the Gate of Augustus gives some feeling of the grandeur of what once was.

By the 6th century BCE Ephesus, under the rule of King Croesus of Lydia was already one of the wealthiest cities in the world, rich in great works of art, a renowned centre of learning and home of the philosopher Heraclitus – '*no man ever steps in the same river twice, for its not the same river and he's not the same man*'. Meaning that all things are changing, and the one fundamental law of the cosmos was that everything was in a state of flux. Women in Ephesus had the same rights and privileges as men and, it is the site of a wonderful Temple of Artemis, another of the wonders of the ancient world.

For a time, it was incorporated into the Persian Empire before being liberated by Alexander. In 129 BCE it was bequeathed to the Roman Empire by King Attalos of Pergamon and by the 1st century CE it was recognised as the most important trading centre in Asia as well as remaining a leading centre of learning. Paul preached here during his third mission, and although he was 'booed' out of the theatre, possibly he was not too popular with the wealthy citizens of this very wealthy city. Both the Virgin Mary and St. John are reputed to have lived here at some time after the crucifixion, her house still stands and can be visited, as does St. John's Basilica built later in the 6th century.

The Emperor Augustus made the city the capital of Asia in 27 BCE and according to the historian Strabo, it was second in importance and size only to Rome. The city remained rich and powerful, until under Emperor Theodosius, Christianity became the only legal religion of the empire. Then the temples and schools were closed, and the rights and freedoms of women curtailed. Worship of the old gods and, scientific thought that contradicted God's omnipotence was forbidden, and the marvellous Temple of Artemis was destroyed by a Christian mob. It did remain an important port in the early period of the Eastern Roman Empire, but gradually fell into decay as the harbour silted up, and here and elsewhere in the Empire the citizens awaited the second coming of Jesus. The strong mystical message of Christianity supplanted reason and logic.

The great old philosophers who had steered mankind towards the path of reason and logic would have been appalled that they had lost out to the drug-like appeal of spiritualism. Which, before long was manipulated to allow powerful kings, sultans and emperors to rule by Divine Right.

The *meltemi* had been gradually building over the last weeks and every mile north was now a battle. The wind hugged the coastline close, bending around the rocky points and blowing into any bay that was not very deeply indented and almost totally protected from the north. The thick pine forests of the south had gone, replaced by low rocky hills sparsely covered with patches of scrub clinging to the thin soil. We spent two nights at anchor outside the harbour at Sigacik Hamami. The cloudless blue sky had returned, and the brightly painted fishing boats in the small stone harbour sparkled in appreciation, while fishermen and their families gossiped, worked on their nets and were pleased to know where we came from as so many had relatives in Australia. We visited the ruins of the ancient city of Teos a short drive to the south, which enjoyed wonderful views over the shimmering ocean, and returned for a feast of the local catch, as a golden sun dropped below the glowing horizon. Pushing on we investigated some deserted bays that looked interesting on the chart but, turned out to be taken over by fish farms. We got as far as dropping our anchor in one of them but, were a bit disconcerted by the sounds of rifle shots coming from some shanties built out over the water. They were almost certainly scaring off birds, but it had that effect on us and we set off again, looking for a more peaceful spot. A little further on, past some fishermen pulling nets, there was a deep bay adjacent to the village of Alacati, which proved to be a beautiful and friendly place and proud of their wine-making tradition. The bay however was one of the windiest places on earth and, as I was not very happy about going ashore and leaving *Sea Dreams* at anchor, we moved on after one night.

Not far away, nestling below an imposing castle on the Gulf of Cesme and opposite the Greek island of Chios, was the village of Cesme, offering a welcome haven from the *meltemi*. There was a comfortable marina enclosed within its own westernised shopping precinct. It was adjacent to the old town, which had a number of very inviting restaurants, where we dined royally on a few occasions as we waited, hoping the *meltemi* would abate enough for us to get on our way. You would like a recipe?

Beef Kofka with Saffron Yoghurt. Mix into a paste the following ingredients; minced beef with finely chopped parsley, onion, coriander, cumin, paprika, allspice, salt and pepper, egg and flour. Form into sausage shapes moulded to skewers. Brush with oil while cooking over a hot plate or grill. Serve topped with saffron yoghurt made from mixing saffron threads in hot milk, combining with yoghurt and coriander. Simple and tasty.

There was a large market not far off with a huge array of vegetables, including some varieties we had no idea even existed. Plenty of good-hearted banter at my ignorance. Everything had the special taste of having been picked ripe that day before dawn and was delicious.

... Cesme Marina from the castle...Chios on the horizon ... a welcome haven from the meltemi...

It was very comfortable in the marina, but the wind was now really howling down the strait between Chios and the mainland, and we started to wonder if we would ever get out. The current plan was that we would meet Charlotte and the kids at Ayvalik, which was still a little further along the coast. On the charts it looked to be an ideal archipelago for us to potter in. But with this wind, we were starting to wonder.

The forecast stayed windy, but eventually we decided we had to brave the magically blue, but boisterous, sea. By the time we were clear of the marina it was blowing twenty-five knots, gusting well over thirty, with a fast-moving chop. We could only make about three knots, so progress was slow, wet and uncomfortable. After clearing some ugly reefs covered with breaking waves and an evil-looking small island which as always seemed to come uncomfortably close downwind as we edged past. Eventually we managed to get a bit of mainsail up and it started to feel as if we would get somewhere. However, by late morning we were tired of the battle and decided to anchor in a reasonably protected bay on the south coast of Kuecuek Island.

There was no sign of life until towards dusk, when we were joined by a fishing boat, who seemed a bit perplexed to have our company. We were also wondering what we were doing in this forlorn and gusty spot. The next day was pretty much the same, only longer and more turbulent and we were very glad to be finally anchored in the northern corner of the bay at Foca.

We had planned to visit the city of Izmir, until recently known since antiquity, as Smyrna. But the wind and the thought of being jostled in a busy commercial harbour persuaded us to keep going north, Ayvalik was not far off now. Aeolus must have heard our prayers. The next day was blue and glimmering, the wind a moderate fifteen knots and for a nano-second we were tempted to go south to Izmir after all. But good sense prevailed, we hoisted all sails and cantered north. Across the mouth of the Gulf of Koerfezi with the Greek island of Lesbos beginning to take shape on our port quarter. The water was still a beguiling sapphire when we anchored in the channel inside Kalem Adasi in the late morning.

To say that the history of Greece has been a tragedy, in no way captures the utter calamity of it all. The collapse of the golden age that laid the foundations of all that is best in western civilisation. The abortion of the intellectual blossoming that had so much still to offer. The bravery of her defence against the invading Persians, the glory of Alexander's empire and the spread of Hellenised culture throughout the Mediterranean. Then the horror and despair that followed for the next two and a half thousand years. The enduring subjugation to Macedon, Rome, Constantinople, and on the fall of that city, to the Muslims.

The tragedy that begot the tragedy was one of the most

devastating wars of history, from which Greece never recovered. The Peloponnesian War fought between Athens and Sparta and their allies, from 431 to 405 BCE.

Once again, the idyllic setting, the now calm blue water and the cloudless sky, gave no hint of what had happened here. We were anchored pretty well on the spot where in 406 BCE the Battle of Arginusae, the most violent battle of the Peloponnesian War, involving over 270 triremes and 50,000 men was fought. The Athenians destroyed seventy-seven Spartan triremes for the loss of twenty-six of their own. On top of victories in a series of smaller battles it should have won Athens the war. But lurid stories of the abandonment of thousands of crews of the sunken Athenian ships left to drown in the stormy waters, filtered back to Athens. An uproar followed and the capricious Athenian mob, in a manner which had already cost them dearly and was a fatal weakness of their democracy, demanded bloody retribution against the admirals of their fleet. Six of the ten admirals involved – including Pericles' last son – were executed and the remainder fled into exile.

With the Spartan fleet gravely weakened, but preoccupied with their witch hunt, the Athenians failed to grasp the chance to utterly destroy their enemy. For some time, the Spartans had been receiving financial backing from the Persian Empire and employing mercenary crews. Within two years they were able to replace most of what they had lost and destroy the Athenian fleet at the Battle of Aegospotami only a few miles north of where we were, effectively giving the Spartans final victory in the Peloponnesian War. The Athenian command structure had been fatally weakened by the purge of their admirals, where-as the Spartans were led by their most brilliant commander, Lysander. Complacent after their recent victories the Athenians were caught off guard and the entire Athenian fleet was either sunk or captured.

Now with a huge fleet, Lysander did not miss his chance and headed south to Athens and its final subjugation. Imperial Athens was no more, democracy had brought its own demise.

By a quirk of fate one of the Athenian's most brilliant commanders, who had also been exiled, was watching the catastrophe unfold. Alcibiades had become a hero as a nineteen-year-old in the first battle of the war and, he went on to win dazzling victories and introduce brilliant innovations while still a young and charismatic man. But he was a man who made both venomous enemies and ardent supporters. He had engineered a disastrous expedition to Sicily and afterwards fled to Sparta to escape a certain death at the instigation of his political opponents. He conspired with the Persians against both Sparta and Athens. He was forgiven again and rehabilitated but, was unjustly blamed for a defeat at the battle of Notium in 406 BCE and banished again. With the Athenians, Spartans and Persians all seeking vengeance, no one had so many dangerous enemies. He was murdered not long afterwards. By whom, no one is sure. But some think it could have been a jealous husband or an irate father.

The power of his charisma is captured in a quote from Plutarch describing the feelings in Athens in the dreadful summer of 403 BCE, while the Spartans still occupied the ruined city.

'Nevertheless, despite their present plight, some vague hope yet prevailed that the affairs of the Athenians were not completely lost so long as Alcibiades was alive'.

But of course, by this time he was long since dead, along with around a third of the population and many, many thousands amongst her allies. The Athenian plain had been ravaged year after year, the city's wealth long gone and perhaps five hundred triremes had been sunk. And this mirrored most of Greece, where the long war had also destroyed the nations intellectual vigour.

Very hard, sitting in the back of the boat watching darkness fall, and not to be moved by these great ancient tragedies and wonder what could have been.

***

The wind was back with us the next day as we motored up the very narrow entrance into the large harbour at Ayvalik. It was indeed as beautiful as we had hoped. Lovely bays, some small villages nearby, the town itself with a large bazaar and plenty of good restaurants serving genuine Turkish fare1⁻ this was well off the tourist route for most westerners.

But . . . but . . . It was blasted by the wind roaring down from the mountainous hinterland. Perhaps it was not the place for a month with the grandchildren. But before we worried about that there was lots we had to explore. Leaving *Sea Dreams* on anchor was not an option so we took her into the marina, a short stroll from the bazaar and restaurants.

This area is dense with history from the earliest recorded times, and for clarity it is probably best to talk about things in some sort of chronological order. In fact, the world's earliest recorded saga from around 1300 BCE is partly set nearby. Jason and the Argonauts, a band of mythological Greek heroes in search of the *Golden Fleece*, sailed through the nearby Dardanelles and on to the Black Sea. Their boat the *Argo* is the world's oldest 'named' boat and was built and the expedition launched from modern day Volos, which we intend to visit in due course - so more later.

Next, the greatest event of Greek mythology/history the Trojan War, is believed to have been fought around 1200 BCE on the Asian shore a few miles away, where the ruins of an ancient city generally accepted as Troy have been discovered. The story is widely recounted in Greek literature, the most famous being Homer's the *Iliad* and the *Odyssey* composed perhaps around 7-8th centuries BCE. The story remains the world's most enduring epic/tragedy and I would be surprised if anyone reading this would be unaware of the details. The great city falls by trickery, is sacked and burned, the brave defenders including King Priam slaughtered after so many have already fallen. Achilles, Hector, Paris, Penthesilea the Queen of the Amazons die in battle, Odysseus is doomed to a decade of trials. Helen full of self-loathing and treachery at war's end has a clouded future with Menelaus. Agamemnon was murdered after returning home.

Of course, post-war, Odysseus was the lead in Homer's tales, and whose landfalls and adventures are the source of endless discussion. But in the end, he is not the one with the greatest part to play in history. This role certainly belongs to Prince Aeneas, a Trojan hero mentioned by Homer and also by Virgil and other Romans writing around 1st century BCE. He is the son of Prince Anchises and the goddess, Venus, and escapes from the sack of the city by sea with a group of survivors. He eventually leads them to Carthage and thence to Italy where he establishes a settlement at Alba Longa. Some hundreds of years later his descendants Romulus and Remus founded Rome. Julius Caesar's family claimed descent from Venus through Aeneas's son, Lulus, and went on to give the great Roman Empire its first Emperors. Romans are often accused of adopting the

Greek gods, but I think this legend, where they actually bring the old gods with them, is a better scenario.

So, our first expedition was to Troy, followed by a visit to the nearby site of the Battle of Granicus. The conquest of Alexander's empire is one of the most famous events of Greek history, and among the long cast of luminaries he is perhaps the greatest. In 334 BCE the first battle of his campaign to conquer the Persian Empire was fought a few miles away. Alexander was one of the greatest military leaders of all time and had had a meteoric ascent to power. He had been born in Pella in 356 BCE, the son of King Phillip II of Macedon and his wife, Olympias, the daughter of the king of Epirus. She was the fourth of Philip's eight wives. Some ancient accounts credit that Alexander was actually fathered by Zeus himself, when Olympias dreamt that her womb had been struck by lightning. From around the time he was twelve or thirteen, he and other noble Thracian youths including Ptolemy, the founder of the line of Egyptian kings who gave us Cleopatra - who would go on to become Alexander's generals and famous 'Companions,' were tutored by Aristotle. In payment Philip offered to rebuild Aristotle's hometown of Stageira which he had previously destroyed and to free the citizens who had been enslaved.

Around this time his father was offered a mighty black war horse with an impeccable Thracian pedigree. His father refused the horse as it was widely believed that the beast could never be tamed. However, Alexander was smitten by the mighty animal and begged his father to be given the chance to train it himself. And so began the most famous relationship between man and beast that history has recorded, and Bucephalus the most famous steed.

At sixteen, Alexander, who was regent of the kingdom while Philip was waging war against Byzantium, defeated a revolt of the Thracian Maedi. In 338 BCE he played an important role in the defeat of Athens and Thebes at the Battle of Chaeronea, which led to gaining control of most of the Greek city states and the announcement by Philip of his plans to attack the Persian Empire. On their return to Pella, Phillip fell in love and married Cleopatra Eurydice, the niece of his general Attalus. The marriage potentially jeopardized Alexander's position as heir, as a child from this marriage would be fully Macedonian, while Alexander was only half Macedonian. At the wedding a feud erupted, described by Plutarch.

'At the wedding of Cleopatra, who Philip fell in love with and married, she being much too young for him, her uncle Attalus in his drink desired the Macedonians to implore the gods to give them a lawful successor to the kingdom by his niece. This so irritated Alexander, that throwing one of the cups at his head, 'You villain,' he said, 'what, am I then a bastard?' Then Philip, taking Attalus's part, rose up and would have run his son through; but by good fortune for them both, either his over-hasty rage, or the wine he had drunk, made his foot slip, so he fell down on the floor. At which Alexander reproachfully insulted over him: 'See there,' said he, 'the man who makes preparations to pass out of Europe into Asia, overturned in passing from one seat to another.'

Alexander and his mother fled, but after six months peace was restored between father and son. But in 336 BCE Philip was assassinated by the captain of his bodyguards and Alexander was proclaimed king by the nobles and the army. He consolidated his power by executing potential rivals to the throne. His mother consolidated her position by having the young Cleopatra Eurydice and her daughter by Philip, Europa, burned alive. This sealed the fate of her powerful uncle, the general Attalus, although Alexander probably already considered him too dangerous to leave alive.

He now needed to take an army south to quell the stirrings of the Greek city-states. At Corinth he had a famous encounter with Diogenes the Cynic, whom Alexander asked what he could do for him. Disdainfully, the philosopher who had been laying naked beside the road, asked Alexander to stand a little to one side as he was blocking his sunlight. A reply that apparently tickled Alexander's sense of humour. Other quotes of Diogenes include.

'The foundation of every state is the education of its youth'

'We have two ears and one tongue so that we can listen more and talk less'

'In a rich man's house there is no place to spit but his face'

After having taken more steps to secure Greece and the northern borders of Thrace, Alexander crossed the Hellespont in 334 BCE with an army of approximately 48,000 soldiers, 6,000 cavalry and a fleet of 120 ships. He defeated a Persian army at the Battle of Granicus, accepted the surrender of the provincial capital and treasury of Sardis, before liberating the Greeks cities along the eastern shore of the Aegean. The next year he defeated a large

Persian army at the Battle of Isus. King Darius fled the battlefield leaving behind an immense treasure, his wife and two daughters and surrendering Syria and the coast of the Levant. In late 332 BCE Alexander marched into Egypt and the following year headed east into Mesopotamia where he again defeated Darius at the Battle of Gaugamela. Again, Darius fled, and Alexander moved on to Babylon, Susa than Persepolis.

The pursuit of Darius continued into Media and then Parthia. Before he could be captured Darius was murdered by his kinsman, Bessus, who was also murdered. Alexander continued marching east into Pakistan, defeating armies at the battles of Jaxartes and Gabai. At this point his empire extended from the Adriatic Sea to the Indus River, but two plots on Alexander's life were uncovered and the reprisals weakened the fabric of the *companions* and the army. In 323 BCE he invaded India, winning an important victory at the Battle of Hydaspes. The demands of his battle weary and homesick army eventually forced him to head home.

As Plutarch describes:

'As for the Macedonians, however, their struggle with Porus blunted their courage and stayed their further advance into India. For having had all they could do to repulse an enemy who mustered only twenty thousand infantry and two thousand horse, they violently opposed Alexander when he insisted on crossing the Ganges also, the width of which, as they learned, was thirty-two furlongs, its depth a hundred fathoms, while on the further side were covered with multitudes of men-at-arms and horsemen and elephants. For they were told that the kings of the Ganderites and Praesii were awaiting them with eighty thousand horsemen, two hundred thousand footmen, eight thousand chariots and six thousand war elephants.

Alexander died in Babylon, where he had intended to establish the capital of his empire, in 323 BCE. There are numerous versions of the cause of his death. The most commonly accepted being from malarial fever or, that eleven days after drinking a large bowl of wine he died with a fever and in agony. Alexander was married three times. Roxana, the daughter of Oxyartes, who he married for love and who bore him a son—Alexander IV of Macedonia, and two Persian princesses he married for political reasons, one of which may have given him another son, Herakles of Macedon. He had a close relationship with his friend and companion Hephaestion, although no ancient writer explicitly indicates it as sexual.

After his death both his empire and the Kingdom of Macedonia were wracked by civil war. The Empire was divided amongst his generals. In Macedonia his son, Alexander IV, and his wife, Roxana, were murdered, while his formidable mother, Olympias, was stoned to death by the families of some of her many victims.

But the legend of Alexander, by no means ends with his death. His body was placed in a gold anthropoid sarcophagus filled with honey, which itself was placed in a golden casket. While it was on its way to Macedonia it was seized by Ptolemy—who was almost certainly his half-brother, an illegitimate son of King Phillip II—and taken to Egypt. Pompey, Julius Caesar and Augustus were followed by many Roman emperors who visited his tomb in Alexandria where it was still on display into the 3rd century CE, before the tomb was sealed on the orders of Emperor Caracalla around 217 CE. Before this time, over five hundred years after his death, his tomb had become the greatest shrine in the Empire and, he had been deified by the Roman Senate and elevated to the Pantheon of the Gods.

There are no verifiable accounts of what became of his body and his tomb after 217 CE. Some theories are; it was destroyed during the periodic invasions of Egypt in the 3rd century or destroyed by the earthquake and tsunami of 365 CE or destroyed by Christians after the pagan gods were outlawed by the Emperor Theodosius in 391 CE.

But there is another theory which is I think, more suitable for the great man and god.

The theologian and historian, St. Jerome, writing a little after the widespread destruction of temples and shrines of the old religions precipitated by Theodosius's edict, first records the discovery of the mummified body and sarcophagus of St. Mark, in the vicinity of Alexander's old tomb. This is a little strange, as all previous historical accounts have him being cremated some three hundred years previously. Hundreds of years later this rediscovered mummified body was taken to Venice and interred in St. Marks's Cathedral. Alexanders body, the body of one of the old Roman Gods, enclosed in the tomb that was once the greatest shrine in the Roman Empire, would have been a prime target for destruction by the Christian mob. All the old temples in Egypt at this time were either destroyed or converted to Christian churches and the old priests driven out or stoned to death. Across the Empire the destruction has left the greatest archaeological record of any historical event. In one of the greatest acts of vandalism the world has ever seen, the last of the Library of Alexandria was burned.

Would Alexander's tomb have been safe from the Christian mob? Certainly not. But could his mummified body have been rebranded as that of the rediscovered St. Mark? Possibly. If so, he still lies in state in Saint Mark's Basilica, Venice.

***

...if you are lucky enough to be tied up at the marina at Ayvalik, it is only a short stroll along the waterfront to many fine traditional restaurants...Ro and a couple of Gulet captains...

Meanwhile, nearly two and a half thousand years later, the wind was still howling down from the northern mountains and battering *Sea Dreams* tied up in the Ayvalik marina. Now, wind can be a good or a bad thing on a yacht. Obviously, you need a bit of wind to sail from one place to the next, but it can become very annoying well before it becomes a gale, particularly if it is also raining. Whether you are anchored or tied up at a quay or marina you cop it much more than someone lounging in a fragrant courtyard or looking through a window that can be pulled closed. If it is hot, a sea breeze will cool things down, but if its already cool a sea breeze will be freezing. Sometimes, if the wind is howling you have no option but to hang on and put up with things. But, if you are lucky enough to be tied up at the marina at Ayvalik, it is only a short stroll along the waterfront to a substantial old brick complex, with a red tiled roof and intricate brick work, that is home to many fine traditional restaurants.

Most of which have verandas with pleasant views to the west over the broad expanse of the bay, and where the wind is moderated to a mere cooling zephyr. A fishing fleet ties up only a short cast away. The food was great, the hospitality warm, the company convivial, and we were only faced with the problem of not upsetting our hosts of the previous evening, by choosing his neighbour. Here is one of many seafood recipes we enjoyed:

Sauté fennel, cumin and garlic. Add tomato paste, *raki*, tomatoes, sugar, thyme, lemon peel, salt and pepper and simmer for 15 minutes. Add more water if needed. Divide the sauce into serve size dishes. Place fresh fish topped with squid and prawns in the dishes. Top with a layer of cheese and a few thyme leaves. Bake for around ten minutes until the seafood is just cooked. Melt butter with chopped chilies, add lemon juice, and spoon over the seafood as it comes out of the oven.

Going back in time again, if you are watching the scattered lights on the far shore in such an ancient place as Ayvalik, after enjoying a fine meal and enough local wine, is easy. But will it be an anti-climax? What can the past here offer, after what it has already given us? The death of Athens and democracy, the world's greatest epic by the world's most famous writer, and the great military genius who conquered the largest empire the world had seen.

Much, much more actually! The world's greatest city and how it was betrayed and rose again. The ultimate union of kings and gods and the rise to power of Christianity and Islam. Two of the most powerful women the world has seen and some of its most powerful men.

Not so far north of where we sat there was once, for nearly a thousand years before the Emperor Constantine the Great founded the new capital of the Roman Empire there, the small city of Byzantium. It occupied the promontory bounded by the south-western shore of the Bosphorus, and the inlet that became known as the Golden Horn. Constantinople was officially founded on 11 May 330 CE. It was the most important city in the world for fourteen hundred years, until in the seventeenth century when it was surpassed by London, the capital of the British Empire. Constantinople ruled the Roman Empire for a far longer period than Rome herself, and then rebranded as Istanbul, was the heart of the Ottoman Empire that had taken its borders into central Europe. Shortly afterwards, the Industrial Revolution and the conquest of the globe by western European fleets, changed the political/geographical map of the world.

Western history has never adequately acknowledged the debt we owe this great city. It ruled a newly created Christian empire for over a thousand years, but has come down to us through histories written in western Europe and Rome that seek to underplay her glory and immense contribution, and delegitimise her as only the *Byzantine Empire.* This is a term that was not applied until the 16th century, prior to that, to the world and the inhabitants of Constantinople, it was the Roman Empire. In our lexicon the term Byzantine has come to be derogative, implying tortuous faithlessness, murder and duplicity. Machiavellian at best. And certainly, there was this aspect to it. Even Constantine, who because of his role in establishing Christianity and creating this great city and is ranked by many as a figure only a rung below Jesus, murdered a wife and a son who he suspected of plotting against him. The numbers of murders, blinding's and decapitations carried out in pursuit of imperial power are beyond counting. Although perhaps not noticeably worse than in many other empires and nations and by no means in the same league as the rules of Stalin or Mao Ze Dung.

Constantine also introduced the political innovation that was to dominate the way Europe was to be ruled for the next millennium and a half. From this point onwards the heads of the Christian churches and the Emperors and Kings of the Christian nations ruled in an uneasy alliance. The Kings' were appointed by God and ruled by 'Divine Right' proclaimed by the clergy. The Kings provided the military power to ensure the clergy maintained a very rich and powerful position in a society where nearly all social contracts were in their control.

Without the bastion of Constantinople safeguarding the Asian border the weak armies of the small states of medieval Europe would have been swept aside by invasions from the east. After the invasion of Europe by the Norse and German tribes and the fall of Rome, the great intellectual, spiritual and artistic heritage of the Greeks and Romans would have been lost forever without the scholars and scribes of Constantinople, despite the flickering candles of isolated bishoprics that governed so much of darkened Europe.

'While western Europe struggled through the Dark Ages, Constantinople blazed with light as a bastion of Roman law, Greek culture and Christian spiritualism'. (Richard Fidler-Ghost Empire).

Over the next thousand years there were hundreds of Byzantine Emperors. Many of these emperors had a greater impact on western civilisation than any of the rulers in the West. Many were able rulers and commanders, but many were not. Some, along with Constantine, were awarded the epitaph *'great'*. Some deserved it, and some did not. To my mind the Emperor Theodosius I who ruled 347- 395, had a huge impact on our civilisation, but fits into the second category. He is revered by the Christian Church and is regarded as a saint by some of its branches, because he elevated Christianity to the position of being the only legal religion of the Empire. All other religions were outlawed and decreed as blasphemous, and the powers of state were devoted to their prosecution and eradication. From 391, for the first time in history people were categorized by their religion, and those not of the faith were regarded as enemies and under church doctrine any act seeking to subvert them, even murder, was justified and indeed commanded.

Theodosius's prostration before Bishop Ambrose of Milan represented, perhaps, the most significant turning point in the history of the Church and its rise to ultimate temporal power. It was the first time that, not just a Christian Prince, but the Emperor himself had publicly submitted to the judgement, condemnation and punishment of an authority which he recognised as higher than his own. Having grasped this powerful weapon, the Church would continue to wield it until the seventeenth century, when the bloody Christian wars of this period saw its grip weakened.

Theodosius was the last emperor to rule over both halves of the empire. Unable to expel the barbarian invaders he allowed settlement of "allies' within the borders, which sowed the seeds of disaster. He needed to recruit barbarians to fight barbarians. He issued decrees that outlawed all religions other than Nicene Christianity, the creed adopted in present day Iznik in 325 and 381, which affirms the co-essential divinity of the Holy Spirit, the Father and Son. His edict resulted in the obliteration of the old religions, but infinitely more important, the destruction of nearly a thousand years of the intellectual, philosophical and scientific knowledge that had been amassed since the time of Thales. This was the greatest act of intellectual vandalism, the greatest intellectual setback in the history of the human race. It would be over a millennium before the darkness could be lifted enough for it to be recognised that the world was not flat, and the second enlightenment ushered in a second age of reason.

The Temple of Apollo at Delphi, Hellenistic Temples throughout the Empire beyond count, were torn down. The Olympic Games was banned and the statue of Zeus at Olympia, another marvel of the ancient world, broken into rubble. The sculpture of Aphrodite at Knidos by Praxiteles the most beautiful and the most important sculptural work of man was stolen, leaving a mystery and loss that has saddened hearts for nearly two thousand years. Following his decree, a thousand years of intellectualism was destroyed as the old gods were being torn down. Any knowledge, any book, any mechanism or any person who denied, contradicted or question the Christian doctrine, was heretical and criminal. The wonderous temple of Serapeum in Alexandria, which housed part of the collection of the great Library of Alexandria was destroyed and the books burned on the orders of Theophilus, Bishop of Alexandria. In 415 CE his successor, Bishop Cyril incited a Christian mob to tear to pieces the greatest female philosopher, mathematician and astronomer of the ancient world, Hypatia.

If there is one event that bookends the end of the Classical Age of Intellectualism, it was this act of despicable barbarianism. In the west, for the next millennium, all the great *scholars* were Christian priests and their subject was mysticism—not science or philosophy. All things were as ordained by the great monotheistic Christian god, whose representatives on earth – the Roman Popes and the Emperors of the Western Holy Roman Empire and the Patriarchs of Constantinople and the Emperors of the Eastern Roman Empire in Constantinople—spent the millennium in mutual loathing and internecine warfare.

So, perhaps Theodosius I was not such a great Emperor.

Although Rome had been sacked a number of times previously

by northern tribesmen, the Western Roman Empire can said to have ended on 4th September 476 with the abdication of the emperor Romulus Augustus in favour of the Germanic general Flavius Odoacer, who proclaimed himself the first king of an independent kingdom which included Italy, although his capital was in Germany. It was not until the Frank, Charlemagne, was crowned Roman Emperor in 800, and when the Duke of Saxony was crowned as the first Holy Roman Emperor in 962 that western political and military power was re-established. Once Charlemagne was crowned there were two centres of Christian power—Byzantine in the east and, the uneasy alliance of the Holy Roman Emperor and the Pope in the west.

***

Less than two centuries after Theodosius the Empire was ruled by two historically and equally famous giants. The Emperor Justinian and his wife, Theodora. There are two descriptions of the Empress Theodora that have come down to us. In one she is cruel, venal and lustful, in the other pious, beautiful and loyal. She was born in Cypress c500 CE and reigned alongside Justinian the Great from 527 to 548. The daughter of a bear trainer and a dancer/actress she arrived in Constantinople as a child. Some say she worked in a brothel while still very young, others that she was just a sexually active actress. She must have been beautiful, for at the age of sixteen she accompanied the newly appointed governor to Libya. She later travelled to Alexandria where she converted to Christianity and by the age of twenty-two was back in Constantinople. Again, accounts differ. Was she a wool spinner living in a house near the palace, or did she meet Justinian in more intimate circumstances? In any case she must have become even more intoxicatingly beautiful and beguiling. By the time she was twenty-five she had married Justinian, the heir to the Empire's throne, and two years later she became Empress of the Eastern Roman Empire. She soon proved herself not just a beautiful dalliance but a wise councillor. During the Nika riots of 532 it looked as if Justinian might be thrown from the throne, but it was Theodora who had the spine to urge the Emperor to fight, advice that perhaps saved the Empire and Europe.

'My lord, the present situation is too serious to allow me to follow the convention that a woman should not speak at a man's council

... (but) flight is not the right course even if it should bring us to safety ... for one who has reigned it is intolerable to be a fugitive ... If you wish to save yourself, my lord, there is no difficulty. We are rich; over there is the sea, and yonder are the ships ... As for me ... royal purple is the noblest shroud.'

They decided to fight, thirty thousand rebels were killed, and the Empire was saved, to last for nearly one thousand more years. Justinian's legal code was completed and would go on to be the basis of the law in the west and many of their later colonies.

Although the city nearly destroyed it was rebuilt to greater splendour with ornaments such as the Hagia Sophia considered the epitome of Byzantine architecture and still one of the architectural wonders of the world. Theodora grew into a powerful figure in her own right, courtiers and officials prostrated themselves at her feet and sought her advice. She was a partner in the development of Justinian's legal reforms, closed the city's brothels, made pimping an offense and expanded women's rights. She died when she was about fifty, the most powerful women of her age. Justinian continued to rule until 565, when he was eighty-three.

Justinian justly deserves his traditional title, 'the Great'. He set out to reconquer the lost western half of the Roman Empire and in this he was largely successful. His generals reconquered the Vandal Empire of North Africa, the Ostrogothic Kingdom (Dalmatia, Sicily, Italy including Rome and Spain) and added the east coast of the Black Sea. He also secured the eastern frontier with the Persians.

But perhaps his most outstanding achievement was the unified legal code, the *Corpus Juris Civilis.* It was this codification of a thousand years of Roman law that was the basis of civil law in the west, although at times in the medieval period and during the Inquisitions it shared the stage with anarchy and canon law.

Could he have achieved so much without Theodora? He didn't think so.

His reign coincided with one of the deadliest plagues in history. Some twenty-five to fifty million people, perhaps a quarter of the world's population, died. The Empire was probably the worst effected, forty percent of Constantinople dying from the disease or famine. Plague recurred in the 6th 7th and 8th centuries and devastation badly weakened both the Roman and Persian Empires in the face of Islam. Also, of interest was an extreme cold-weather event in 535-536, perhaps the coldest in human history, which also brought widespread crop failure and famine. Tough times indeed, eased a little by his annual income of some forty tons of gold.

Two centuries later Constantinople, the greatest city in the world was saved from a Muslim invasion by a secret weapon, that enabled the Christians to utterly destroy a huge invasion fleet and, win one of history's greatest victories.

Muhammad, an Arabic tribesman, was born in Mecca in 570 CE. His tribe worshipped Allah, the supreme God, and a number of his daughters who were lesser goddesses. As a young man he travelled in trading caravans between Mecca and Syria where he was introduced to Jewish and Christian teachings. One night the Archangel Gabriel revealed to Muhammad that he was the prophet of God and he was to spread his divine word, by sword if necessary. After Muhammad died in 632 CE campaigns were launched against the plague weakened Roman and Persian Empires. *'We went to meet them with small abilities and weak forces, and God made us triumph and gave us possession of their territories.'*

Muslim power spread rapidly, westward along the North African coast and northward to Constantinople. The city was unsuccessfully attacked in 674-78 and in 717-18 it was attacked again. Initially by a 100,000 strong army and a fleet of 1800 war galleys, which was later reinforced by another army and a further 800 galleys. In one of the greatest military disasters of all time only five galleys survived the siege. At this time Constantinople was ruled by Emperor Leo III, who proved to be a most astute diplomat and antagonist. Although his skills certainly helped save the city, it was the mighty walls and one of history's greatest and most secret military inventions that decimated the Muslim fleet. It became known as Greek Fire and was the precursor to the modern-day flame thrower and mounted in the Roman galleys was capable of spewing a flaming liquid on the opposing galleys. The mechanical aspects such as the pump to propel the liquid and the metal work of the weapon had been well understood by Greek engineers for centuries, but the chemical composition of the liquid has remained one of history's mysterious secrets—though of course there have been many imitations. It enabled the Romans to control the Sea of Marmaris for several hundred years – until gunpowder and canon again changed the nature of warfare. Of course, there were serious limitations in employing

Greek Fire but the particular nature of the Sea of Marmaris suited it. During the sailing season the wind and current are always from the north and ideally suited for sorties from the secure port inside the Golden Horn. The timing and conditions could always be at the Roman's choice, and many of the vagaries of a battle at sea were taken out of play.

After this great victory the Empire went on to reclaim all of what is modern day Turkey. By 867 the so-called Macedonian Dynasty had reinvigorated the Empire. It was in an expansionist phase and stimulated a revival of the arts, sciences and philosophy.

...a quiet spot on the Asian shore of the Bosphorus...

***

There were continuing threat from across the borders and rarely a year without a military campaign. And in 1054 came the terminal crisis of the Great Schism between the Roman and Orthodox Churches, that was to split Christianity into two mutually despising camps for the next five hundred years. In 1071 an army was destroyed in Anatolia and the Emperor Romanus Diogenes captured and ransomed. It was the Empire's greatest disaster in 750 years. But within a hundred years it had reconquered most of Asia and was enjoying another renaissance.

During the First Crusade (1096-99) the Empire included most of the Aegean coast of modern-day Turkey. But the Crusaders and Popes were as antagonistic to the Byzantines as they were to Muslims, not-withstanding that from 1100 onwards there was sporadic warfare between the Empire and the Turks. Critically, relations with Venice over trade, and with the Papacy over doctrine grew more and more feral. Another bout of the plague devastated the city. In 1176 the Seljuk Turks were victorious in Anatolia. In 1187 the Saracens capture Jerusalem, which triggered the Third and Fourth Crusade (1202-4).

If you were to search history for the acts of greatest betrayal, the Fourth Crusade would most definitely make the short list. We touched on this crusade, which was mounted on the instigation of Pope Innocent III, in Volume One as it was leaving Venice. But just to recap. A prince of the Empire, Alexios Angelos, had offered the crusaders a fortune if they would depose the current Byzantine Emperor and place him on the throne. Its military leaders included Boniface of Montferrat, Baldwin of Flanders, Richard of Dampierre, Guy of Conflans, the Castellan of Bruges, the Seneschal of Champagne. The army was provided by the Kingdom of France including Burgundy, Blois, Champagne, Flanders, Saint-Pol, Ile-de-France, Amiens and the Holy Roman Empire, including Montferrat, Hainaut, Halberstadt. Reading through this list, it is pretty obvious that this crusade should be really known as 'The Frank's Crusade', although the ignominy must be shared with Venice and Rome.

The fleet comprised fifty war-galleys, dominated by the three most powerful vessels a float, the Paradiso, Aquila and Pellegrina. There were two hundred and forty troopships, seventy supply ships and one hundred and twenty cavalry transports.

'To the soldiers from France, Belgium or Germany, Constantinople was more than just a city, it was a myth and a mystery. The Russians called it Tsarigrad, Caesar's city, the Vikings Mickle Garth, the Mighty Town, and it had long before entered the legends of the west. Young men grew up with a vision of it. The city on the seven hills, the grand repository of classical civilisation – the greatest city of them all, rich beyond imagination, stuffed with

treasures new and ancient, where the wonders of ancient learning were cherished in magnificent libraries, where the supreme of Santa Sophia, the church of the Holy Wisdom, was more like a miracle than a work of man, where countless sacred relics were kept in a thousand lovely shrines, where the emperor of the Byzantines dressed himself in robes of gold and silver, surrounded himself with prodigies of art and craftsmanship, and lived in the greatest of all the palaces among the palaces of the earth, the Bucoleon. It was the City of the World's Desire. It was the God-Guarded city. It was the city of the Nicene Creed – 'Maker of heaven and earth, and all things visible and invisible!' (Byzantium – A Short History. John Julius Norwich)

The fleet eventually dropped anchor below the mighty walls of Constantinople, which in a thousand years had never been breached and had protected not just the city itself, but all of Europe. If an army could not cross the Bosphorus the only route to Europe was around the north of the Black Sea. The crusaders soon found that threats alone were not going to put a new Emperor on the throne, the only way to the vaults of the treasury would be to storm the impregnable city. The future of the crusade was on a sword edge. The army would starve, the Venetians faced bankruptcy and the Latin clergy would be thwarted. The crusaders proceeded to lay siege to the city and the bitter fighting began. At first it seemed that the crusaders would die before the mighty walls were conquered.

But the remarkable Venetian Doge, Enrico Dando, who was ninety-six years old and blind, led an assault that stormed the city walls from the rigging of their ships. The city was captured but the rewards promised by Alexios Angelos could not be paid. He was overthrown and a new Emperor installed, but he refused the promises of his predecessor. The crusaders stormed the city again. A savage and brutal sack followed, and a vast fortune was taken by the Crusaders.

In the words of a witness, Nicetas Choniates:

'They smashed the holy images and hurled the sacred relics of the Martyrs into places I am ashamed to mention, scattering everywhere the body and blood of the Saviour ...As for the profanation of the Great Church, they destroyed the high altar and shared the pieces among themselves ... they brought horses and mules into the Church, the better to carry off the holy vessels, and the pulpit, and the doors, and the furniture wherever it was to be found; and when some of

these beasts slipped and fell, they ran them through with their swords, fouling the church with their blood and ordure.' And

'A common harlot was enthroned in the Patriarch's chair, to hurl insults at Jesus Christ; and she sang bawdy songs, and danced immodestly in the holy place ... nor was their mercy shown to virtuous matrons, innocent maids or even virgins consecrated to God...'

The Empire was dismembered and much of it was distributed amongst the crusader lords, ensuring there would then be little to oppose the spread of the mighty Ottoman Empire. Subsequently the Ottomans captured Constantinople in 1453, and in 1529 and 1683 besieged Vienna, the capital of the Holy Roman Empire. If Vienna had been captured perhaps all of Europe would have fallen to the Muslims. The Venetians were rewarded with a number of strongholds, including Corfu which they ruled until 1797 and later Crete.

Many scholars believe that the sack of Constantinople was a greater loss to Western civilisation than the burning of the library at Alexander in the 4th century—also by Christians—or the sacking of Rome in the 5th century. Militarily and politically the damage was beyond calculation. The Empire was left powerless to defend itself from the Ottomans and halt the expansion of Islam, as well as placing the most strategically important city in the world in their hands.

Unlike in the case of the sacking of Zara there were no excommunications!

After the fall, the Balkans, Bulgaria, Serbia and Thessaly remained in turmoil and anarchy. Turkish pirates and marauders spread through Thrace and Bulgaria. By 1362 most of Thrace had gone and in 1371 the Serbian army was destroyed. In 1373 the Byzantine Emperor was forced to accept vassalage to the Ottoman Sultan. The old empire was effectively no more, although the Emperor still held court in Constantinople. In 1387 Thessalonica was captured by the Ottomans.

***

Then. On 5 April 1453 the twenty-year old Sultan Mehmet II, the most powerful ruler in the world, a multi-lingual scholar whose mother had been a Christian slave in his father's harem, led his eighty thousand strong army to the walls of Constantinople. Quite probably, on the way he would have camped close to where we sat at our table in Ayvalik, and enjoyed the same view across the harbour, and dreamed the greatest of all Muslim dreams—the capture of Constantinople. I wonder if he knew of Alexander and visited the near-by battlefield? He brought with him huge bronze cannons that had been cast by European armourers and which had already given him control of the Bosphorus. His huge armada was anchored beneath the walls of the city. Shawn of its Empire, nearly bankrupt and with less than seven thousand men to defend its walls, the city was only a ghostly shadow of what it had once been.

On 6 April the cannon opened fire and a portion of the wall was breached. But repeated assaults by the Muslim army were repulsed and during the night the wall was repaired. Mehmet decided that he needed to destroy a much wider section of the wall, so that he could use his huge numerical superiority on a wider front. The bombardment continued uninterrupted for the next forty-eight days. Meanwhile, enough Muslim galleys to give them control of the Golden Horn, were dragged on large cradles running on iron wheels and tracks over the hill separating the Horne from the Sea of Marmaris. This exposed another long stretch of the city's sea wall.

By late May the city was facing starvation, there was no sign of a relieving fleet, and many omens were fore-shadowing disaster. It seemed to the defenders that God had deserted them. In the darkness of the early hours of 29th May a major assault was launched. By daylight the walls had been taken, by noon the streets were running with blood, the city was being ransacked, its citizens raped and slaughtered.

As Mehmet wandered through the ruins of the Palace of the Emperors, founded by Constantine eleven and a half centuries before, he is recorded as reciting the lines of the Persian poet Saadi

.

'The spider weaves the curtains in the palace of the Caesars;
The owl calls the watches in the towers of Afrasiab'.

There are many rumours as to the fate of the Emperor Constantine XI, but most likely he died fighting beside his soldiers and was buried in an unmarked communal grave. The Turkish flag depicts the crescent of a waning moon, reminding all that the moon was in its last quarter when Constantinople fell.

Mehmet reigned until 1481, extending his Empire westwards as far as Bosnia and unifying Anatolia. He was a social and political reformer and is still regarded as a hero in modern day Turkey. He was married four times as a teenager and again when he was twenty-five, but his most famous romance was with Radu—the beautiful—Prince of Wallacia, brother of Vlad Dracula. He seems to have been easily upset when rebuffed romantically. It is recorded that he once demanded that his chief minister send him his fourteen-year-old son for his pleasure. When he was refused, he ordered the heads of the minister and his son to 'be placed on the banqueting table before him'.

In 1520, a thousand years after Justinian and Theodora, Constantinople, now known as Istanbul, was ruled by another couple whose fame and love has also been remembered by history. Sultan Suleyman the Magnificent and the Hurrem Sultan, also known as Roxelana. Suleyman the Magnificent, mighty Sultan and warlord definitely had a romantic side. Who amongst us would not be envious of this poem of love and praise of Roxelana?

'Throne of my lonely niche, my wealth, my love, my moonlight.
My most sincere friend, my confidant, my very existence, my Sultan, my one and only love.
The most beautiful among the beautiful ...
My springtime, my merry faced love, my daytime, my sweetheart, laughing leaf ...
My plants, my sweet, my rose, the only one that does not distress me in the world ...
My Istanbul, my Caraman, the earth of my Anatolia
My Badakhshan, my Bagdad and Khorasan
My woman of the beautiful hair, my love of the slanted brow, my love of eyes full of mischief ...
I'll sing your praises always
I, lover of the tormented heart, Muhibbi of the eyes full of tears, I am happy.'

Well, perhaps it is a bit on the soppy side.

Her story is a remarkable one. Roxelana began life as the daughter of an Orthodox priest living in a village in the Ukraine. As a young girl she was captured by Crimean Tartar raiders and sold into the slave trade. Her beauty was a very valuable commodity and she was taken to where it would attract the highest price— Istanbul. Here she caught the eye of Suleyman's mother—the Valide Sultan—who bought her as a present for him. She is believed to have been fifteen when she became Suleyman's concubine around 1520.

He became entranced with not just her beauty, but also her intoxicatingly cheerful nature and her wise advice—which he came to rely on more and more. She bore him five sons and in 1533/34 they were married in a magnificent ceremony. Never before had a former slave been elevated to the status of formal spouse, but she was also awarded the title of Haseki Sultan, the first consort to hold the title. She was Suleyman's chief adviser of state affairs and foreign policy and was recognised internationally as one of the most powerful women in the world. She was painted by Titian—La Sultana Rosso 1550—inspired music—including Joseph Haydn's Symphony No.63, an opera by Denys Sichynsky—ballet, plays, novels and more recently TV series. She died in 1558 and her mausoleum is adjacent to Suleyman's in the courtyard of the Suleynabiye Mosque. But within three centuries of Roxana enchanting Europe and while Suleyman was the most feared warlord in the world who appeared to be on the cusp of conquering all Europe, the Ottoman Empire was in serious decline and in 1914 it had become embroiled in World War I.

Back on *Sea Dreams*. Prior to our visit to Ayvalik we had spent quite a lot of time in Istanbul. We had ended a cruise from China there in 2006 and visited again the year we arrived in Turkey on *Sea Dreams* and left her in Marmaris for the winter. We had done a great loop around the back country, on their excellent bus service, and at the end spent a fortnight in the city. There after we would stay for a while whenever we flew in or out on the way to our boat. We never tired of wandering the streets, palaces and churches, discovering new restaurants, haunting the markets, inspecting the walls and vast underground caverns, and cruising to the Black Sea and the Sea of Marmaris in whatever was available. We have become fascinated by her story and must admit it is yet another place we have fallen in love with.

***

We had one more place we had to visit before we took *Sea Dreams* to sea again. The wind was still howling when we headed off by car for Anzac Cove on the western side of the Dardanelles. The wind was ripping down the channel as we crossed over, but by the time we reached Anzac Cove it was almost perfectly still. We had been back here a couple of times over the years, being driven down from Istanbul by drivers intent on scaring us witless. There is a memorial at Anzac Cove—and a reproduction not far from where we live in Canberra—with Kemal Ataturk's engraved words and despite our familiarity it almost always moves me close to tears.

...Mustafa Kemal Ataturk ... small informal memorials to him everywhere in Turkey...

Those heroes that shed their blood
And lost their lives
You are now lying in the soil of a friendly country
Therefore, rest in peace.
There is no difference between the Johnnies
And the Mehmets to us where they lie side by side

Here in this country of ours,
You, the mothers,
Who sent their sons from far away countries
Wipe away your tears,
Your sons are now lying in our bosom
And are in peace
After having lost their lives on this land they have
Become our sons as well.

The Dardanelles Campaign and the subsequent evolution of the Anzac legend has become a central tenet of how we Australians see ourselves as a nation. The bravery, loyalty and self-sacrifice of the men, and women who fought there have ennobled us for over a century. We honour and mourn them. But the campaign, of which the Anzac landings were the second act, was not just a defeat but a disaster. This has been recognised since before our soldiers were pulled off the beaches, leaving thousands and thousands of their dead comrades rotting in the shell-torn hills. Failure and death have added poignancy to the tragedy.

But how would we feel if we knew that all these lives were thrown carelessly away on an enterprise of which the planning, equipment, logistics and implementation was so bad that there was never any chance of success? And that this was recognised by all the competent military and naval experts who reviewed the plans before they were implemented.

But perhaps there was still a noble and vital reason for the sacrifice. But what if there wasn't? What if the lives of all our men were thrown away as a mere political gesture?

The historical rationale for the campaign was that it was needed to break the stalemate on the Western Front, and as a corollary, take pressure off Russia. Certainly, Russia's enthusiasm for the war was wavering and a separate peace which would release over a million German troops to the Western Front would be a disaster. But while Russia continued to believe there was a chance of achieving her greatest historical ambition, the control of the Bosphorus, she would continue to fight.

On the other hand, other than defeat by Germany, the last thing Britain wanted was Russian control of the Bosphorus, giving its fleets unhindered access to the Mediterranean and changing the whole economic and political balance of Europe. Since the 18th century Britain and Russia had confronted each other on the borders of Asia, and they had fought the Crimean War over Russian expansion southwards. Thwarting Russian expansionism had been the second great constant in British foreign policy. At the outbreak of war, it had practically ushered two modern German warships into the Bosphorus, seemingly as insurance against a Russian assault.

The Gallipoli campaign was also a bloody disaster for the Turkish forces who suffered a quarter of a million casualties defending their country. Prior to the war Turkey sought to align itself with the allies but had been diplomatically rebuffed by Britain, who subsequently impounded two state of the art 'Dreadnoughts' which had been built in England and had already been paid for—leaving Turkey vulnerable to Russian ambitions to control the Bosphorus and pushing her into the German camp.

Why did Britain shun Turkey? Was it because Britain recognised that for Russians to fight alongside the allies in a war against Germany, she should be encouraged to dream of gaining Constantinople? By late 1914 the quandary for Britain and France was how to maintain the illusion of supporting Russia's ambitions, while at the same time keeping them out of Constantinople.

On 1 January 1915 a request for military assistance to relieve pressure on the Russian army in the Caucuses was received in London. However, even while this was being considered a major Turkish debacle was unfolding following a Russian victory at the Battle of Sarikamish, which rendered any military intervention at this time unnecessary. Never-the-less after discussing the request with Winston Churchill, Lord Kitchener replied

'Please assure the Grand Duke that steps will be taken to make a demonstration against the Turks'.

On 3 January the First Sea Lord, the very experienced and well-regarded Admiral Fisher informed Churchill that a naval attack on the Dardanelles could not succeed, unless it was supported by a large number of troops on both the Asian and European shores. Admiral Frederick Tudor, the Third Sea Lord gave the same advice and Admiral Jackson told Churchill he would be *'mad to try and get into the Sea of Marmora without having the Gallipoli peninsula held by our own troops and every gun on both sides of the Straits destroyed.'*

Despite this advice, approval for a naval assault was given by the

War Council on 13 January and a fleet dispatched to *'bombard and take the Gallipoli Peninsula with Constantinople as its objective.'* This was an absurd order, even Churchill the main protagonist for action had already conceded that little could be achieved without ground forces. A long-range bombardment on 19 February had little effect on the Turkish forts, which had among them over two hundred modern Krupp 6-inch and 14-inch guns, which were mobile, well concealed and protected from naval fire.

Meanwhile on 16 February criticism of the futility of a purely naval assault had reached such a pitch that the War Council agreed that 18,000 British and 34,000 Anzac troops should be placed on stand-by. The French Government agreed to provide another 20,000.

It was not until 18 March that a serious naval attack was made on the Straits. A fleet including thirteen battleships was ordered to force their way through to the Sea of Marmora. In one of the greatest debacles of British naval history, it was driven off before they could even reach the narrows. Their losses included three battleships sunk and three badly damaged, while the Turkish losses were a few artillery pieces. Their strong minefield was left untouched. The attack was a disaster, its total futility exposed, a futility that had been widely and vociferously recognised by a wide circle of naval experts. In terms of comparative losses, it was the worst result in British naval history, with perhaps the exception of the battle of Medway, which had been fought against the Dutch navy when the fleets were still comprised of sailing ships.

The navy played virtually no further part in the fighting.

Sixty-five days elapsed between the first naval bombardment and the assault across the beaches by allied troops on 25 April. Troops had been put on standby on 16 February and on 23 February General Birdwood was sent to assess the situation. His response was the same as that of the senior naval officers. The navy could not force the passage alone and would need to be supported by strong land forces. On 12 March Kitchener appointed General Sir Ian Hamilton to prepare a Mediterranean Expeditionary Force and he arrived at the island of Lemnos on 17 March and the next day made a preliminary reconnaissance of possible landing sites on the west coast. By this stage the Turks had had a month's warning of an impending invasion, any element of surprise was gone and, troops were digging-in and laying barbed wire.

At this time no operational or logistic planning had been carried out and there was virtually no military intelligence available about Gallipoli and the Turkish forces defending it. Various commanders had suggested that between 130,000 and 200,000 men would be needed as part of a combined operation but, only 75,000 poorly equipped soldiers scattered all over the Mediterranean had been allotted. General Hamilton advised Kitchener that only a combined attack stood any chance of success, but subsequently no plan for such was considered by the War Council.

General Hamilton arrived back on Lemnos on 8 April from overseeing the shambolic preparations in Egypt and wrote to Kitchener that his commanders could now see all the difficulties with *'extraordinary perspicacity'* and *'would each apparently a thousand times sooner do anything except what we are about to do.'* And *'the truth is, every one of these fellows agrees in his heart ... that the landing is impossible.'*

On the morning of 25 April, the landings went ahead, unsupported by naval action, and the anticipated carnage ensued. The allies managed to land 30,000 men, suffered 20,000 casualties and gained a foothold. A British journalist Ellis Ashmead-Bartlett noted:

At Anzac any further advance is out of the question ... no army has ever found itself dumped in a more impossible or ludicrous position, shut in all sides by hills, and having no point from which it can debouch for an attack, except climbing up them.'

The total casualties were Britain, 73,485. Australia, 28,150. France, 27,000. New Zealand, 7,991, India— 4779. Ottoman Empire, 251,309.

Virtually no competent naval officer thought an unsupported naval attack could succeed. No competent military officer thought an unsupported military assault could succeed. No combined operation was planned or implemented when it was only this option that had any chance of success. Why was this shambolically conceived, organised and implemented campaign ever allowed to proceed? Why were the lives of so many brave, determined and loyal soldiers thrown away?

Was it all just *'...a demonstration against the Turks...'* to keep the Russians happy?

It was with sombre thoughts that we drove back to Ayvalik. Sombre, bordering on disgust by thoughts that so many young men's lives may have been carelessly thrown away by those for whom they fought.

During our travels in Turkey we began to realise the regard in which Mustafa Kemal Ataturk, who was the commander of the Turkish troops at Gallipoli and, later President from 1923 to his death in 1938, was held. There were photographs and small informal memorials to him everywhere—in offices, in parks, amongst the paraphernalia of shoeshine stands and homes. Mostly private demonstrations of love, respect and affection for someone who had died seventy-five years before.

He was a tough commander at Gallipoli who shared the trenches with his men and was prepared to give his life as an example, to save his country.

'Men, I am not ordering you to attack. I am ordering you to die. In the time it takes us to die, other forces and commanders can come and take our place'. (Orders to 57th Infantry Regiment, Gallipoli 25 April 1915).

'If you don't have ammunition, you have bayonets! FIX BAYONETS!' (The same day).

Apart from his role at Gallipoli he led the Turkish forces in the so-called Turkish War of Independence, which preserved the nation from partition after the war, and went on to create a secular state and a dynamic modern country out of the ruins of the old Ottoman Empire. He was one of the great statesmen of the 20th century, and one of the few whose honour is still intact.

'In the face of knowledge, science, and the whole extent of radiant civilisation, I cannot accept the presence in Turkey's civilised community of people primitive enough to seek material and spiritual guidance of sheiks. The Turkish Republic cannot be a country of sheiks, dervishes and disciples'. (Ataturk 30 August 1925).

'To the women. Win for us the battle of education and you will do yet more for your country than we have been able to do. It is to you that I appeal.

To the men. If henceforward the women do not share in the social life of the nation, we shall never attain our full development. We shall remain irremediably backward, incapable of treating on equal terms with the civilizations of the west'. (Ataturk 4 October 1926).

...no army has ever found itself dumped in a more impossible or ludicrous position, shut in all sides by hills, and having no point from which it can debouch for an attack, except climbing up them...

~ THE AEGEAN ISLANDS ~

After lots of research it had been decided that our rendezvous with Charlotte and her boys, Hubie, Ru and Ferdi arriving from their home in Annecy in the French Alps would be at Diaporos Island on the Sithonia Peninsula in northern Greece. Ro had been assured of warm and gentle weather with no *meltemi,* white sandy beaches, great restaurants and all the vital indulgences required for our eldest daughter. After being misled by this sort of talk for most of my life, I was a bit dubious that the Greeks would be any more honest than all the others who had lied to me about the weather—but what could we do? It meant that we would have a run across the centre of the Aegean while the *meltemi* was at its strongest—but that was a cheap price to keep the girls happy. After that, it would be all downhill. Thank Zeus!

Not a moment too soon as far as I was concerned. If you are toiling on land, going uphill and downhill are both hard work but, at sea the downwind part is generally just plain good. For a start you can actually head towards where you want to go, none of this bothersome 'tacking' which can take you miles from where you want to be. When going downwind and the wind is gentle, all is serene, there is plenty of time to contemplate the joys of life and the sea. As it picks up so does the speed and the excitement. The exhilaration of harnessing its power, the flow of adrenalin from the knowledge that the waves gambolling past like playful Labradors nipping at your heels, could shortly become snarling Dobermans. We generally pull the sails down before it gets to this and look for a peaceful anchorage.

But first to the Greek island of Lesbos a short hop across a channel from Ayvalik. It is one of the larger Greek islands, close to Turkey but remote from Athens. It is quite famous, but not so much a holiday magnet as many of the southern islands. Since our visit it has been overrun with migrants and large refugee camps, which have largely destroyed the life on the island as we experienced it.

The capital, Mytilene, was an attractive port, with the usual Greek harbour lined with restaurants and groups of men drinking coffee and solving the problems of the world. The odd black-robed priest with two or three of—someone's—wives and a horde of young children. The island is justifiably famous as the home of the traditional Greek ouzo, which is interwoven with life on the island *'it has accompanied the islanders in their lives, giving courage, happiness and hope. It has been the drink of revolution.'* It is around 46% alcohol and on the island is distilled by *traditional methods,* scented and flavoured with anise and various herbs depending on the maker's taste. Most Greek tavernas offer a glass gratis at the end of a meal, as a means of guaranteeing happy customers—so we all have a debt of gratitude to this wonderful place.

...a small harbour on the north coast of Lesbos ... as the height of summer approached the rugged mountains were sprinkled with the green of olives and vineyards among the hardy scrub clinging to the ridgelines ...

Historically Mytilene has a somewhat rough reputation. In addition to the Barbarossas, the famous pirates who we will meet in a moment, it has been a renowned haven for brigands and marauders for much of its history. And it was for this reason that a young Julius Caesar was here in 81 BCE. Caesar feared for his life under the reign of terror of the dictator, Cornelius Sulla, and had thought it prudent to leave Rome while Sulla was in power. Mytilene had revolted against Rome and was also accused of aiding pirates. The twenty-year-old Caesar thought joining the army sent to punish the city would be a good career move, which could also keep him alive. It proved to be even better than that. In bitter fighting on the city walls his actions earned him the Roman's highest accolade for bravery, the Civic Crown. Otherwise known as the 'Grass Crown' it was awarded on the recommendation of the common soldiers fighting alongside. It entitled the recipient to many privileges, including membership of the Roman senate and to be recognised by applause on public occasions. A perfect launching pad for a young man with high ambitions.

The island itself was lovely. Dry as the height of summer approached, rugged mountains sprinkled with the green of olives and vineyards among the hardy scrub clinging to the ridgelines. Panoramic views across the water to the Turkish mainland or the distant horizon to the west, castles and cathedrals and bits and pieces of antiquity secreted here and there. From Mytilene we skirted the southern coast, poking our nose into two large bays, Kolpos Yeras and Kallonis Kolpos in search of calm anchorages, only to find that Aeolus still had his eye on us. Strong katabatic winds whistled over the mountains along the north coast and made for nervous nights.

In the 6th century BCE Lesbos was home to the poet, Sappho, who composed lyric poems written to be sung while accompanied by a flute or lyre. She was, and still is regarded as one of the world's greatest poets, writing about and capturing a world far different to ours. Reading her work does take you to her far distant time and place, to discover the emotions and passions we still live with, are timeless. Her works have primarily been seen to be for the enjoyment of women, but personally, I think that puts men in a very bad light. If her works are not universally loved, even without music, there is definitely something badly amiss with the world.

'Ode to Aphrodite'.

'*...and thou, gracious Vision,*
Leaned with face that smiled in immortal beauty,
Leaned to me and asked, 'What misfortunes threatened'
Why had I called ...?
What my frenzied heart craved in utter yearning,
Whom its wild desire would persuade to passion?
What disdainful charms, madly worshipped, slight thee?
Who wrongs you, Sappho?'

The Garden of the Nymphs.

'*Here reclined the Nymphs at the hour of twilight,*
Back in shadows dim of the cave, their golden
Sea-green eyes half lidded, up to their supple
Waists in water.
Sheltered once by ferns I espied them binding
Tresses long, the tint of lilac and orange;
Just beyond the shimmer of their bodies
Roseate glistened;
Deftly, then, they girdled their loins with garlands,
Linked with leaves luxuriant limb and shoulder;
On their breasts they bruised the red blood of roses
Fresh from the garden.'

Anacreon's Song

'*Sing the song while I, in the arms of Atthis,*
Seal her lips with a lover's fervor,
Breathe her breath and drink her sighs to the honeyed
Lull of melics'

After Sapho graced the island, it was another two thousand years before it produced two citizens of equal, perhaps even greater fame —but at the other end of the spectrum of humanity. In 1462 Lesbos was captured from the Genoese by the Ottomans. One of the Turkish officers was Yakup Aga who took as a wife, Katerina, the widow of a Christian Orthodox priest of Mytilene. This is probably a sanitised version of events, which omits how Katerina actually became a widow and the form of the proposal of marriage. In any case the union produced two daughters and four sons. Three of the brothers became notorious pirates who played important roles in developing Ottoman naval power all over the Mediterranean. The eldest, Oruc Reis became known in the west as Barbarossa, as did a younger brother Hayreddin and they took control of Algiers on behalf of the Sultan. From here they inflicted almost unimaginable damage on shipping and coastal villages and cities in the Western Mediterranean. Between 1530 and 1780 it is estimated that around one and a quarter million Europeans were enslaved by Ottoman pirates, the numbers killed at least as much again, the numbers displaced and starving uncounted, the destruction completely incomprehensible.

***

We had been waiting, optimistically, for a break in the weather. So, on a morning when less robust winds were forecast, we cast the beautiful island of Lesbos behind and set sail for Lemnos, more or less halfway to the coast of northern Greece. It was a broad reach the whole way, the wind fifteen to twenty knots on our beam, the water sparkling, laced with dancing white crests, the sky a cloudless blue. We reefed the genoa and mainsail and danced along at seven to eight knots, leaving the helm to the autopilot. Bliss. We spent an interesting hour or so crossing the busy shipping route in and out of the Bosphorus. At one time there would have been over a dozen cargo ships in sight, and more on the radar, all travelling at different speeds and with absolutely no intention of doing anything whatsoever to avoid a slow-moving Australian yacht.

Before long the mountains of our destination were in view and in late afternoon we were skirting around the south coast, the bare ridgelines framed by a still cloudless pale blue sky. The boisterous waves of the crossing began to flatten as we got into the lee of the land. In World War I the allied headquarters for the Gallipoli Campaign was located in the huge bay of Moudros and at times up to three hundred warships were anchored here. We nosed into the bay and by the time we anchored the sun was setting and there was not a boat to be seen. The only signs of life were the scattered lights of a small village on the distant shore. Knowing its history, there was for us a haunted feel. The thousands who came through heading to hell, the thousands who came back physically and emotionally scarred, leaving the bodies of their mates behind. The senior officers who sent so many to their death would have lounged around here. Some in comfortable cabins aboard some warship, the less important among the tent city around the shoreline.

Lemnos first appears on the historical record as the first port of call for Jason and the Argonauts on their search for the Golden Fleece—the oldest saga in western literature. But it is quite a long hop from their start point at Volos to here, and it would be surprising if they did not have a break at the charming Sporades Islands on the way. Anyway, they did stop here to discover, to their pleasant surprise, that the island was inhabited only by women, lustful women. This made the stopover longer than planned and by the time the sailors left a new tribe had been created. Why was it inhabited only by women? They had killed all their men because of complaints about the girls' body odour and, had also cavorted with those loose harlots from Thrace. The same fate was planned for the Argonauts, but they were too smart for the girls, or just lucky, depending on what version you like. The island sits on what was once the main trade route between Constantinople and Europe and was strategically important for all the great maritime powers of the middle ages—particularly Venice and Constantinople.

In the morning we motored around to Mirina, the capital of the island and anchored in the small harbour below an imposing Byzantine castle. While it was still cool and clear we strolled through the delightful town and struggled up the hill to the top of the castle walls, to be greeted by yet another unforgettable view. Peeking over the horizon, eighty kilometres away, was the mighty pyramid of Mount Athos. Below, the colourful houses of the village were watched over by an imposing monastery on the facing headland. Tough brown hills rolled away to the north and east, interspersed by patches of garden and vines. In the evening we enjoyed excellent seafood at the *Taverna Glaros,* overlooking the marina. The fish was straight off one of the boats beside our table. Our wine was from local vines, a local cheese, *Kalathaki Limnou,* for which the island is famous and made from goat and sheep milk, a lush salad with figs and olives. All very simple, very fresh and very tasty—the smell of the sea, the aroma of the wood fires. Spoils you for everything else really, including the pretensions of much of cosmopolitan dining.

As usual we were up while the sun was still thinking about it. But, by the time we were outside with our sails filled nicely by the fresh northerly, its rim was peeping over the stern horizon. As the sun rose, so did our spirits, the sea shed its greyness and became its blue and sparkling best and white caps began to dance among the waves.

...fish was straight off one of the boats beside our table... wine was from local vines... a local cheese, Kalathaki Limnou, made from goat and sheep milk... all very simple...the smell of the sea, the aroma of the wood fires...spoils you for everything else really, including the pretensions of much of cosmopolitan dining...

The sun climbed higher, the great circle of our horizon hardened into a clear line etched across the rim of the pale blue sky, and dead ahead the pinnacle of Mount Athos began to rise into view. The wind stayed steady, giving us a broad reach with the occasional burst of spray flicking over the starboard bow. Breakfast, lunch, the overwhelming majesty of the mountain growing before us. By mid-afternoon we were under its dominating bulk, awed by its might and the beauty of the monasteries, great and small, sprinkled among the mighty crags.

Mount Athos Holy Mountain is a self-governing monastic republic dedicated to prayer, chastity and pure untarnished Orthodoxy. St Euthymius of Salonica established the first monastery in the 9th century. Some two hundred years later there were already many monasteries, but the monks had earned themselves a licentious reputation by debauching the local women who came to sell things the monks enjoyed, as well as food and wine. Their doings came to the ears of the devout Byzantine Emperor, who decreed that henceforth nothing female—no woman, cow or bitch could enter the limits of the Holy Mountain. At the council of Florence in 1439 it was the Athonite monks who refused to agree on uniting the Catholic and Orthodox Churches in return for Western military assistance against the Ottomans. This insured the purity of the Orthodox doctrine but, preserved the debilitating religious schism between East and West and within two decades, the fall of Constantinople. This blind pride in their creed, and suspicion of others, probably still defines their theology.

'They have long memories on Athos, and if the monks have never forgiven the Papacy for authorizing the ransacking of Constantinople during the Fourth Crusade over eight hundred years ago, they have certainly not forgotten the 19th century bibliophiles who decimated the libraries of Athos only a century ago ... the Abbot thinks the present Pope is the Antichrist and his mother is the whore of Babylon ...' William Dalrymple. From the Holy Mountain.

These days there are a number of organised tours of the peninsula and the monasteries. They will enable you to peer back in time for over a thousand years into a most remarkable institution, set in such breathtaking beauty, that for this reason alone, you will have memories for as long as you live.

The sun was starting to slide behind the Thracian mountains as we carefully edged into the narrow entrance to the bay behind Diaporos Island. Not too many yachts come here. Unless you are actually circumnavigating the Aegean, it is very much out of the way, and quite a challenging sail if you are coming north along the Greek coast against the prevailing winds. But if you do arrive one way or the other, you have found paradise. Most days you can avoid having to share one of the dozen or so anchorages with anyone, other than perhaps one of the local fishermen in their small brightly painted boats. On the adjoining mainland there are a couple of villages for supplies and a few tavernas on a sandy beach where the water actually laps at the feet of your table. You are out of the worst of the *meltemi,* although there is the odd thunderstorm in late summer and the occasional north westerly barrelling down from the Thracian hinterland. Mount Olympia, where all the old gods hang out from time to time is not far off, so you have to expect a bit of hubris to come your way. The water is exquisite, the sandy bottom a gleaming pristine white, making the chore of diving down to inspect the anchor a pleasure.

Everyone we met was relaxed and friendly. This included the local police who could not be bothered interrupting their afternoon game of cards to complete the normal formalities for arriving yachts. A local, who we did not meet until we later sought him out to thank him for his generosity, sent half a case of his own wine out to *Sea Dreams*. He had seen the flag and had a brother in Melbourne. An English family we met had been returning to the island for thirty years after being adopted by a local farmer. We also spent some happy times with Bruno Germanaz, a retired Michelin star chef, and his delightful Australian wife, Judy, on their lovely yacht *Pacific Pearl* where Bruno cooked us up some scrumptious feasts.

...most days you can avoid having to share one of the dozen or so anchorages with anyone, other than perhaps one of the local fishermen in their small brightly painted boats...

We spent the best part of a month here, and had serious thoughts, again, of migrating and buying a getaway on one of the islands. We probably would have but, kept coming back to the main stumbling block. Would it be remotely possible that we would live long enough to complete the long, intricate and baffling process of acquiring a house in Greece? And ensuring there was not some ancient covenant over the title, which meant some relative of the brother of a previous owner two hundred and fifty years ago, had the rights to the grape harvest, or the olives or any of the problems associated with fights over who really owned the property etc. Title records are not too flash in much of Greece. In any case, we became distracted by guests.

Godfrey and Kirsty Esmonde arrived from Australia, followed by Charlotte, Hubie, Ru, and Ferdie from Annecy. With the team on board we started heading south again, calling into the wonderful Porto Koufos, where a narrow entrance through steep rocky headlands leads to perfectly protected anchorages. One is tucked up in the western corner adjacent to a couple of hospitable tavernas. Their seafood comes from the fishing boats operating out of a small jetty and their inexpensive wine from the extensive vineyards in the surrounding hills. Very much my sort of place. At the other end of the bay was a quite posh resort with fine dining, beauty parlours, spas, masseuses and hairdressers—a bit expensive and full of gold-chained eastern European oligarchs, but otherwise perfect for the princesses on board. There were lots of water sports for the younger members, so with a couple of trips to the ancient city of Thessaloniki and Pella the birthplace of Phillip II and Alexander the Great thrown in, everyone was happy most of the time.

With autumn rapidly approaching, the French family headed home, to be replaced by the Welsh choir of Ro's nephew Andrew Rosewarne and family. We enjoyed another pleasant sixty mile downwind run to a bay on the west coast of the island of Kyra Panagia, the northernmost of the Sporades Islands. A calm night with no other yachts in sight. In the morning the breeze began picking up a little from the northwest and we planned a peaceful amble across to neighbouring Alonnisos island. We were only halfway across the intervening channel when the gentle breeze began to snarl a little, bringing with it streaks of chasing cloud. The day was suddenly sullen, and we were very happy when we found some shelter in the lee of the island. The wind continued to build, we brought in the sails and hugged the coast looking for a snug spot to anchor. By the time we reached Ormos Milia, a deep sandy bay with protection from the north and west, the wind was gusting over forty knots and the forecast was for stronger winds overnight. I thought two anchors would be best.

I have often boasted of our mighty thirty-five kilogram 'spade anchor', which in terms of my affection for things onboard, comes only slightly after my wife. It is probably big enough for a yacht twice our size. Generally, if it is dug in on a good bottom with plenty of our heavy chain out, there is very little chance of us going anywhere. But we do carry a couple of spares, including a twenty-five kilogram Delta tied to the pull-pit for emergencies or for those rare occasions where a second anchor seems a sensible idea. The most common method of deploying two anchors is to drop them the same distance in front of the bow, but some distance apart, so that the chains run back at an angle of around forty-five degrees. This requires a bit of mucking around when you are setting them, makes them hard to pull up and, if the wind changes, they will probably get tangled. But Bruno—a Frenchman, I must admit—had shown me a far better way. The primary anchor is set with, say, thirty metres of chain. The second anchor is attached to the primary anchor chain by two or three metres of chain and lifted overboard so that it hangs off the main chain. A length of floating rope has been attached to the head of the second anchor. The main anchor chain is let out, taking the second anchor with it, so that the two anchors are in line, say, forty and seventy metres from the bow. Very effective holding and easy to retrieve the second anchor. Simply pull in the chain. When the floating rope appears, pull the second anchor onboard and unshackle it. Continue retrieving the main anchor.

Anyway, when the somewhat sleepless night of fifty knot winds was over, we were all glad we had gone to the extra trouble. Andrew, who spends a lot of time sailing off Wales and circumnavigates Ireland most years, said the wind was as bad as he had ever experienced at home.

In ancient times when galleys used to follow the Greek coast north towards Constantinople the Sporades Islands were known as 'the gateway to the winds.' Beyond here they entered the zone of the *meltemi* that blew a near constant gale during the summer sailing season. There are five major islands, with forested mountains decorated by picturesque white villages and lonely churches, and several, mostly deserted smaller islands. The most southern island

Skiathos is a lively and sophisticated *destination* with a direct airline service, so there were plenty of people around. Thankfully, they were mostly beautiful young things, not a soccer hooligan to be seen. We found a secure anchorage an easy dinghy ride from the waterfront esplanade, which is boisterous and fun after dark with a few dozen restaurants and lots of shopping. Skiathos was the backdrop for the movie, *Mama Mia*. Again, we thought we would like to live here, but the rapidly approaching autumn brought good sense and we reluctantly continued on.

When we arrived at Volos, we found a bustling university town with a number of hospitable restaurants and tavernas along an even more boisterous waterfront, which we enjoyed very much. The town was dominated by the magnificence of Mount Pelion, one of Greece's most spectacular mountains. Its slopes are densely covered with forests of beech, oak, maple, chestnut and plane trees. Hiking trails and stone paths lead through the lush greenery and breathtaking views, to mountaintops, springs and sparkling streams, captivating villages, orchards, coves of vibrant blue and deserted beaches. In winter there is skiing on the higher slopes. Traditional local cuisine specializes in hearty stews including *spentzofai*, a spicy dish of pork sausages, peppers and vegetables. The higher regions produce wines blended from Messenlikola Black, Sirah and Carignan, while on the lower slopes are more likely to be Roditis or Savatiano. As everywhere in Greece local, family and house wines are available in most restaurants.

It was once home to the *Argo*, the famous ship that carried Jason and the *Argonauts* on their search for the Golden Fleece. This saga is the oldest story in western literature and the *Argo* is the world's oldest named ship. The tale has been told since c1300 BCE. Jason's father, Aeolus, was usurped by his brother, Pelias. To safeguard his kingship of Iolcus, Pelias made sure that all of Aeolus's descendants were murdered, however by a ruse the baby, Jason, was spirited away to the forests of Mount Pelion, where he was raised by the wise centaur Chiron. Jason grew into a strong and able young man and was advised by an oracle to return to Iolcus. On the way home he won the support and affection of the goddess, Hera, who decided to help him reclaim his rightful throne.

When Jason arrived at Pelias's court, he found that his uncle was honouring the god, Poseidon, in the company of a number of other kings. This circumstance saved Jason's life, and instead Pelias swore to give him the throne if he succeeded in bringing home the Golden Fleece, a task that was universally believed to be a warrant of certain death. The Golden Fleece was located in the far distant land of Colchis where it was guarded by a dragon that never slept. Jason accepted the challenge and commissioned the building of the *Argo*. It was capable of making the voyage to what was the end of the known world and could carry eighty warriors. He assembled, with the aid of Hera, a band of mythical heroes, whose fame eclipses even that of the mighty warriors of the later Trojan War. It included Heracles—Hercules—a great-grandson of Zeus and the greatest of the Greek heroes, Theseus, who had defeated the minotaur, the huntress Atalanta, and the musician, Orpheus, whose names are as familiar to us now, as they were to the ancient Greeks three thousand years ago.

The Argonauts set off. After their adventures with the women of Lemnos, they sailed on to the land of the Doliones than battled the Gegeines, a tribe of six armed giants—who would have been very handy on a yacht for changing navigation lights etc. In Thrace they were confronted with the Harpies, then pressed on through the Symplegades, huge rock cliffs that crushed all who tried to pass through and eventually reached Colchis. King Aeetes of Colchis promised Jason the fleece if he could perform three tasks. Plough a field with fire-breathing oxen, then sow dragon's teeth which sprouted into warriors, who he then had to kill. And then take the fleece from the dragon who never sleeps. With the help of Hera and Aphrodite and the king's daughter, Medea, who had fallen in love with him, he was successful. But he was forced to flee with Medea when the king changed his mind about the fleece. They managed to escape by cutting up Medea's brother and throwing the pieces in the sea to slow down King Aeetes' pursuit.

The trip home was long and dangerous. Zeus sent storms as punishment for cutting up Medea's brother, they had to pass the Sirens—the same group who later tempted Odysseus—the giant Talos hurling huge stones. This was at Crete, because of the storms they were well off course! Eventually Jason made it back home, but as with most things Greek there were still tragedies and heartbreak to come.

While waiting out the wind in a lovely anchorage behind the

island of Dhiaporos on the Sithonia Peninsula we had become friendly with another cruising couple, Pippa and Rod from New Zealand. As winter approached, we decided not to rush back to our base in southern Turkey, and on Rod's recommendation booked *Sea Dreams* into a shipyard at Volos for the winter. A bit of research uncovered the fact that the shipyard was probably on the site where the *Argo* was built. Is it possible that this is the oldest shipyard in the world, in operation for over three thousand years?

Possibly. Certainly, there were more wrecks—seemingly from every epoch of history—than seaworthy yachts. And, we were 'pulled out' on a rickety trailer by an ancient tractor that looked as if it predated industrialisation, and it had to be hitched to an even older beast to get the job done. First impressions were certainly not good, but our doubts were assuaged by Gregory, a charming and handsome young man who had taken over from his parents and waived dismissively at the surrounding wrecks as a mere product of a bygone era. If we had any sense, we would have put *Sea Dreams* back in the water and braved the windy passage back to southern Turkey. But home was calling, and we had had enough of hanging on an anchor in violent winds with the yacht yawing savagely on a rigid anchor chain and threatening to throw herself ashore, for one year.

Once *Sea Dreams* was safely—we hoped—ensconced ashore and propped upright by a motley collection of poles, which Gregory assured us were safer than steel cradles in an earthquake we got to talking. He offered some great prices for a few jobs on the boat— repainting the hull, replacing the anchor chain and swivel and a few other bits and pieces. The prices were too good to be true, but despite our age and bitter experiences we were still basically optimists by nature and told him to go ahead. He promised all would be shipshape when we returned in the last week in April the next year.

We then spent two agonising days working our way through the bureaucratic mazes of customs, the police, the Port police and the Taxation Office before heading south to Athens, via one of the most famous sites in European history. The narrow pass between the sea and the mountains where the battle of Thermopylae, between 300 Spartans—assisted by 700 Thespians and 400 Thebans—and the Persian horde of King Xerxes was fought in 480 BCE. Modern estimates of the size of his army are in the hundreds of thousands, while ancient numbers are in the millions. The Greeks held off the invaders for seven days. Herodotus records that their weapons were smashed and broken from the slaughter, but they fought on with their bare hands and teeth and died to the last man as they were finally overwhelmed. Their example inspired Greece to their later decisive victories at Salamis and Plataea.

The battle is still honoured by two memorials on the site. The Leonidas Memorial, in honour of the Spartan king who fought and died beside his warriors. It is engraved with his response to Xerxes demand to lay down their weapons. One of history's most famous, one that has rung down through time and inspired countless others. *'Come and get them.'*

The second carries a verse from the poet Simonides and is one of history's most inspiring warrior epitaphs.

'Go tell the Spartans, stranger passing by,
that here, obedient to our laws, we lie.'

Unfortunately, the narrow defile and the images it has conjured has vanished. Today there is only a wide plain between the hills and the distant sea.

***

While we were home in Australia we stayed in touch with Gregory and he was fulsome in his praise of himself and how work was progressing. We returned to Europe in April for a much-anticipated stay in Venice with Charlotte, and we had only just settled in when we started getting emails from Gregory, suggesting we delay our arrival in Volos as he was running a little behind schedule. We managed to get a couple of extra days in Venice but in the end, we had no option but to head to Volos where there was plenty of accommodation that did not require us to entirely mortgage our future.

We checked into the same hotel on the waterfront and then set off to see what was happening with our yacht. I was feeling a bit irritable as my left knee, which was going to be replaced at the end of the year, was killing me. As was my jaw, where it turned out I needed root canal surgery. My irritability was transformed into a desire to throttle Gregory by the sight of *Sea Dreams*, sitting forlornly amongst the wreckage of the shipyard, apparently untouched and covered in a thick layer of dust. A check of the machinery revealed that nothing had been serviced, there was no sign of the new anchor chain. The one sign of progress was that it looked as if the hull had been sanded in preparation for painting, but it was so dusty it was hard to be sure.

An acrimonious meeting with Gregory. The weather had been bad, he explained with a shrug of the shoulders and no hint of remorse. Three weeks later we finally hit the water. The water maker did not work, and the generator impeller had not been changed and disintegrated as soon as it was started. More delays and a strong feeling of apprehension about the main engine. However, the hull looked fantastic and the new chain was good. I had used the delay to have my root canal surgery. This involved six visits to the dentist, a lady who operated her surgery singlehandedly behind a locked door with a peep hole, presumably to safeguard her drugs from the university's students. She was also the receptionist and dental nurse and carried out long and voluble conversations, over her mobile, with her husband, the local undertaker, while she had me strapped in.

I was very impressed by her work. Her operations caused only mild discomfort, and as I have an exceptionally low tolerance of pain, this was very pleasing. But after two weeks at sea the filling fell out and I spent the rest of the year with a large tender cavity. Once again, the price had been too good to be true. From the above it would be easy to imagine we were not enjoying Volos. This was not so and by the time we left we were, perhaps not in love, but certainly infatuated. We had a couple of great tours through the surrounding mountains, some excellent meals with perhaps a little too much to drink along the waterfront at night, to dull the pain of my ongoing surgery—of course.

However once *Sea Dreams* was afloat, we were anxious to get going. But, a big but, as it turned out. We still had to clear ourselves and the boat through the many layers of the local bureaucracy. Customs found a 900 Euro levy that had lain unused on the statute books for centuries—or at least since the EU was illegitimately born—and we were sent off to the Finance Department to pay it. They said we could not pay it unless we had a Greek tax file number. The Tax Office said we could not have a file number unless were residents. Immigration said we could not become residents until we had a residence and a tax file. These voluble circular arguments, in shouted Greek and English lasted the whole of one day, as we trudged between the various departments, spread out as widely as possible all over the city – while my leg was getting sorer and sorer. Finally, a file with the number 000000 was created for us by an imaginative clerk and we were able to pay—in cash of course—and we were given an effusive farewell. In retrospect we should have offered cash to the Finance Department in the first place, and it would probably have been over in five minutes.

Relieved to be finally underway, but still sad to be leaving the seductive bedlam of Volos, we headed south across the gulf to the broad expanse of our Aegean. A lovely day's run back to the familiar waters of Skiathos, where we spent the night, and then south towards unexplored mysteries. Nightfall of following day found us anchored in a cove adjacent to the village of Linaria on the island of Skyros. We spent the night on board and dinghied in to explore the island the next morning. The quay was just coming to life, and there were a handful of yachts anchored stern-in which looked as if they were nursing sore heads.

The island has at least two strong connections with antiquity. Theseus, after surviving all his adventures, including the Minotaur and the search for the Golden Fleece, finally met his end when he was thrown off a cliff by the local king. Achilles was here, enjoying a love affair and trying to avoid the Trojan War when he was tricked into fighting by Odysseus. He left a son behind when he sailed off to war. In modern times, the poet Rupert Brooke died here on 28 February 1915 while on his way to Gallipoli. He is one of the most admired poets of World War I and was once described as the most handsome young man in England. Perhaps his best-known work is:

The Soldier
If I should die, think only this of me:
That there's some corner of a foreign field
That is forever England. There shall be
In that rich earth a richer dust concealed;
A dust whom England bore, shaped, made aware,
Gave, once, her flowers to love, her ways to roam;
A body of England's, breathing English air,
Washed by the rivers, blessed by suns of home.
His tomb overlooks the sea and bears the following inscription.

*'Here lies the servant of God, Sub-lieutenant in the English Navy,
Who died for the deliverance of Constantinople from the Turks'.*

When we returned from tramping around the island and had selected the table with the best view back over the bay to *Sea Dreams*, Ro was made much of by the aging Lothario who was the proprietor. In fact, after his attentions while serving a fine dinner, I was relieved when she agreed to return to the boat with me.

The next day was a beautiful reach, a steady fifteen knots abeam and we scooted across the shimmering water, touched here and there by flecks of white. The grey mass of the island of Limni gradually sank below the starboard horizon and for a while we had the universe to ourselves. No sign of land, no yachts, no freighters, not even a bird interested in sharing our fate. I was trolling a line astern with what was reputed to be the world's most enticing lure, but as usual no fish were enticed. What would happen to Greek tavernas, I wondered, if I could catch my own fish.

We arrived at the snug harbour at Psara at the same time as the afternoon ferry, and we only just managed to find ourselves a spot to anchor with some protection behind the breakwater wall. Not much protection from a southerly though, if any of the gods felt like kicking us.

After settling in we strolled through town then followed a path leading south along a ridgeline to a high headland, with distant views in every direction. Late afternoon, the sun edging towards the horizon and bouncing warmly off the golden water. The breeze now only a gentle flutter. But again, the beauty belies yet another tragedy —at times it feels as if every square metre of land in the Aegean has been soaked in blood. And you are reminded, time and time again, just how brutal Greece's history has been.

In 1824 Greece's battle for independence from the Ottomans was underway, and across the far-flung land, in islands, villages and the rugged mountain ranges, Greeks, after over two thousand years of subjugation, were yet again sacrificing their lives for freedom. In June an Ottoman fleet arrived to put down the rebellion, and the islanders made their last stand in an old fort near where we now stood. Eventually the Turks stormed the walls. Seeing they were defeated the islanders exploded a great cache of gunpowder, sending themselves and many of the two thousand invaders to their doom.

Some of the population had managed to hide in the hills, but those that were captured were killed or sold into slavery. The island remained in Turkish hands until it was liberated by the Greek navy in 1912 during the First Balkan War. Many of the children orphaned in 1824 were gathered together and educated in the Orphanotropheio of the priest Theophilos Kairis, where the memories of their heritage were kept alive. A century later their descendants were among those who returned.

With a gentle wind on our beam we had a beautiful morning's sail across the intervening channel and anchored in a narrow bay on the island of Chios, not far from the beautiful old town of Mesta. There was one other yacht, a cluster of fishing boats, a couple of tavernas and a scattering of cottages. All was peaceful and well protected. In the afternoon we took the dinghy in for a poke around, and on the way home decided to give the outboard motor its first run of the season. It refused to start. Now, there is no doubt that outboard motors are unreliable and temperamental bits of rubbish, and if one decides not to work, I am the last person on earth to coax it back to life. I checked the fuel and the fuel line, that the spark plug was clean, and the carburettor was not flooded. Experts say these are what cause stoppages. However, they rarely solve the problem for me, despite the lots of advice that is always available on our boat. I think outboard motors are like horses and can sense when the rider doesn't know what he's doing. After we rowed back, I wasted an hour or so proving Einstein's theory of insanity—something along the lines of repeating things that do not work. Oh yes, and I probably did tell the motor what I thought of it, and Gregory from the Volos boatyard for that matter, for not servicing the bloody thing.

I was about to take a break when a youngish man, off a British registered yacht, rowed over and offered his assistance, which we gratefully accepted. He did exactly what I had already done fifteen times, but one pull of the starter and the motor emitted a throaty purr and ran with a steady beat. He stopped it, it restarted. He stopped and restarted again. Ro was gushingly impressed. I thought, one more pull and I would have had it, but also tried to look grateful. Most importantly we met Andy and Stef who have been friends ever since, and that night we enjoyed the first of many waterfront dinners together. The next day Ro dropped some precious knick-knack overboard in twelve metres, which is about eleven metres deeper than I can dive. Andy noticed the mishap and arrived with his scuba gear. Life can be hard at times.

On our way north the previous year we had spent a couple of nights on the island while *Sea Dreams* was safely tucked away in the marina at Cesme, on the adjacent Turkish coast. What we had seen had made us resolve to spend more time there on our way back south. Being a large rich island close to the Asian mainland has given it a long and tumultuous history. While on the island we had hopes of finding more clues to that great unknown, one that during our decade of sailing in the Mediterranean we had already gone to great lengths investigating. *'Who invented red wine?'* We were optimistic that we might find a clue here, for we knew that the Greek Historian Theopompus (c380-315 BCE) had offered the suggestion that it was actually discovered on Chios. But we were treading carefully. He was writing some six thousand years after the event, which is not exactly firsthand and, has been described by other historians as a *'man who wrote slander, not history'*. We realised we would need more evidence and could not accept his opinion at face value. But Chios has been inhabited since around ten thousand years BCE and most experts think red wine was invented around six to seven thousand years BCE. Most give the credit to Georgia or Iran. But who knows? Certainly, Chian wine—as it has been known by us connoisseurs—has been synonymous with excellence since the earliest times and was already exported to Gaul, Egypt and Russia by the 4th century BCE. So indeed, perhaps we were as close as we had come, so far, to the man who invented our favourite drink. But we made doubly sure we left no stone unturned. We investigated the ancient and artistically decorated village Pyrgi and dined around the old waterfront at Chios Harbour, where the ancient galleys would have been loaded with great clay amphoras full of the precious drink, riding low in the water as they set sail for distant ports. Alas, there were no new clues, but looking at the history it still looks a possible candidate.

By at least the 12th century BCE it was ruled by a monarchy and there is evidence of trade with the Greek mainland and the Levant. By the 7th century BCE, it was minting coins and had elements of democratic rule. But after that, even by Mediterranean standards, its history has been a bloody one. In 546 BCE it was incorporated into the Persian Empire and that began two and a half thousand years of fighting for its life. Against the Persians on several occasions, the Athenians during the Peloponnesian and Social Wars, the Macedonians, Romans, Byzantines, Genoese and in 1566 the Ottomans. During the Greek War of Independence, it was devastated by the Massacre of Chios in 1822 where the whole island was expelled, killed or enslaved by the Ottomans. It also, eventually rejoined Greece after the First Balkan War in 1912.

It was a brisk dawn when I came on deck. Already a fresh breeze had *Sea Dreams* tugging at her anchor chain, anxious to be off and the shoreline still held the soft grey of the last of the night. Behind the hills, the wispy clouds being chased southwards their tails tinged with pink, promised a boisterous day at sea. We were planning to be snuggly anchored in the port of Pythagoreio, on the south coast of Samos in time for drinks. I started the motor, checked the vital dials on the instrument panel, peered intently at the waterflow coming through the exhaust, and went forward to haul the anchor and to layer the chain in the anchor well as it came onboard. All, of course, under Ro's watchful eye.

After an exhilarating run under our large genoa, we were comfortably anchored in time to watch a golden sun sink below the shimmering horizon. Pythagoreio is built on the site of the ancient city of Samos. In those times it was a rich and powerful nautical state, but today it is just a beautiful Greek village, spilling down from the hills behind to a stone esplanade surrounding the startling blue water of the protected harbour. Yachts and fishing boats were moored stern-in to the promenade, overlooked by plenty of friendly tavernas and restaurants offering a wide choice of local wines and seafoods, cooked as they have been for thousands of years. In other words, it was heaven.

Nearly all Greek islands claim close connections with the gods, and this is certainly the case with Samos. According to legend the Queen of the gods, Hera was born under a sacred Lygos tree on the island, and she and Zeus celebrated their wedding nearby. From the 8th century BCE, a series of temples dedicated to her were built here and became important sites in the cult worship of Hera. Archaeological digs have discovered offerings from all over the Greek world and ivory carvings from Egypt. Unfortunately, earthquakes and the Byzantines have left only the ruins and, it is probably best to try and remember it as the historian Strabo (c64

BCE-24 CE) saw it.

'As one sails towards ... the Heraion which consists of an ancient temple and a great shrine ... the temple which is open to the sky, is likewise full of the most excellent statues. Of these, three of colossal size, the work of Myron stood on one base; Antony took these statues away, but Augustus Caesar restored two of them, those of Athena and Herakles ...'

There are nearly as many opinions of the goddess as there were mistresses of her husband Zeus. According to the Greek poet, Hesiod (c700 BCE) their marriage was *'after his seductions of the goddesses Metis, Themis, Eurynome, Demeter, Mnemosyne and Leto. Zeus then made Hera his blooming wife: and she was joined in love with the king of the gods and men and, brought forth Hebe and Ares and Eileithyia.* However, in Pindar's Olympian Ode it is claimed that the couple first slept together for three hundred years, contributing to culmination of the great love between the two. And to confuse things more, Homer describes her as jealous and conspiring, rather than affectionate and loving.

The observant reader will have already noted a connection between the name of the village and the famous mathematician, Pythagoras (c570-495 BCE) who was born here. As well as being perhaps the most famous ancient mathematician he was a philosopher who applied his theories to everyday issues, such as rules for living in harmony with others— 'yes, you are right, dear'- and, the natural world and the physical and psychological importance of diet.

The island was also the birthplace of another ancient scientist of almost equal standing, if not fame. **Aristarchus of Samos (c310-230 BCE) an astronomer and mathematician was the first to recognise that the sun was the centre of the known universe and that the earth and the other planets rotated around it**. He also suspected that the stars were other bodies like the Sun. Do I need to mention Galileo and the Roman inquisition of 1615 again, which found such thought was 'foolish and absurd in philosophy, and formally heretical since it explicitly contradicts in many places, the sense of the Holy Scripture'.

But we were here not only to honour the memory of these great man, or even just to follow Lord Byron's advice about enjoying the island:

'Fill high the bowl with Samian wine! ... It made Anacreon's song divine:'

No, we had come to visit another of the ancients' remarkable engineering feats. In the 6th century BCE, probably during the reign of Polycrates the famous tyrant of Samos, the thousand metre long tunnel of Eupalinos was constructed as an aqueduct to carry water under Mount Kastro to the city. It is history's first recorded example of using a geometrical approach to dig a tunnel from two ends and meeting in the middle. So, after lunch the next day we took ourselves off to the truly remarkable tunnel, paid homage to Hera and came back to the waterfront as the sun was getting close enough to the horizon, for us to obey Lord Byron's instructions about Samian wine, which along with everything else we had seen, was etched in our minds.

The wind was up when we left and with the motor ticking over and the mainsail reefed, we beat against it to the northern tip of Fournoi Island before turning south again and running under the genoa through the channel between Fournoi and Thimena islands. We passed below a magnificent blue domed monastery perched on a high bluff on Thimena, before turning into a deserted bay on the western shore of Fournoi and anchoring. Not a soul to be seen, though a small flock of goats fossicking along the waterfront stopped for a while, before ambling off. The chimes of the bearded leader's bell just audible over the sound of the wash on the rocks.

The wind was still fresh the next day and we were snugly anchored in Kampos Bay on Patmos Island before lunch. We lingered between a few anchorages in this area before finding ourselves in the port below the great monastery overlooking the island and a vast expanse of sea. It was only a short dinghy ride, propelled by the now efficiently operating outboard, to the harbour waterfront. It is Christian tradition that it was here John the Apostle was given a vision from Jesus, which is recorded in the Bible as the Book of Revelation. The cave in which he is said to have lived is below the monastery and is a popular destination for Christian Pilgrims. Ro bravely toiled up and down the mountain, but I judged it beyond the ability of my agonising knee and decided to rely on a full report over dinner. As most of the waterfront's patrons were here to save their souls, the tavernas lacked much of the exuberance and *joie de vivre* of the normal Greek harbour.

We crossed the channel to Leipsoi Island and chose a good spot to anchor in the attractive harbour. At twilight, as we were just preparing for an expedition ashore an attractive young woman from the Port Police arrived and politely told us to move elsewhere, so that the afternoon ferry could come in. She assured us there would still be a table for us on the quayside if we were a few minutes later. Which there was, a nice blue table and seats right on the edge of the quay, with the water lapping below our feet. Delicious char-grilled octopus tentacles, a bounteous salad and a carafe of the local red served by a charming local girl with relatives who ran a similar restaurant in Darlinghurst, in Sydney. The outboard started first pull for the longish strip back to the boat.

As usual it was hard to leave, but after a couple of days we bestirred ourselves and set off to explore some possible anchorages on the south of the island. They seemed a bit narrow for us, so we crossed the channel to Leros where there were a number of bays on the north of the island. They seemed too exposed to the north, so we kept running down the west coast and eventually tucked up into the north east corner of the large bay of Lakki, off a small village. The bay is reputed to be the largest and deepest in the Mediterranean. Italy had occupied Leros, along with all the other Dodecanese islands, except Kastellorizo, after 1911-12 Italo-Turkish War and was not returned to Greece until 1948.

When the sun was an appropriate distance from the horizon, we went into explore and to enjoy the hospitality of a small restaurant on the quay. It was quiet, with only a few other patrons. We were just thinking about rowing back to *Sea Dreams* when we got to chatting with a couple of the young sailors from the large naval base on the opposite shore. Of course, before long they wanted to know how I had been lucky enough to have such a beautiful wife. When I professed that many years ago, I had been a dashing army officer, they gave me a very sceptical look. But we started talking about things military and got onto the fighting on the island between the Germans, Italians and the Allies late in 1943. I confessed guiltily, that I knew nothing about what was, actually, the Aegean Campaign of 1943, and they offered to take us to the war cemetery the next day.

It was in a beautiful spot beside the water on the other side of the island. *'The land on which this cemetery stands is a gift of the people of Greece for the perpetual resting place of the sailors soldiers and airmen who are honoured here'.*

It marks the resting spot of only a handful of the thousands who lost their lives. The casualty toll was. Italians 5,350. British 4,800. German 1,184. The British also lost 113 aircraft, 4 cruisers, 10 destroyers, 7 submarines, 10 other ships. Probably not as bad a Churchill's naval assault on the Dardanelles, but up there. There is no accurate record of the number of Greek civilians killed, wounded or rendered homeless and starving by the conflagration.

And who was the architect of the imbroglio?

Churchill had been keen to attack the Greek islands for some time, but the Americans saw better uses for the scarce resources that would need to be committed and, thought that Churchill may have been thinking more of post war politics than defeating the Germans. The campaign was launched without sufficient forces, and crucially, once the British failed to capture Rhodes, the Germans had total air superiority.

Churchill displayed his normal bravado.

'Good. This is a time to play high. Improvise and dare.'

Once again showing a cavalier disregard for the lives of his soldiers, and the campaign became commonly known as Churchill's Folly. Perhaps, one of Churchill's follies would have been more apt.

Major Lord Jellicoe, Commander SBS—Special Boat Service— politely gave Churchill his view.

'I happened to be among the lucky ones who managed to escape and found myself, a few days after our defeat in Leros, at the British Embassy in Ankara. I had barely arrived there when I was told that I was urgently required in Cairo. I took a train to Adana and from there flew to Cairo. There was a car awaiting me in which I was whisked off towards the Pyramids. We stopped at a stately house where I was informed the Prime Minister was staying following the Teheran Conference. It was then early afternoon and I was promptly ushered into the room where I found Winston Churchill in bed, taking his customary post-prandial rest. Without further ado Winston asked me for my impressions of why things had gone so wrong. ... I felt it had been a folly to embark on the Aegean campaign ... if we were not in a pretty sure position to capture Rhodes and its essential airfields at the start.' He goes on to say that, *'the Leros campaign, given the circumstances, was a sad mistake.'*

After the war cemetery the young sailors drove us up to the Castle of Panagia, which was built in the 11th century and still dominates the whole island from its site on the summit of Apitiki. They had a story to tell that tickled my fancy. In the 15th century the castle was occupied by the Knights of St. John and it was besieged by the Muslims a number of times. On one desperate occasion in 1409 the fighting force was reduced to one young squire, who saved the castle by dressing the women and children in the armour of the dead and wounded knights and parading them on the battlements. Seeing the large number of defenders, the disheartened invaders sailed off. But after the fall of Rhodes in 1522 it finally passed to the Ottomans.

From the battlements we could make out the nearby island of Farmakonisi. Plutarch describes that Julius Caesar, while still a young man was captured by pirates and held prisoner on the small island. When the pirates demanded a ransom of twenty talents Caesar burst into laughter. Did they not know who he was? He was happy to pay fifty—perhaps he was not just being egotistical, but just making himself more valuable to keep alive. Caesar sent companions off to raise the money and remained with only one friend and two servants, treating his captors with light-hearted jocosity. If he wanted to sleep, he commanded them to be quiet, he joined in their games, read them poems and speeches and called them illiterate savages if they did not applaud loudly enough, even threaten to crucify them. Eventually the ransom was paid. Caesar sailed off to Miletus, assembled a force and returned to Farmakonis. Where he captured most of the pirates and, crucified them.

We left the young sailors still shaking their heads about my luck in winning Ro, and had a brisk run along the west coast of Kalymnos island to the remote bay of Vathi. It was deserted when we arrived, with no sign of life ashore, but just before dark we were happy to see a fishing boat tucking up close to the rocky head of the bay. Gale-strength winds were now being forecast, it looked as if the *meltemi* could be beginning, so we left early and berthed at the Kos marina by mid-morning. We filled our diesel tank and, hoped gentlemen's winds would return. After a few days the wind did drop off and we continued south, visiting the islands of Nisyros and Tilos before arriving at Rhodes.

Rhodes is another one of those islands that has been a crossroads of the world since it was first inhabited around 4000 BCE. Along with the other islands lying close to the Asian shore it has had more than its fair share of lustful and rapacious attention. These days it is still very popular with those seeking both the natural beauty and enjoyments offered by all the Greek islands, as well as the history left behind by the great crusader fortifications and centuries of Ottoman rule. The city sprawls around the old ports and is a bustling and cosmopolitan place with lots to see and do and plenty of shaded terraces to philosophise on.

We avoided the crowded harbours and marina and anchored in the bay south of Rhodes Marina. It was protected from the northerlies and handy to everything. Of course, the thing that Rhodes is most famous for is the Colossus of Rhodes. The construction of this great statue was commenced in 292 BCE. It was built to pay homage to the Sun God, Helios, and to celebrate the defeat of the siege of the city by an invading army from Cyprus. The besiegers were forced to leave behind much of their equipment, some of which was sold or used in the construction. Iron was recast to form the skeleton of the thirty-three-metre high statue—about the same height as the Statue of Liberty and bronze recast into glimmering plates that created the sculptured figure of the god. For fifty-four years it stood on a fifteen-metre high marble pedestal overlooking the harbour entrance until it was toppled by an earthquake. Ptolemy III of Egypt offered to pay for the reconstruction of what all recognised was one of the wonders of the ancient world. But the oracle of Delphi is said to have advised the Rhodians that the statue may have offended Helios—although I think it more likely that it offended the spiteful Poseidon, who was after all, the god responsible for earthquakes!

According to Strabo the statue lay on the ground for eight hundred years. It was still so impressive that it attracted visitors from all over the Mediterranean. Pliny the Elder recorded that it was so large that few people could wrap their arms around even the fallen thumb. In 653CE an Arab army captured Rhodes and, it is reported by Theophanes the Confessor, that the bronze was melted down and sold to a Jewish merchant who carried it to the East on nine hundred camels.

After the old crusading order of the Knights Hospitallers had been expelled from Cyprus they established themselves on Rhodes in 1307. They fought off a Mamluk fleet in 1444 and an attempted invasion by the Sultan Mehmet in 1480. This was a close call, and the knights realised that if they were to survive in the hostile situation in which they found themselves after the fall of Constantinople, they would need an impregnable fortress. By the time they were attacked by the newly enthroned Suleiman the Magnificent in 1522 their defences were second to only Constantinople. By December, both sides had fought themselves to a virtual standstill, and the vastly outnumbered knights realised that there were simply too few off them left to be able to dream of success. When Sulieman offered them a deal, they could leave with their arms and all the wealth they could carry, they decided to leave and live to fight another day.

The few surviving knights sailed westward and eventually established another mighty fortress on Malta. Sulieman's knightly recognition of the Hospitallers bravery had a profound effect. Forty-two years later, at the Great Siege of Malta, the knights destroyed a mighty Ottoman army and denied Suleiman the key to the door of Europe and perhaps saved the West from conquest. Another great benefit of Sulieman's gesture was that enough of the city's architecture was left standing for the new Ottoman rulers to be able to create what is today a marvellously unique ambience.

***

In July we took the short hop to Marmaris and the Turkish coast to wait for the *meltemi* to abate and to stock up with what we needed to cross back over the southern Aegean to Crete. As I have already mentioned, our 'Pilot' expressed the opinion that only idiots would take a yacht anywhere near Crete before mid-September, so we were in no rush. During July and August, the *meltemi* blows down the centre of the Aegean at thirty knots or more, day and night with barely a pause. This is manageable on our yacht, but uncomfortable, and with just the two of us on board any breakages to either ourselves or the yacht can become a serious problem. Also, many of the island anchorages have poor holding, with shallow sand over rocky bottoms making it difficult for the anchor to dig in securely. This can lead to restless nights, the wind howling in the rigging and reminding you the yacht could be on the rocks any moment Aeolus chose.

In late August we were back on the beautiful island of Symi, with its small, bustling and colourful port, pretty pastel cottages and rocky coastline indented with small bays. For many people, possibly everyone who has ever visited, this is their favourite Greek island.

The water is intensely blue, the sky mostly cloudless in summer and the *meltemi* somewhat muted on its eastern side by the island's mountains. Although it is only accessible by sea there is always a bustling throng in the streets of the port, and plenty to occupy ladies intent on 'warding off sorrow', by shopping in the waterfront boutiques. And the young and not-so-young men keeping an eye on them. The island was also once a crusader stronghold and their castle, built around 1309 still watches overall. I wonder what the old knights with their vows of poverty and chastity, would make of modern Symi?

We had intended to moor alongside in the harbour, but as usual it was full, and we could not find a spot close by that was shallow enough to anchor in. So, we took ourselves off to the nearest anchorage in the rocky bay at Pethi a few miles south and, caught the bus back across the hill so we could complete the formalities for checking back into Greece. We were in a hurry now as it looked as if there was a good weather window approaching, earlier than we expected, and we wanted to get going.

Have I mentioned that checking a yacht in or out of Greece is always a trial?

Ha! In Turkey it is just a matter of giving your documents to an agent and paying a small fee. In Italy they don't care if you check in or not as long as you don't interrupt the siesta. The French? Well you can never be sure with the French. They may ignore you, but arrest and imprisonment should never be discounted. But in Greece it is a tortuous process in which you must battle your way through many layers of Greek bureaucracy. Just in case you have forgotten, it requires multiple visits to the Port Police, customs, the (real) police and the Taxation Office, few of which are manned by officials who can understand me and few of whom I can understand because of both poor hearing and poor language skills. Which is why it's always best for Ro to accompany me and to try to keep the channels open. Of course, all islands and officials operate on different sets of rules and regulations, which are kept in loose-leaf files in folders stored in the bottom drawer of someone else's desk. Which is locked. And the 'someone else' is on holidays.

And no, I am not the only one who has these problems.

Symi...with its small, bustling and colourful port, pretty pastel cottages and rocky coastline indented with small bays...for many people, possibly everyone who has ever visited, this is their favourite Greek island...

Having survived the hair-raising bus ride over the hill into town we set off to do battle with the bureaucrats. Naturally the bus drop-off was a long walk from the Port Police, on the other side of the harbour and my knee was killing me. At the Port Police station, we discovered that it had been converted into a crowded youth hostel, with many swarthy-looking young men of Middle East and Pakistani appearance lounging around. Some, as you would expect of the idle young, still in their sleeping bags. On closer investigation we discovered that there were some uniformed police behind a counter inside the station, and as they seemed unoccupied—the default position of Greek authorities—we enquired if we could check in.

'Impossible. We will be busy for days processing all these migrants,' said one policeman, his legs crossed comfortably on his desk and gesturing towards the lounging young men. 'You will have to go somewhere else. Rhodes perhaps.' Now this was serious, we would miss our 'weather window'. Our appeals were met with an unsympathetic smile and shrugged shoulders. Even pleas from Ro left them unmoved.

We left and over a cup of coffee regrouped. Rhodes was out of the question. It would take at least a day going backwards to get there. It was renowned as being the most difficult of all ports in Greece to check in or out of. Apart from giving us a better angle with the *meltemi*, this was part of the reason we had come to Symi. So, we decided to bend the rules a little bit, and head for Crete and hope no one asks why we had come halfway across the Aegean before checking in.

That decided, we risked our lives again on the bus, hurried back on board, pulled up the anchor and headed off, anxious not to miss our 'window'.

'Where are you going?' asked a yacht anchored near us.

'Crete,' we answered.

'Oh. Have you been there before at this time of year?' In a sceptical tone, waving us off.

A few very windy weeks later we realized why.

If we made good time, we would be anchored in the harbour at Halki before late afternoon. However, courtesy of our old friend Aeolus, what was forecast as a lovely sail with the wind on our beam turned out to be into twenty-knots pretty well on the nose. Nevertheless, with the mainsail sheeted in tightly and the motor at 1500 revs we managed to make seven knots in the right direction. Before long Symi was a smudge on the horizon and we were alone on the tossing sea. Later the angle of the wind improved, we managed to get some genoa out and our destination climbed over the hazy horizon.

Halki turned out to have a lovely harbour with a nice-looking quay. We carefully selected a quiet spot well away from the ferry terminal and retired below for showers before heading ashore for dinner. I must confess that when we are anchored, I normally turn off the VHF radio—which really should be left on for safety reasons—because the continuous babble in Greek can become irritating after five seconds or so. I was about to pour myself a wine while waiting for Ro to finish dressing when there were shouts of,

'Ahoy, *Sea Dreams*. Anyone aboard?'

I scrambled topsides to find an English dinghy alongside.

'Port Police are trying to get you on the radio. You best give them a call.'

I thanked my helpful neighbour as Ro came up. We are both very law-abiding citizens—well, Ro is Irish—and our reactions were of horrified guilt and panic. How could the bloody cops have got onto us so quickly for bypassing Rhodes. Bloody hell, what will they do. Where's the nearest Australian embassy. I'll call my lawyer brother, Richard.

Trying to sound calm and unworried I called the police.

'Would we mind moving a bit further away, sir, as a very large ferry is due in shortly'.

Standing to attention and saluting over the radio. 'Of course not, sir'.

We were up early the next morning, the water still dark, the sun just beginning to colour the eastern sky. The wind was still blowing a fresh twenty knots once we were outside the anchorage. Ahead the sea was empty, to the south the smudge of Rhodes was beginning to appear. We set the reefed main and genoa and surged forward, the sun came up and the water sparkled, whitecaps danced around us, the wind was fresh on our faces. A beautiful mug of coffee in the cockpit with the cook, the smell of breakfast, the joy of life.

We were aiming to anchor on the southwestern end of the island of Karpathos about fifty miles away, but thought if we had a very good run, we might make Kasos a further twenty miles on. The *meltemi* funnels through the passages at both ends of Karpathos, between Rhodes on the east and the islands of Kasos and Crete on the west. In the windy months they are mostly gale force or more and the seas steep and uncomfortable. The wind stayed around twenty knots and we had a marvellous morning's run. By midday we were off the main town of Karpathos and thought we could easily make Kasos in the afternoon. We charged on, the wind freshening as we neared the cape on the southwest tip of the island. We reefed our sails some more.

Then, with almost no warning we were hit by a solid wall of wind. On our nose. A cacophony of noise, the wind a gusting bruising thing that shuddered the sails, rattled the rigging and laid us over. It was storm strength, blasting down the channel ahead and swinging east-ward around the approaching cape, and hitting us with battering power.

It only took us a second to realise that we weren't going any further out into that. The sails came in, the motor came on and we backtracked to a small bay tucked under the cape. The wind was still a gale, blowing over the narrow sandy isthmus of land that formed the bay. We nudged in as close as we dared and dropped the anchor into a soft sandy bottom and let out eighty metres of chain. The anchor dug itself in and we felt safe enough, but somewhat disconcerted by the wreck of an old steal coastal trader on the beach behind us – which had obviously dragged from where we were now anchored. Before dark we were joined by two fishing trawlers, the only boats we had seen all day, who nosed right up to a small wooden jetty and took lines ashore.

It was a bleak miserable spot - the water grey and the windswept land without charm. But it was a lot better than being out in what we had just escaped from. The night was no better, nor was the following day, but as dawn was breaking on the next, it seemed to have dropped off enough to investigate the channel.

The wind was not too bad for the first hour or so, but by the time we were approaching the lee of mountainous <u>Kasos</u> island it picked up again. We went close in to try and find some protection from the gusts that blasted off the mountains, tearing spray and fume from the sea within touching distance of the shore. It was a bleak and lonely prospect, the grey rocky slopes of the mountains, the dark tossing water and not a sign of man or ship.

By mid-day we were approaching a possible anchorage at <u>Helartos</u> Bay and we nosed into a narrow entrance on the remote south-western tip of the island. It was smaller than we liked, and the surrounding terrain was rocky and sandy, and looked as if it had been mined. There were a couple of dilapidated buildings.

As we were tossing up whether to stay or go on to Crete our old friend Aeolos, the god of the winds, intervened. The sun broke through the grey sky and the wind abated to a comfortable stiff breeze.

Was he helping us, or playing with us?

We crossed our fingers and plunged out into the infamous passage before us. How quickly things change at sea. The afternoon was delightful. A fresh northerly, the waves dancing and playful once again – their sullen ill humour of the morning forgotten. The grey mountains of Crete began to climb above the hazy blue horizon, and crept closer and closer. The sun cruised calmly across the great blue expanse of the unclouded sky.

...Kasos...a bleak and lonely prospect, the grey rocky slopes of the mountains, the dark tossing water and no sign of man or ship...

We edged through the rocky reefs and islets close to the south east coast and anchored off a white sandy beach at the head of a large bay. The wind was still fresh, but we were protected. The sun set, the western sky began to flush, our mighty anchor settled deeply in the sand, we opened a bottle of wine and toasted Crete—home to the earliest Western fables. In fact, Icarus and his old man must have flown over not far from where we were now anchored, when they escaped from King Minos all those years ago.

Crete has also had a violent and fractured history. It has changed hands many times. The first recorded civilisation in the Mediterranean was the Minoan from the 20th to the 15th centuries

BCE. After that it was part of the Mycenaean Empire of mainland Greece until the 13th century BCE. It was part of the Roman and Byzantine Empires—although from 820 to 961 CE it was captured by Muslims and was known as the Emirates of Crete. It was obtained by Venice in 1221 CE after the sacking of Constantinople during the Fourth Crusade. And there was still a lot of agony to come.

Two days later we anchored in the bay at the delightful town of Agio Nikolaos. Having completely forgotten that we were more or less in Greek waters illegally, I was a bit nervous when we reported to the Port Police. But all was well, a smiling welcome and no suggestion that it was a bit strange to be checking into Crete from Turkey.

We really are a pair of pushovers. It only took a short stroll through the town before we were hopelessly smitten. It sits astride a peninsula. On the north there is a harbour connected by a small channel to a picturesque lagoon formed from a flooded volcanic crater. Small fishing craft in traditional colours are moored around the esplanade, which is lined with restaurants and tavernas. On the southern side of the peninsula there are a couple of beaches and the marina which was to be the winter home of *Sea Dreams*.

The whole town had a well-loved and cheerful feel: tree-lined boulevards, colourful flowers, sculptures and lots of good shopping and more restaurants. There were more good restaurants within walking distance of the boat than anywhere else we had found in the Med, perhaps in the world. A great range in menus and fusions.

We were not the only ones to be captivated. It has been the setting for lots of movies, although that does not seem to have spoiled it, including: *He Who Must Die, The Moon-Spinners, The Lotus Eaters* and *Not After Midnight*. That night we had the first of what would be a number of memorable dinners in the town - baked mussels stuffed with herbs and grated cheese, and salmon and prawn rolls in a honey sauce. The next night, a simple vegetarian in a small family affair in a back street. In the coming days, good fish, good Italian and Greek and some excellent take-away from a small place overlooking the marina.

Several days later, we took *Sea Dreams* a few miles up the coast to the large enclosed bay of Spinalonga and anchored off the village of Elounda. The anchoring was excellent, protection in all winds and with terrific restaurants on the adjacent shore. It was time for one of the highlights of our sailing year. Charlotte and her two eldest sons, Hubie and Ru were joining shortly from Annecy, and we needed facilities to keep everyone happy. Some of Greece's finest resorts are located along the nearby coast with spas and beauty treatments for the girls. For the boys we had water sports—we were still carrying two kayaks tied to the safety rails, that I tripped over and swore at whenever I went forward to do the anchor—fishing expeditions by day and ferocious no holds barred poker tournaments and chess at night.

The strong and near constant winds were back with us and we were glad to be somewhere safe, although it was far from snug. Bit of a worry getting to shore and back in the dinghy and kayaks at times, but with our great Spade anchor firmly dug in, there was no danger of the boat going anywhere.

As you sail into Spinalonga, you come past the great fortress the Venetians built on an island at the narrow entrance to the bay. It was one of the mightiest strongholds they built in the Eastern Mediterranean to protect their colonies and trade routes. No-one could enter without running the gauntlet of its deadly cannons. After a long and bloody war Ottoman armies conquered Crete in 1669 and it was not finally recovered by Greece until 1913. In more recent times the old fort was a leper colony, but these days it is only a tourist attraction. Standing on the ramparts it is easy to feel part of all that has gone by; to see the old galleys furling their flapping sails and rowing in from the dangerous waters, the gunners looking out over their cannons, archers at the ready, and realise once more that history has few happy endings.

In due course we decided to return to the delights of Agios Nikolaos and we took *Sea Dreams* into the fine marina at the edge of the town. And, it was now another very special time of the year again. In fact, the most important week of the year—the week both Ro and Charlotte celebrate their birthdays. These happy events are always preceded by weeks of sly hints and oblique questions to ensure proper preparations are in hand; bookings at suitable restaurants have been made, cards and presents bought etc. I'm sure all households are familiar with the routine. So, we had a great week, including memorable nights at the *Paradosiako, La Strada and Chrisofyllis*—with their great honeyed prawn and salmon rolls— restaurants and more good nights on board as we fought out the finals of the No Holds Barred European Poker Championships.

But then, in no time at all, we were waving Charlotte and the boys farewell, and it was time to explore Crete by road.

Greece, particularly Crete is a wonderful, wonderful country to explore by car, except for the cities and large towns where anarchy generally prevails, and it is much safer and enjoyable to find some other means of transport. The countryside and the views are spectacular, the mountains majestic, the panoramas of the sea and the rich verdant valleys send the spirit soaring. There are some great highways built at huge expense with EU money, beautifully engineered bridges sweeping over vast chasms and tunnels through soaring mountains. But many of the back roads in Crete can be terrifying: narrow, mountainous, no safety rails, precipitous drops, crumbling road edges, blind corners, poor signage and road markings.

Don't let that put you off if you do have the chance to explore this magnificent country. It is full of surprises that will exceed your expectations. However, you should be aware of the following opinion of Greek drivers that was passed on to me by a long time British resident, who was actually an honorary member of one of the many Greek men's clubs that meet every morning in every town square in Greece, before adjourning for an aperitif, lunch and a snooze.

Following road rules is seen as a weakness of character by Greeks of all ages and sexes, who mostly drive with the patience and consideration of tantrum-throwing toddlers coming off a sugar high. Seatbelts in cars and helmets on motor bikes—which may be carrying a parent and two or three young children—are regarded as an assault on freedom of expression and the vibrant exploration of life. Remember, you may be the only driver on the road who is sane, sober and with a legally obtained driver's license awarded after having passed a road test. Traffic lights, lane markings and pedestrian crossings are regarded as guides for drivers with lesser flair and ability, who don't really have a life. Double white lines, speed signs and road warnings are challenges, tests of your masochism or liberation. Flashing warning-lights on cars are generally an indication the driver is driving illegally or parked illegally and has God's permission to do so—so up you!

There are a wide range of hire cars available and in the light of the above you can see the sense in hiring the safest you can find—forget the expense. Whereas cars in most countries are hired with the petrol tank full and the ash tray empty, your car in Greece will have the petrol tank empty and the ash tray full, so your first priority should be to fill up the tank. In many areas, petrol stations are widely spaced.

We gingerly negotiated our way out of town and onto the highway heading west. It was a two-lane road with overtaking lanes here and there. It took us a while to adjust to the fact that the overtaking lane was superfluous, as Cretan drivers overtake at any time by merely driving astride the central line, giving oncoming traffic the choice of a front-on collision or edging onto a rocky edge beside a precipitous drop. This concept made us both a bit nervous—although it was good training for what was to come. It was late morning by the time we reached the capital of Crete, the ancient city of Heraklion, an hour or so up the road from Agios Nikolaos. It did seem longer and, having been quite shaken by the drive, we thought we would have a coffee before choosing a place to stay for a night or two. After that, there were a number of things we were anxious to explore.

We loved the waterfront with its fine old buildings, welcoming restaurants and the remains of the grand fortifications that enabled it to endure a long and bloody siege by the Ottomans. In fact, it was the second longest siege in history, twenty-one years from 1648 to 1669. This was only a hundred years before Captain Cook and Governor Phillip were nosing around Australia, so we should be grateful it was these gentlemen and not a Muslim fleet led by some bloody Barbarossa. We spent the rest of the day exploring the town and the still standing defensive walls, then had dinner overlooking the great fortress that nearly saved the city and all Crete.

Several decades after the Christian victories at the Great Siege of Malta in 1565, and the Battle of Lepanto in 1571 had saved the western Mediterranean, the balance of power in the eastern Mediterranean had swung back in favour of the Ottomans. Most of the European nations were preoccupied with slaughtering each other in the bloody battles of the French Wars of Religion, the Eighty Years War and the Thirty Years War, and the strain of containing Islam and defending the sea fell heavily on Venice and the Knights of St. John. Venice's mighty fortresses at Koroni and Methoni on the south coast of the Peloponnese, had long since been captured, as had most of her empire in the Aegean Sea. But her greatest prize, the jewel of her empire, Crete was still hers.

But its safety had become largely dependent on a fragile truce, which allowed the Venetians to trade with the Ottoman Empire and to continue to bring the riches of the Silk Road to Europe. But there was no truce as far as the Knights of St John, now operating out of their great fortress on the island of Malta, were concerned.

In 1644 they captured an Ottoman convoy on its way from Istanbul to Alexandria. Onboard were pilgrims heading for Mecca, including women of the Sultan's harem and important members of his court. Most were slain, but three hundred and fifty men and thirty women were taken to be sold as slaves. The ship carrying them stopped over for a few days at a port on the south coast of Crete, where for some reason a number of sailors and some captives were disembarked. Naturally enough the attack enraged the Sultan, and when he heard where some of the captives had been taken, he accused the Venetians of being complicit. This was vehemently denied. But there was a powerful faction in the Ottoman court that believed this was a perfect pretext for breaking the truce and there was more to be gained through war than trade. Negotiations continued for the best part of a year, but in the end the decision was for war. Although at this stage no declaration was made.

A large fleet of around four hundred and twenty vessels, carrying some sixty thousand troops was dispatched from Istanbul on 30 April 1645. But instead of heading straight to Crete it sailed to the Peloponnese port of Navarino, where it remained for three weeks. The Ottomans implied that the fleet was waiting there for suitable weather to sail on to Malta, where it would take vengeance on the Knights of St. John. This ruse worked and the Venetians were surprised when the fleet was sighted off the north west coast of Crete on 23 June. They landed west of the beautiful Venetian city of Chania and attacked the small island fortress of St. Todero. In a sign of what was to come, the commander blew up the fort, the garrison and himself, rather than surrender. The Ottomans advanced and captured Chania after a siege of fifty-six days, then repulsed an attack from an allied fleet trying to retake it.

In November the Ottoman commander, having put his army into winter quarters on the island, returned to Istanbul to report to the Sultan. The Sultan judged that things were not moving quickly enough and had him beheaded.

This got things moving and by early 1648 all the island apart from Heraklion was in Ottoman hands. It is thought that during this phase of the war nearly half of the Cretan population had already perished from warfare and plague. The Ottomans now had the benefit of controlling the resources of the island, although resupply from Istanbul was still vital. The Venetians were totally dependent on resupply and reinforcement by sea. Christian ships prevented Ottoman efforts from concentrating an overwhelming force, and their efforts were also disrupted by the Sultan's growing insanity and his propensity to cut off so many heads—until he was replaced by his son. As was the custom, all his other sons were strangled so they could pose no future threat to the throne. This does seem a bit ruthless, but there would certainly have been a number of English kings who would have thought it was a good idea.

The Ottomans were strong enough to maintain the siege, but not strong enough to capture the city. The main war effort was now at sea, with a number of desperate sea battles and raids. The Venetians gambled that their best defence was to blockade the Dardanelles and in this they were largely successful. In 1651 they were victorious in a major sea battle near the island of Naxos and in 1656 inflicted the worst Ottoman defeat since Lepanto. After 1648, and the end of the Thirty-Year War between the Catholics and Protestants in Europe, reinforcements began to trickle into Crete. The long friendly relationship between the French and the Ottomans soured and French reinforcements in support of Venice arrived in 1660.

The siege continued to eat up men on both sides. Assaults against the walls and the fortresses, bombardments and counter bombardments, tunnelling, mining and raids against strongholds held by the Ottomans. Plague killed thousands on top of the misery of existing in a beleaguered city, or worse, living in tents and trenches outside the city in the stifling heat of summer or in winter, when gales roared down from the snow-capped mountains.

In 1665 the Ottomans received nine thousand reinforcements and in 1667 a whole new army. Reinforcements from all over Europe continued to bolster the besieged city, and considerable sea power was deployed. During the next two years seventy thousand Muslims were killed, along with thirty-eight thousand conscript Cretans who fought for them. Behind the walls thirty thousand defenders died. At times it looked as if either side could be victorious. With relations still sour with Istanbul, the French became heavily involved and it was this that undid the allies. The pride of the French navy, the nine-hundred ton *St Therese* exploded killing most of the crew and causing havoc among an allied fleet. This was the catalyst for the French fleet and their ground forces to throw up their hands and abandon the cause.

Behind the city walls the Venetians were left with only a few thousand fit men and scant supplies. In September 1669 they surrendered and their four and a half centuries of rule in Crete was over, although they were allowed to keep their fortress at Spinalonga. The defeat marked the end of Venetian greatness and left the city nearly bankrupt. The Ottomans were also badly damaged by the long struggle, and it was a big factor in the decline of the Ottoman Empire in the 17th century. An interesting footnote has recently been discovered in the Venetian archives. The Venetians had developed a liquid made from the spleen and buboes of plague victims which they could spray on the Muslims to spread the disease. They claim it was never used, although I'm sure the age-old method of catapulting the corpses of plague victims into the forces of the opposition, would have been used by both sides.

So ended a long and bitter war. In history it has been overshadowed by the bloody Thirty Years War. But in some ways the long-term effects were just as significant. It also highlighted, once again, how the bitter religious differences in Europe hamstrung the Wests response to the unrelenting and deadly threat of Islam. In the end, by 1669 the population of Crete had been decimated: from two hundred and sixty thousand to eighty thousand.

Knowing about the siege certainly makes you look at Heraklion in a different light. Such a beautiful old city, but it has certainly seen more than its share of sorrow, and it is hard to enjoy the sunset along the ancient quay without melancholy intruding.

But there was another place we had to see before we checked out of our comfortable lodgings. The Palace of King Minos of Knossos is a few miles inland. It was rediscovered at the beginning of the 20th century by the British archaeologist Arthur Evans and, it is here where the story of European civilisation probably started. Other Minoan settlements, tombs and cemeteries have been found all over Crete, and in addition to the palace at Knossos there are large multi-storied palaces at Phaistos, Malia and Zakros. The absence of fortifications is an interesting feature, perhaps indicating a Spartan-like dominance of the island. A wide range of military artefacts; ornate swords, daggers, armour and helmets suggest a strong military caste.

The palaces appear to have been first built around 2000 BCE and rebuilt around 1700 BCE after earthquake damage. Their final destruction was around 1450 BCE and there are still a few theories as to the cause: a tsunami following the eruptions of the volcano on Santorini, earthquake and fire or invasion or a combination. All the palaces exhibit sophisticated design features: light wells, theatres, drainage, large halls with frescoes, statutes, colonnades and staircases. There is considerable religious art depicting the worship of bulls, sacred bull's horns and the sport of bull leaping which are related to the old Greek legends of Theseus and the Minotaur, Ariadne and Icarus. Their sophistication extends to their sea-born trading routes which linked Egypt, the near East and Greece and the islands.

There was a literary tradition—firstly hieroglyphic and then Linear A scripts. What secrets will be revealed when they are eventually deciphered?

'Robert, I'm sorry, there is a God' or perhaps

'Red wine is good for you and was invented by Nikos.'

Despite our huge advances in science and technology, it is hard not to wonder just how far we have actually come in the last three and a half millenniums. There is a nobleness and spirit about these Minoans and their tales, that was much richer than we have these days. How do today's 'Hollywood Superheroes': Spiderman, Superman, Batman and Wonder Woman for goodness sake, measure up against the ancient heroes: Daedalus, Androgeus, Theseus and Ariadne?

Who will be remembered longest?

How does our art, our so called 'installations' and the meaningless daubs of Markus Yakolevich Rothkowitz - otherwise known as Mark Rothco and selling for around $100,000,000 a daub —and Jackson Pollack really compare to the 'Bull Leaper from

Knossos', the dancing frescos and magical pottery?

We spent another day contemplating the ruins and another night studying the old fortress at Heraklion under the light of a full moon and illuminated by a few too many carafes of local wine. Then we reset our time machine for the 20th century. For Australians, the story of another almost forgotten campaign began in Greece and came to the harbours of Heraklion and Chania. Winston Churchill has a history of flamboyant military adventures. Often they displayed a somewhat cavalier attitude to the lives of the soldiers involved—the Gallipoli landing, the fall of Singapore, the raid on Dieppe, the Aegean Campaign, perhaps even the Italian campaign, perhaps even World War II itself for that matter—Pat Buchanan's 'The Unnecessary War': How Britain Lost Its Empire and the West Lost the World, is an interesting and not so controversial take that springs to mind.

In March 1941 Australia agreed to send troops to Greece to oppose the threatened German invasion. The Australian Prime Minister and the Australian commander in the Middle East, both thought it was a risky move that could end in disaster but agreed with Churchill that Greece should be supported. It was a great risk for a good cause.

But in the end, it was a calamity. The Australian 6th Division was among allied troops who arrived in Greece from the Middle East in early April 1941 and were unable to stop the German advance southwards through the centre of the country towards Athens. After a month of fighting the allies were evacuated by ship. Some, including the battle-weary Australian infantry and an artillery regiment, were taken to Crete. They were disembarked at Heraklion and Chania to bolster the defence of the strategically important island. Disastrously, most of the equipment they would have needed to fight the well-armed Germans was lost in the withdrawal or had to be left on the docks in Greece. The men were armed with little more than their personal weapons and by the end of April there were forty-two thousand allied soldiers on the island.

On 20 May the German invasion began with paratroop landings along the north coast. Ralph Honner, a company commander with the 2/22 Battalion, later to be one of the heroes of the Kokoda Trail and father of a companion of mine in Papua New Guinea many years later, recorded his impressions of the invasion.

'(It was) a spectacle that might have belonged to a war among the planets. Out of the unswerving flying fleet came tumbling lines of little dolls, sprouting silken mushrooms that stayed and steadied them, and lowered them in ordered ranks into our consuming fire. And still they came, till all the fantastic sky before us was filled with futuristic snowflakes floating beneath the low black thundercloud of the processional planes – occasionally flashing fire as if struck by lightning from the earth.'

The successful parachute assaults enabled the insertion of main force German units, including artillery and elite mountain troops. The Germans were now better armed and enjoyed overwhelming airpower. After a week of savage fighting the Allies positions along the north coast were untenable.

Ted Randolf of the 2/7 Field Ambulance.

'A sickly-sweet smell drifted through the area getting stronger until one could taste it in the mouth. The smell was of the dead. I can still taste it. Once it is with you, you never forget it.'

By 26 May retreat and evacuation was the only option. Some were evacuated from Heraklion. At Retimo the 2/11 and 2/1 (Australian) Battalions were cut off and most of the men captured, although some were able to escape into the mountains. Around ten thousand allied troops made an arduous fighting withdrawal over the mountains to a bay at <u>Sfakia</u> on the south coast, where they were evacuated by the Royal Navy. Among those saved was my friend David Henry's father, Major Arthur Henry. Disastrously the gallant men of 2/7 Battalion which had fought bravely in the battles near Chania as well as on the retreat, had to be abandoned. Without food and ammunition, most were captured. Some soldiers who were cut off and were able to avoid capture escaped into the mountains. With the assistance of brave Cretans, who faced the firing squad if they were caught helping, many were able to survive. Between June and September around 600 allied soldiers were rescued by naval ships from remote bays around the coast. But of the Australians on Crete when the invasion began forty percent were either killed, wounded or taken as prisoners of war.

The Greek venture was an ill-conceived disaster, but it did have huge unforeseen strategical ramifications. It forced Hitler to delay his invasion of Russia by a couple of months, and ultimately this could have been the difference between victory and disaster on the eastern front. Hitler was beaten, Stalin and the USSR, Mao Ze Dung and the Chinese Communists became probably bigger threats to the democracies than Hitler would have ever been.

So, we had plenty to mull over as we continued west along the coast for Chania, for many centuries one of the Mediterranean's great beauties. The road took us through the area where much of the early fighting in 1941 took place. It twisted and turned through broken country, hard mountains and small fertile valleys. A nightmare for soldiers on foot carrying their wounded and heavy packs in the dust and heat of summer. By car it was a delightful few hours with a salad for lunch in a small restaurant surrounded by olive groves. There was a fine view along the coast and the sparkling ocean and to the south, the hard peaks of the White Mountains.

Chania is also very hard not to fall in love with and even on a crowded summer's day it still had a noble aura. The old paved streets, the fine Venetian buildings and the walled Venetian port have an ageless grace. It is easy to imagine the bustling scene of five hundred years ago. Galleys entering past the old lighthouse, the streets a babble of tongues, riches and spices from all over the known world being bought and sold. All testimony to Venice's wealth, power and cosmopolitism. Soon to be crumbled beneath the Ottoman's boot.

Around us was the area that saw the major clashes of the Germans and allies in 1941, before the fighting withdrawal to the south coast. We could find no memories of that, but we did a few days later in the mountains.

But first we wanted to drive to the north-western tip of the island and, see if we could catch a glimpse of the island of Antikythera which lies some twenty miles off the coast. It is hard to know what you can and cannot expect to see in the Mediterranean. Some days mountains forty miles away will be clear, but on hazy days things only a few miles distant, invisible. We could not see the island, only vast panoramas of sea, sky and mountains.

Antikythera lies on the route the galleys followed between the Peloponnese and Crete. In 1901 sponge fishermen discovered a small wooden box in an ancient sunken galley, and to my mind this could be the most amazing archaeological discovery of all time. The Antikythera Mechanism as it has become known, is an ancient analogue computer and it has taken over a hundred years for scientist to unlock its secrets. It is about the size of a shoe box, with dials and knobs on the outside and a complex assembly of precisely machined bronze gear wheels within. By winding the knobs on the side, the positions and eclipses of the sun, moon, and planets could be determined for any chosen date and would be displayed on the dials. Amazingly, carbon dating places its construction at around early 3rd century BCE. The precision of its working components was not matched again until the manufacture of astronomical clocks in Europe in the 14th century CE, seventeen hundred years later. Even more amazing when you remember that even in 1632 Galileo and the Catholic Church were still having a very ugly argument about whether the earth rotated around the sun or vice versa.

Was this machine a singular marvel or were they common and, who created them? Was Archimedes the only creator of these wonders or were there others? Why and when did the knowledge and ability to produce these computers disappear? Did the censors of the early Christian church outlaw them?

How would the world have been changed, if scientific knowledge had forged onwards from this base, rather than this vital step being lost for a millennium and a half. Perhaps the industrial revolution and the age of computers could have arrived fifteen hundred years earlier? The universe could already be ours, or of course we could have already blown ourselves up.

Of all the marvellous secrets of the ancient world, this could be the most teasing. And it makes you wonder, if the secrets of this machine were lost, what other ancient marvels have also been lost or destroyed and forgotten? Recently there have been discoveries of sophisticated relics on the coast of the Black Sea, dating from around 5000 BCE, pre-dating the Mesopotamians by over a millennium and the Minoans by three.

Up until now, by keeping an eagle eye on the twisting roads and treating all approaching vehicles as dangerous German Stukas, we had survived without incident, a few scares but no crashes. We now headed into the White Mountains to cross to the south coast. They are the spine of the island, a hard-rocky range with bare peaks that shimmer in the heat of mid-summer and, are shrouded in mist and snow in winter. A hard land that has bred a tough and resilient population, that has never stopped resisting the many invaders of their island. We have Greek friends in Tasmania who came from here after the war. Tough and hardworking folk, generous and loyal to their friends and great businesspeople. I think they now own half of the state!

At the small mountain village of <u>Vouves</u> we stopped to admire possibly the oldest olive tree in the world. Believed to have been around for some three thousand years, its trunk is a squat gnarled thing that looks every day of its age. But the foliage is as fresh as spring, and it still produces fine tasty olives that are very much in demand. It is an inspiring drive, a unique Cretan experience. Dramatic scenery, small villages with populations of a few dozens in houses of rock and cement and clustered around red-tiled domed churches. Some in small fertile valleys, others clinging to rocky hillsides and perched on the edge of precipitous canyons with views to the distant, wide blue and windy ocean. Some with a sparse covering of trees, others within dense forests. Flocks of goats and sheep picking over hard pasture that in winter is covered with ice and heavy snow.

The village of Askifou clings to a shallow pass that is the gateway to the south coast. There was hard fighting here as the allies withdrew and fought to hold off the advancing Germans. A repeat of many battles fought over the centuries against Venetian, Turkish and Egyptian invaders. At Kares, overlooking the Askifou plateau there is a small war memorial with heart wrenching memorabilia and photography of the war. After some hours on the twisting, winding roads we arrived on the southern coast, trembling, but grateful to have landed. Much of the southern coast is almost an empty quarter. A hard rocky coastline with a stony plain backing on to the high, bare russet brown mountains. Between the barren headlands there are pebbled beaches with white walled villages spilling to the water's edge.

From the hills the small port of Sfkia looks exposed and vulnerable. It was here on 31 May 1941 that 9,000 exhausted allied soldiers, who had fought their way back across the mountains, were trapped and praying for evacuation. It is impossible not to feel the hopelessness and fear that they must have felt. Almost out of food and ammunition, carrying their wounded, the Germans on the overlooking hills and in the sky above, as they waited for darkness and the hope of escape on RAN destroyers.

We paused for a night at <u>Loutro</u> with its white boxed houses and a shallow rocky boat harbour half protected by a stone jetty. A few fishing boats and great rooms with nice terraces overlooking the azure sea. At <u>Frangokastello</u> with the evocative Venetian fortress at the lonely and windy end of their empire, overlooking a beach and small fishing boat harbour, and at Koraka with a pebbly beach and a tiny harbour behind a stone breakwater.

Wine has been made in Crete for over four thousand years. On the eastern coast at Kato <u>Zakros,</u> near where we anchored when we arrived on the island, a wine press has been discovered that is around three thousand five hundred years old. It is also here that the world's first Alcoholics Anonymous was established in 1599BCE—don't Google this.

...<u>Frangokastello</u> with the evocative Venetian fortress at the lonely and windy end of their empire, overlooking a beach and small fishing boat harbour...

Between the ancient olive tree, the Minoan palaces, the oldest wine press and people who loved leaping long horned bulls, you would have to think that the man who invented red wine, could have been a Cretan.

After arriving at this spot in our still undamaged hire car, we felt our circumnavigation complete. We toasted this accomplishment with a wine from one of the local vineyards and headed back to *Sea Dreams* at beautiful Agios Nikolaos.

***

The next year we arrived back from Australia in early May to continue our voyage back to the Ionian Sea. It is another accepted wisdom—blessed by Aeolus—that the *meltemi* does not begin to blow until late June, so we were planning on having a couple of months to peacefully explore those Cyclades islands we had missed when we had come eastwards a few years previously. Our taxi driver, who brought us from the airport to Agios Nikolaos, said that it had been very windy, but all that was over now, and the weather would be marvellous.

'Oh, is that so!' I thought, recalling Charmaine Clift's advice about Greeks wanting only to give you good news. For the last couple of years or so I had complained bitterly about having to limp around so much on my agonising knee. I don't think I've mentioned it, have I? Over the Australian summer I had been given a new one, courtesy of the Department of Veteran's Affairs, and I could now swagger through Agio Nikolaos with the careless insouciance of a Greek lothario, attracting admiring glances from the young ladies we passed—in my dreams—while we stocked up with food and wine. After one peaceful sunny day with moderate breezes, while we were getting things ready to go, a strong north-westerly with all the features of a *meltemi*, howled over the hills to welcome our guests. Mark and Remy Towers, who we had purchased *Oceania* from many years before, were coming along for the first few weeks. In the past we had spent a lot of time sailing on *Oceania* in company with them and their beautiful new yacht *Knot Again* in the Coral Sea. So, we had overstocked *Sea Dreams* ample cellar in preparation and were ready to go. But for the wind. We sent Mark and Remy away in a car, but that night they were back pale and shaking after a day on Cretan roads, begging instead for the dangers of the deep. The next morning, we edged cautiously along the coast to our lovely anchorage at Spinalonga, where we would be ready to sally forth to Santorini, our first island destination, as soon as weather permitted.

After a couple of days, the wind eased and not long after the sun was up, Crete was only a shadow on the southern horizon. We breakfasted and admired the arrival of a beautiful Mediterranean day. The great blue dome of the sky spread, clearing the horizon of whites and pinks and the golden sun dispelled the few flimsy clouds. The wind was a brisk breeze from the southwest, the sails were full, pulling us onwards as the boat cleaved a clean passage through the shallow swells of the rich blue sea.

All cares were left behind. Sunlight, sparkling waters and paradise lay before us. Santorini is probably 'the' picture postcard of the Greek islands. It is a high rocky crater, always surrounded by the bluest of blue seas. There is rarely a cloud in sight in summer. The villages running along the rim of the crater are gleaming white terraces with entrancing decks and pools overlooking the breathtaking panorama. All enhanced by the three hundred and sixty-five blue domed churches—okay to Google this—dotted here, there and everywhere. We were desperate to visit Santorini because Remy had set her heart on it, but it is probably the worst island in the whole of the Mediterranean to find a spot to anchor. We had convinced ourselves that if we tried hard enough there must be a spot somewhere. There is a small marina on the south coast, but the entrance was too shallow. We investigated other possibilities, but they were too deep, too open to all winds and had bottoms of rocky lava which were impossible for anchoring. Ro and I had visited the island a number of years before, so were not as disappointed as Remy.

It seems to be generally accepted that the volcanic explosion that tore apart this ancient island three and a half thousand years ago, to create what is here today, was responsible for causing a tsunami that destroyed the Minoan civilization. Not too sure about that myself. Perhaps it damaged and weakened it enough for the Mycenaean's to finish them off? There are also theories that this might have been the site of the fabled city of Atlantis and that seems reasonable.

There was not a lot of daylight left when we gave up looking for a reasonably safe anchorage, and headed for the lovely island of Ios, a few miles further north. We found a deserted bay on the southeast corner of the island, and I have to say Remy was a pretty good sport about it. Just brushed a tear away and got on with life. Although I did notice her jotting down something in her diary. Ios is famous for being a place to come to for a good time—although most Greek islands fill the bill in this regard. It has lovely white beaches and picturesque coves protected from the full blast of the meltemi, pretty whitewashed villages with tavernas full of boisterous fun and lots of young men lured here by the flocks of golden nymphs. There is plenty to explore: old churches, fertile valleys with groves of vines and olives, stunning outlooks.

Now, if that is not enough to justify a visit to the island, there is the tomb of the world's most famous writer, Homer, sitting in a place as mystically beautiful as he deserves.

Before long, a forecast of stiff southerlies, encouraged us to move to the more protected anchorages at Milos, a day's sail to the west. We skirted along the mountainous north coasts of the islands Sikinos and Folegandros which looked pretty bleak from the water, although the sailing was spectacular. In the mid-afternoon we anchored behind the Pollonia Peninsula on the north coast of Milos. The clear water here was delicious, the first touch of summer's warmth over a sandy bottom. There were no other yachts, only a few small fishing boats pulled up on the beach. The next morning the wind had gone and, we drifted as much as sailed around to the large bay in the centre of the island and anchored off the village of Adamas. Milos, like Santorini, is the crater of an extinct volcano. But Milos is much more attractive for a yacht, with anchorages all around the inside edge of the flooded crater. Much of the island is covered with fertile volcanic soil that will grow just about anything, but there are patches of rocky lava and solidified white ash.

On 8 April 1820 one of the world's most famous pieces of art was discovered within the ruins of an ancient city on the island. The sculpture by Alexandros of Antioch of the Goddess of Love, known these days as the Aphrodite or Venus de Milos, is believed to have been created between 130-100 BCE. There are a number of tales of how the statue was spirited away from the then Turkish-held island to the Louvre. The most colourful involves a dashing French naval officer fighting off Turkish brigands and presenting it as a gift to the French King, Louis XVIII.

There are some very interesting villages around the island. The fishing village of Klima at the entrance to the bay and Pollonia on the east coast are both captivating and dining on fresh seafood accompanied of course by local wines like Assyrtiko, Savatiano, and Serifiotiko which are among the vines growing on the island will leave memories to savour from the rocking chair on your verandah. And to be fair, Adamas is also magnificent, a little more boisterous as the daily ferry calls here, but with a wide selection of good eateries.

Remy had not forgotten her promised visit to Santorini, and as the ferry ran a daily service, she persuaded Mark that it would be a good idea to spend a couple of nights there. When she returned, she had that self-satisfied, smug look, that girls have following a successful shopping expedition. After a week on Milos we headed north and poked our nose into a couple of small bays on the eastern side of Kimolos island and, finding nothing to our liking we continued to Sifnos where we anchored in Ormos Vathi. The bay was almost fully enclosed with only a narrow entrance to the west, the water was clear with a good sandy bottom. Perfection was completed by three or four low key tavernas on the shore.

There was also a small eye-catching waterfront church with its own stone jetty, which rekindled my thoughts on careers in the Church. If you are also thinking along these lines, there are some things you should be aware of.

In most places, but particularly in Greece, the number of churches in any area is in direct proportion to the wealth of the area. Same sort of thing as where you choose to site a goldmine, or an oil well there needs to be gold or oil underneath. For instance, in the light of there being three hundred and sixty-five churches on the small island of Santorini, I will leave it to you to work out if it was a wealthy island or not. Generally wealthy places like Santorini are pleasant to live in, which partially explains why I have rarely encountered a happier group of men then the Greek Orthodox clergy. They can always be found, in any of the hundreds and hundreds of delightful villages all over Greece, black robed, happy and relaxed. A bit overweight with Olympian beards, enjoying a coffee or wine or two in the town square, normally in the company of a few pretty women and a number of children who all appear to be closely related.

But if you do happen to tire of village life, there are some famous religious communities you can join. The holiest, of course, is the self-governing Monastic State of the Holy Mountain in the vicinity of Mount Athos in northern Greece, that I mentioned earlier. This has been home to around two thousand monks and a collection of twenty monasteries, some of which are very large and sumptuous, since 800CE. No females are allowed within the borders of the state, however not all worldly pursuits are outlawed. Prior to the 2008 financial crisis one of the monasteries amassed a fortune estimated somewhere between one and two billion dollars by property speculation geared on the title of a worthless swamp. It is rumoured the abbot was offered the position of Treasurer of Greece, but in the end, they could not afford him.

Another alternative to the stress of parish life would be to join one of the monasteries sitting on the awe-inspiring limestone pinnacles at Meteora in the Plain of Thessaly in central Greece. It is hard to imagine grander platforms from which to contemplate God's works. We had visited Meteora, during our sojourn in Volos the previous year.

And yet another career path for priests can involve one of the small magical churches dotted all over Greece, on high mountain ridges, on promontories with magical views overlooking miles and miles of ocean, in forests and groves in isolated valleys. There are at least hundreds, perhaps thousands of small churches with a beauty and serenity that is supernatural. They are too remote to be bothered by any pesky parishioners, although it is possible that a lost traveller or a ship-wrecked sailor may scratch at your door occasionally. And to cap things off, there is no need to endure any hint of penury, as the Greek government pays a handsome salary to all Orthodox Priests. So, despite my agnostic and indulgent nature, I can sometimes imagine myself enjoying the life of an ascetic in one of these outposts of heaven. Although, I probably would not fit in at Mount Athos.

But time was slipping by. Mark and Remy left after exploring Sifnos and we continued on our way. A night at Serifos with a panoramic view over the turquois water to the majestic mountain-top village, its narrow stone streets winding to the blue domed church surmounting it all.

On to Kythnos where we anchored with our stern tied ashore in a lovely, but narrow bay not far from Loutra. We do not like being tied to shore all that much, it puts you at the mercy of later arrivals who can drop their anchor over yours or drift down on top of you, usually late at night when an unexpected wind comes up, invariably causing bedlam. If you are swinging on your anchor the process for leaving in an emergency is easy. You just pull up the anchor keeping your bow into the wind and motor off.

However, in this situation we felt we had no option. If we anchored in the middle of such a narrow bay, we would interfere with the arrangement for boats tying to the shore. We went in for an early dinner at a quite smart restaurant and came home just after dark to find yachts moored stern ashore on both sides. But it was a calm evening, no wind was forecast, all would be well.

...small magical churches dotted all over Greece, on high mountain ridges, on promontories with magical views overlooking miles and miles of ocean, in forests and groves in isolated valleys...

However, Aeolis must have been having a restless night and decided to amuse himself — although it could easily have been that miserable bastard Poseidon. After midnight the wind started to get-up a bit, and before long, it was blowing strongly from the starboard side, putting a lot more pressure on the anchor and the shorelines. All were drawn taut as bowstrings, quivering under the strain.

It blew harder.

Slowly our upwind neighbour started to sag down towards us as his anchor was dragged sideways over the sandy bottom. Wavelets were now pounding on our hull. It was obvious that we would need to move soon, before he was on top of us and we were pushed onto the rocks. We hurried to recover our leeward stern line, leaving us hanging on the windward line and the anchor chain.

Meanwhile our downwind neighbour had attempted to leave but had jammed the stern of his boat onto the bow of his downwind neighbour. We would now have to clear two boat lengths, forty metres or so, before we could let our boat swing with the wind—meaning we needed to go out as fast as we possibly could.

There was now much shouting, in a number of languages on both sides of us, and the wind seemed to be getting worse. We would have to cast off our stern line and hope it ran free as we quickly recovered it. Then motor out fast enough to clear our neighbour but not over-running our incoming anchor chain, which could cause it to jam on the keel or jump off its bow roller and jam.

I cast off the stern line, pulled it onboard and sprinted forward to the anchor winch.

Ro gunned the motor and edged forward, as fast as she dared without running over our anchor chain, while watching our stern start to swing towards the jammed boats.

'Faster,' I shouted, even though we were starting to drive over our own chain. We had to risk a jam, otherwise a collision was certain. More shouting and swearing on all sides. Torches waving madly.

Out we shot. Would we make it. Yes, no, oh God, no, yes, we will.

Then calamity as the chain was pulled off the roller and jammed on the pulpit. Now we could go nowhere, we just had to let the wind swing us and hope we cleared the downwind yachts. Then pray the anchor held and, try to get the chain back on the roller.

Around we swung, clearing the bow of the outward yacht by inches and continuing to swing out into mid-stream. After another anxious moment the anchor held, pulled taut as a steel bar.

That was the worst part over. But to get enough leverage to pull up the anchor chain required balancing on the tip of the pulpit, with both hands on the chain as the boat bucked in the waves and the wind tore at me. This is much in excess of my normal pay grade, but terror gave me strength and Ro timed a thrust forward to give a moment of slack chain to work on. A back-straining pull, and the heavy 12mm chain came back over the bow roller.

Now all we had to do was motor slowly forward, pulling in the chain and keeping control of the bow once the anchor started to lose its grip on the bottom.

By the time we had anchored under the lee of a headland a few hundred metres away, a grey dawn was seeping through the surrounding hills. The water was still rough and leaden, and our two erstwhile neighbours were still locked together, like giant metallic praying mantes entwined in a deadly embrace. We went across in the dinghy to help pull them apart, and after a couple of hours they were free—with only a few scratches and some bent stainless steel to tell the tale. After a late breakfast we had a nap and wondered why we did it. Later there was much bonhomie as the yachts involved in the saga shouted farewells—at times during the night it had seemed that we were enmeshed in World War III.

After a few wines in the calm twilight we decided not to sell *Sea Dreams* after all but, spend a couple of days exploring the island and visiting the hot mineral baths. Then continue on to Poros, hire a car and explore the Peloponnese. I was always rather a fan of Sparta, and Ro claims she was a member of the Spartan Club at her boarding school. A claim I find quite dubious in light of her kind heart—most of the time—and abhorrence of cold showers. In due course we set off, rounding the northern tip of the island in the company of a couple of other yachts, which as the day passed gradually grew imperceptibly smaller and smaller until they were only tiny white patches on the immense ocean, then disappeared and we were alone.

The islands of the Cyclades sank behind us and the great mountains of Greece climbed out of the blue haze of the horizon. In the late afternoon we crossed our track made five years earlier when we were heading east to Turkey. As twilight approached, we slipped through the narrow passage between steep forested hills, into magical Poros. We started making arrangements for our road trip around the Peloponnese and made certain of a few days of calm weather so *Sea Dreams* would be safe unattended. We had two anchors deeply in-bedded in the lovely glutinous bottom. When the day arrived, we picked up our car, emptied the ash tray and sought out the closest petrol station. We programmed out trusty Tom-Tom so that 'Jane', with a pleasant upper-class English accent, could direct us and Ro would have someone to argue with other than me about being on the right road, and headed off to Mycenae. Our winding route took us along the shore of the Saronic Gulf, we drove through a fertile plain growing all manner of fruit, olives and grapes, with panoramic views across the shining blue water on one side and the steep mountains on the other.

At the small fishing village of <u>Palaia Epidavros</u> we inspected their very impressive theatre, carved into a hillside in the 4th century BCE and afterwards enjoyed a salad on the quay of the picturesque harbour. In ancient times it was an important port, at one time supplying twenty-five ships for the Trojan War. We were already behind schedule as we turned into the mountains, following a road winding through a lush valley which eventually brought us to the city of <u>Nafplion</u> at the head of the Argolikos Gulf.

Jane had been providing clear directions and she and Ro were still on good terms.

Nafplion has been an important port since ancient times and in the middle ages was a busy Venetian port, and the great castle they built still dominates all around it. Later the Ottomans during their long over-lordship used it as an administrative outpost. We did not have enough time to do justice to the quite noble architecture and the marbled square with an interesting market at the centre of the town and, put it down as a spot to revisit in *Sea Dreams*.

We hurried off to inspect the massive ancient royal castle at nearby Mycenae, built on a high rocky prominence looking over a magical vista of fertile plains and high distant mountains. Even after three thousand years it still exudes a feeling of might and majesty. The great rock walls and stone chambers disdainful of the ordinary folk who now trespass, still wait in sulky silence for the return of the great warriors who strode around them—laughing, arrogant, lustful, prideful and boastful. It is impossible here to do any sort of justice to the history of this mighty fortress, the empire it ruled, the heroic sagas it spawned or the wealth in gold, precious stones and archaeological treasures that lay buried here for thousands of years.

There are any numbers of books and television documentaries which I recommend. Then perhaps you too will brood on how and why this mighty place, which was once so great, collapsed for reasons no one can yet adequately explain.

The Mycenaean Civilisation dominated the Greek mainland, the islands and parts of today's Turkish Coast in the second millennium BCE. It was a rich and powerful society ruled by a warrior caste and a supreme king. Its most famous ruler was King Agamemnon, who led the Greek army to Troy to recover Helen the wife of his brother Menelaus, king of nearby Sparta. Helen, the most beautiful woman in the world and another daughter of the lusty Zeus, had famously eloped with Paris, a prince of Troy. So began the Trojan war, that has given us the immortal legends of the mighty Achilles, the wily Odysseus and so many others.

Now we were running really late and by the time we reached our hotel perched high on the mountains overlooking the mythical Spartan Plain, Ro and Jane were beginning to be a bit tense with one another. The roads off the highway had been narrow, winding and confusing. Even for Jane. But nothing that a fine Spartan red did not fix while we were admiring the panoramic scene, as the shadows of the mountains crept over it and darkness enveloped all, leaving only the lights of some solitary farmhouses far below.

Very little remains of the actual ancient city of Sparta which—I think unique amongst the Greek cities of the epoch—was built without fortifications. The Spartans were confident they could defeat any army that marched against them without the help of walls, and who would be mad enough to assault them in any case? Only a few scattered stones remain.

By around 650 BCE the Spartans had become the dominant land-based power among the Greek city states. Its ascension marked the end of the so called 'Greek Dark Ages', which began after the unexplained collapse of the Mycenaean Empire five hundred years before. Its pre-eminence ended in its defeat by Thebes at the Battle of Leuctra in 371 BCE, only a few decades after it had triumphed in the Peloponnesian War and left its great rival Athens in ruins.

In between it forged the reputation which made their name synonymous with bravery, fortitude and loyalty and will have this meaning until the sun sets on us all. The highlights most will be familiar with; the Battles of Thermopylae and Plataea which saved

Greece and the Western World from the Persians, and victory over Athens in the Peloponnesian Wars which were for Greece what World Wars I and II were for Europe twenty-five centuries afterwards.

One story which captures the supreme self-belief of the Spartans.

In 414 BCE at the height of the Peloponnese War, the Greek city of Syracuse in Sicily beseeched the Spartans to send an army to break a long running and bloody siege by a great Athenian army of forty-five thousand men and two hundred and sixteen trimarines. The Spartans sent one man. The general Gylippus, who inspired a great victory and a calamitous defeat for the Athenians.

The Battle of Leuctra which pulled the curtain on Sparta, was also significant for the effect it had on the development of warfare. Traditionally in Greek battles, elite troops were placed on the right flank, eight to a dozen men deep. There were a number of reasons for this. One was, if the elite were fighting the weaker elements of the enemy, it was unlikely to be routed or decimated in the first clash and, the whole army destroyed. I cannot imagine this would have been great for the morale of the badly-equipped farmers on the left flank, who always drew the well-armoured noblemen of the opposition.

After three hundred years of the other cities being cleaned up by the Spartans, the Theban general Epaminondas decided to try a different tack. He stacked the left flank of his army with his cavalry and best warriors to a depth of fifty men and armed them with 12ft pikes—against the Spartan's 8ft pikes—while holding back the rest of his line from the initial engagement. His left flank - better armed and much heavier mass—destroyed the Spartan right flank before the weaker elements of his army were committed to the battle. The Spartans were routed, their aura of invincibility destroyed. Sparta fell, never to rise again.

Philip II of Macedon had been held as a hostage in Thebes at the time and had talked to the Theban commanders and had studied the battle. He and his son Alexander modelled some of their hallmark strategies on Epaminondas's ideas—hence the 'refused flank' or 'oblique order', coordinating the phalanx with light infantry, cavalry, archers and javelins, and concentration of force at the critical point. Philip lengthened his pikes—*sarissas*—even more to 18ft and armed not just the first three ranks but the first five ranks of the phalanx with these deadly implements making an almost impenetrable hedgehog. The evolution of the longer pikes had the same effect as the longer-range English bow against the French crossbow, the long-range Mongol curved bow against the European mounted knight, or breech-loading rifles against muskets.

Alexander was probably the world's first great military genius, particularly in his ability to deceive his enemies, inspire his men, his use of cavalry as a shock weapon in close co-ordination with his light and heavy infantry, his archers and javelin throwers. He led from the front and left behind him a compendium of the principles of warfare.

Some, particularly, have remained with me and still give me a chuckle. In my previous life as an infantryman, I was somewhat disdainful of the cavalry, which is of course, a mutual feeling between the two arms.

'A horse must be a bit mad to be a good cavalry mount, and its rider must be completely so.' And, *'A cavalry man's horse should be smarter than he.'*

Just to come back to that other genius, Napoleon. He thought he appreciated the principle of concentration of force, and indeed he did in a strategic sense. But he fell short in a tactical sense when his armies continued to march their infantry in dense columns against Wellington's thin lines of red coats. In a way, the same principal as Epaminondas, but technology had created a fatal flaw in this tactic. All the soldiers in Wellington's lines could bring fire to bear repeatedly on the front and sides of the advancing columns. Only the narrow front of the French could reply. The result: Wellington destroyed French armies time after time and, did not lose a single battle.

The next morning, Ro and I were very happy to be in this Arcadian valley, the chalice holding the great Spartan legend. We followed the same route as the eloping lovers, Helen and Paris, down the Eurotas river to the sea and the pretty village of Gythio from where legend has the lovers embarking to Egypt before sailing on to Troy. We had a coffee on the warm and sleepy waterfront. Then along a hair-raising road to Porto Kagio a small cluster of houses and a short stone jetty, and on to the often storm-blasted Cape Matapan with a vast outlook over the ever changing sea.

We continued following the coastal road as it wound north along the Gulf of Messiniakos, through Limeni, Stoupa and on to

Kalamata, the famous home of olives, as darkness was falling. We were tired but awed by the country we had driven through. The mountains, valleys, villages and the mighty sea. After such beauty I am afraid Kalamata was a bit depressing. By the time we had driven through the town centre and arrived at the very comfortable Elektra Hotel and Spa on the western fringe near the waterfront, we thought we had seen enough. We called the couple keeping an eye on *Sea Dreams* in Poros and had an excellent meal in the hotel dining room. After deciding the Kalamata wine was as good as the olives, we were revived enough to step outside. But around the corner we discovered a haunted crumbling high rise that looked as if it had survived the battle of Stalingrad and could well have been used as a set for the movie and we decided we would go to bed after all, rather than risk being mugged.

...anchored in our usual spot near the northern shore...a quiet place with a few tavernas adjacent...Ro, Charlotte, Stephen, Hubie, Rufus, Ferdi...a couple of minutes by dinghy into the town...

Further west around the coast are the two, once mighty Venetian fortresses at Koroni and Methoni built as part of the chain guarding the ports of the empire. From here their galleys would head up the Aegean for Constantinople or east to Crete and Egypt. But as the Ottomans began to advance through the Mediterranean, they became known as 'The Eyes of the Serene Republic' until they themselves were captured and the great castle at Corfu became the last redoubt before Venice and Malta in the Western Mediterranean.

We headed back to Poros and *Sea Dreams* along the very expensive highway paved with Euro gold and were safely on board before sunset. We were anchored in our usual spot near the northern shore, adjacent to the Greek Naval Academy. This is a quiet place with a few tavernas adjacent but only a couple of minutes by dinghy into the town itself.

In previous visits the academy had a rather deserted look, as do most Greek government offices despite half the country being on the government teat.

But now we were bemused by a number of heavy whaling launches, manned by young rowers pulling leaden oars, that circled us for hour after hour with no apparent purpose. They were not racing, certainly not enjoying themselves, what could they be learning? Their heads would droop, the laboured oar strokes would become slower and slower, the launches slouching to an almost stop between each pull.

What in earth were they doing, we wondered? Then, looking back many years I realized they were just being 'bastardised'. In the age-old fashion of the services, they were being taught respect, to unquestioningly obey orders and know their place in the world. Eventually most would survive and go on to be happy warriors, and if they were lucky, perhaps idle yachtsmen. Which led my thoughts back, over half a lifetime, to my second tour in Papua New Guinea and to the great mist-shrouded mountains on the border with Indonesia.

~ THE BORDER MOUNTAINS OF PAPUA NEW GUINEA 1971-72~

The first European to approach within sight of the great central massifs that straddle the border of Papua New Guinea and Indonesia, where the mighty Fly and Sepik rivers begin their tumultuous journeys to the oceans, was the Italian explorer Luigi D'Albertis.

...a tribal warrior below the Hindenburg Wall...and soldiers of the Pacific Island Regiment 1972...

On his 1876 voyage up the Fly River he managed to reach a point some four hundred miles from the coast.

On the way he recorded. *'At last I have seen the lofty mountains of the interior of New Guinea. I have seen them like giants of different heights towering one above the other and extending from the principal chain down the river. My mind is on the rack. I feel like Moses in sight of the Promised Land, destined never to enter it.'*

The mountains that he glimpsed, mostly hidden behind curtains of mist and cloud, became known as the Star Mountains and the Hindenburg Range. Near the border they are mighty crags of splintered limestone, rising to around 4000 metres and surmounting dense, tangled, dripping moss forests. I had come across Luigi D'Albertis' account of his voyage up the Fly River when I was young. It had a profound effect on my interest in the country and our decision to go back there in 1971, five years after graduating from the Royal Military College.

We agreed to a posting to Wewak provided we could take it up before Georgina's impending arrival prevented Ro flying, and provided I could take some of the long period of 'leave' I was owed, to settle in. We knew that Moem Barracks at Wewak was a tropical paradise, and we would enjoy life living in the large airy tropical bungalows surrounded by gardens overlooking the sea, that came with the job. We were assured the Wewak hospital had excellent facilities, doctors and staff and we would also have some domestic help.

A lovely holiday in a tropical paradise while waiting for the birth of our second child. It sounded perfect after the frenetic pace and separations of the last three years. In due course we flew into Wewak on the north coast of PNG, a bit over a hundred or so miles from the border with Indonesia. The town is situated on a promontory jutting out into the sparkling blue waters of the Bismarck Sea. Moem Barracks, home to the 2nd Battalion Pacific Islands Regiment was on another promontory, fringed with golden beaches and palm trees, a few miles to the east. The married quarters, sitting on high foundations in the style of old classic 'Queenslanders' were in lush gardens on a rise a hundred metres or so back from the water. They were a short stroll from a modern airy Officer's Mess and enjoyed a peaceful shady ambience, with local gardeners working quietly amongst the flowery shrubs.

Not far away the mighty Sepik River, a gushing torrent in the high central ranges, becomes a languid brown monster as it nears the coast. The river and its crocodiles are both central to the tribal culture of the region and its artistic tradition which is as rich and vibrant as any in the world. Each village is a gallery of tribal art, each with their own style, traditions and story. Life revolves around the river. Men in dug-out canoes, hunting, trading—the canoes themselves an echo of the mighty war canoes of not so long ago. Women fishing or hauling garden produce.

Around a third—two hundred and fifty—of the island's languages are spoken in the region. But it is knitted together by trade and the river, and its vast network of tributaries have facilitated social and cultural interaction. But rituals, genealogy and history still differentiate one group from another. Head hunting was a defining cultural practice—young men could only come of age by taking a head. Which must have added a degree of fission to 'social and cultural' interaction. Heads taken in battle would have the flesh boiled away and then be painted and decorated as trophies to be displayed in the men's houses. Perhaps not all were cannibals, but most old village men can remember that the flesh tasted a bit like chicken, and the term 'long pig' for humans was a common one. Isolated acts of cannibalism still persist to this day. The men's house — 'haus man'—is always the dominating building, no less so than the churches in the villages of Europe. Here ceremonies to please the spirits were performed, the crocodile was worshipped as a water spirit and young men underwent extremely painful initiation ceremonies and symbolic scarring and tattooing.

The Portuguese explorer, Jorge de Meneses, was the first recorded European to sight the north coast of what was to become known as Papua New Guinea, in 1526-27. In 1605 Luis Vaez de Torres explored the south of the island. The Dutch established Hollandia and took possession of the west of the island in 1828, and in 1884 Germany formally annexed German New Guinea, the northeast of the island. It was not until 1888 that the British formally annexed British New Guinea, the southeast. In 1905 Australia was given administrative control of British New Guinea and, in 1920 the mandate was extended over the old German area by the League of

Nations.

When we had arrived, we were met at the airport and chauffeured to the barracks at Moem. Unfortunately, we were told, we would need to 'camp' in a temporary married quarter for a couple of weeks until our permanent home was ready. Oh well. Not the end of the world. But what a great place for a month's leave. Lovely beaches, a tennis court near the Mess, the town looked interesting, some old army mates for me to catch up with and new friends for Ro to make, as on arriving at Moem she knew not a soul. Perfect.

Unfortunately, my new Commanding Officer told me things had changed. No time for leave. I was to immediately take over the battalion outstation at Vanimo near the Indonesian border and I would be there for three months. No families were allowed.

'But ... but ... but, what about my heavily pregnant wife and my young daughter? Sir'.

'The army comes first, Major Peterswald.'

'But we've been put in a temporary married quarter away from anyone she knows, and she will have to move again.'

'I'll lend her a Land Rover.'

'But sir, I have had virtually no leave for three years and we were really counting on some time together. I hardly know my daughter.'

A steely-eyed stare. 'Report to me for final orders before you get on the plane tomorrow. You know the army must come first, Rob.'

What I should have added, but didn't have the backbone to, was:

'Of course, sir. But since we were married four years ago, Ro has put up with moving home five times in the back of a truck between pretty shoddy rentals in Port Moresby, before we could get a married quarter. Then moved again to Lae within a few months, while she was pregnant, and then had to fly home from Lae three months early and stay with her parents. Then moved into a rental while I was on pre-Vietnam training and was away for the birth of Charlotte. Then I was overseas for twelve months and she was back with her parents, again. Then we went to Wagga Wagga where we were put in a miserable mouse-infected fibro shack where she didn't see me from 7a.m. to late most days of the week. Then we moved here so we could enjoy a break for the birth of our second child. And now you want her to have the child alone and move houses again into the bargain. Have you counted how many moves she's had to put up with?'

The CO was a good soldier who had won a military cross in Korea and had been a successful commander of the Australian Army Training Team in Vietnam. But he was a hard man, who I had gotten to know in my first posting to PNG. He rejoiced under the nicknames 'God' or 'Russ', or sometimes when he was particularly abrupt, another, which was inspired by a man who also once had a small neatly trimmed dark moustache.

So, the next day I flew to Vanimo, leaving a pregnant Ro and Charlotte to fend for themselves. Vanimo also sat on a small promontory with another beguiling view over the ocean but was much smaller. Just one trade store and a small 'club' tucked into the beach below the village—a mixture of old thatched houses and more modern 'administration-style' homes constructed from European materials. The small cluster of buildings of the army 'outstation' was on the beach a couple of hundred yards from the club.

The 'outstation' was 'manned' by my new command, 'A' Company. Myself and four other officers, five senior NCOs and around a hundred soldiers. Many years later Ro and I had a holiday at a Club Med in Tahiti, and it had about half the ambience of my new domain. It was delightful, a 'House Wind' on the shore above a white beach, wide verandas overlooking the sea, a small Officers' Mess with a bar, dining room and a billiard table, a kitchen staffed by a few competent cooks. There was a fishing net permanently strung off the beach, and I continued the practice of having a couple of 'duty divers' to ensure a regular supply of reef fish and lobsters.

In the village was an Assistant District Commissioner and a few Patrol Officers and wives, all of whom enjoyed 'sundowners' most days at the club or sometimes, as visitors to the mess. If my very pregnant Ro and three-year old Charlotte were with me, soldiering would have been great. My routine, if I was in the barracks, was very relaxing. Up at six, a five-kilometre run with the soldiers, a swim— perhaps checking the fishing net—breakfast. Stroll to my office and complete any paperwork over a cup of coffee—fifteen minutes or so—stroll around the barracks to make sure all was ship-shape, put my head into the Q-store and Signals Centre—another fifteen minutes or so. Wonder what to do for the rest of the day until five. Then drinks and dinner, billiards then a good book. Some days were not quite so frenetic.

Thankfully, most weeks I could get away from the tedium by

visiting or accompanying the platoons that were either on border patrols, training or on civic action work. The reason there was an outstation was to maintain a military presence on the Indonesian border, and to keep members of the 'The Free Papua Movement' (Organisasi Papua Merdeka or OPM) and any Indonesian soldiers who might be hunting them, on the Indonesian side of the border. The OPM had been established in 1963, after Indonesia was granted control of the former Netherlands New Guinea by the United nations in 1962. It was integrated as part of Indonesia in 1969 after a somewhat controversial 'free vote'. OPM has maintained several armed groups in the mountains on the west of the border between PNG and the Indonesian provinces of Papua and West Papua ever since. Groups were known to be crossing into PNG to avoid the Indonesian army. The insurgents claim that 500,000 Papuans, which I assume must be a pretty gross exaggeration, have been killed, and thousands raped and tortured by the Indonesian military. OPM has remained active and as recently as 2018, thirty-one civilian construction workers were killed in the Nduga area of Papua. 13,000 are reported as living in exile in PNG, and the border patrols continue to this day. The OPM have threatened raids against PNG businesses and, understandably, are seen as a threat to the country.

It was while I was escaping boredom, visiting one of the platoons as they toiled along the muddy overgrown trails that wound their way through the coastal ranges, twenty or so miles south west of the barracks, that I had a Eureka moment. It occurred to me that taking these soldiers into the bush and training them to be reliant on European rations was not all that clever. Most came into the army with well-developed hunting and gathering skills, but we never gave them the opportunity to maintain and enhance such a vital skill. So, I immediately introduced regular 'survival training' just about every time we went bush. Calling it survival training gave it a more acceptable military connotation than, 'hunting and gathering', but that is what it was—and it turned out to be also incredibly popular with the soldiers. As well as being great for morale, it was an effective way of thoroughly reconnoitring a wide area, rather than just plodding along a formed track.

The jungle is full of food if you know where to look. In some areas there are old gardens, but even in untrodden jungle there are coconuts, bananas, sago, yams and of course, snakes, possums, tree kangaroos, freshwater fish—300 species: prawns, crabs, crayfish and a million variety of birds. We would generally have a bit of a talk by a soldier from the area we were in, and there would be much whooping and boasting if the days scavenging was successful—no firearms allowed, of course. I was generally well fed. I really loved those freshwater crays—raw or cooked on a stick—supplied by those soldiers who took pity on me. Everyone learned something, even me, though I'm pretty sure I would have been only able to hold off starvation for a couple of extra hours without plenty of help from the soldiers.

I hadn't thought it a great idea to tell old Russ about our experiment until I saw how things worked out, but word got around and I think he was actually impressed when he came to check things out. Not sure whether this was what got me my next job. But two years later I was posted to the Jungle Training Centre in Queensland, recognised as the world's preeminent jungle training institution, running Survival Training.

Nevertheless, Russ and I did have 'words' a couple of times. A month or so after arriving at Vanimo, Cha came down with a fever and he was reluctant to let me fly back to give Ro some support. A little later, who should fly into Wewak than my old CO in Vietnam, Genghis Kahn himself. He was swanning around as an escort for the Chief of Defence. There were drinks in their honour at the mess, and as men generally are, he was delighted to find Ro there. As an afterthought he even asked of my whereabouts. When he found out I was in Vanimo, he was very happy to be able to offer her a seat on their plane the next day. The Chief of Defence thought it a great idea also —he had followed rugby when I was at Duntroon and we were on nodding terms. That is, he would acknowledge my existence with a nod. However, word soon leaked out and both the CO and the Commander of the PNGDF, a Brigadier who thoroughly endorsed the 'no families rule' were aghast. After the cocktail party a good friend of ours, the adjutant Michael Hughes, was dispatched with a message to Ro from the Brigadier. 'Tell Mrs Peterswald that unless she wants to be married to a major for the rest of her life, she better think of a good excuse for not getting on that plane tomorrow.'

Eventually, both the Brigadier and Russ moved on and the 'no families policy was changed. The next year the Assistant District Commissioner and his wife offered us the use of the old DC's rustic timber residence high on the hill with panoramic views of the ocean not far from the barracks. We had a wonderful few weeks there, and lots of visits from those who had not been able to come to this bit of paradise under the old rules. Some of our favourite old photographs are of Charlotte and Georgie bathing in an old tin tub in front of the cottage and playing in the pristine water at the beach.

But that was all in the future. Meanwhile, our rotation at Vanimo ended and the company returned to Moem Barracks at Wewak to prepare for an imminent patrol in the Milne Bay area, at the other end of the country. Ro had successfully moved into our new married quarter, which befitting our relatively senior status, was in a salubrious spot close to the mess. She was now very, very pregnant but was surrounded by a group of new friends who were most supportive. Two weeks after I had left them and flown to Milne Bay, Georgie, whose blonde hair and blue eyes made her a popular attraction for the milling crowd of 'one-talks'—often carrying spears and bows and arrows—who hung around the hospital wards, was born. Mother and daughter were good, and the day after the birth I received a 'Morse code' message to that effect. We had no voice communication over the old HF radios at the time. So, I didn't actually get to speak, or see any photos for that matter, of mother and daughter for another month.

Back to the jungle. We had been given a very interesting task. A week or so around Milne Bay doing the usual civic action jobs, three weeks training in the uninhabited jungle peninsula at the southeast extremity of the island—including 'hunting and gathering, of course'— and then a cruise and hike along the south coast back to Port Moresby on a 'Landing Ship Large'.

The tribes around the south-eastern coastal regions are very much a maritime people. Their traditional outrigger canoes are very impressive and have probably been in use for thousands of years and, are perfectly capable of extended ocean cruising in suitable conditions. The oldest known watercraft, a hollowed-out log preserved in a peat bog, was discovered in the Netherlands not long ago. Peat has remarkable qualities of preservation and some mummified bodies of humans thousands of years old have been discovered in a number of locations in Europe. Anyway, the hollowed-out log is around 10,000 years old. Undoubtedly there would have been earlier craft than this, perhaps just rafts made from buoyant logs, perhaps there were even oceangoing canoes with outriggers, similar to those in the photographs, older than the Netherlands' log. Some academics have suggested that the Australian aborigines, rather than arriving in Australia on foot 60,000 years ago, came by boat. But I'm not sure what they were smoking while developing this hypothesis.

In due course we made our way through to the south coast at Orangie Bay after crossing some arduous country—particularly the last couple of days which were through tidal mangrove swamps. These were excellent for foraging, lots of fish and crabs, but bloody difficult, wet and muddy to wade through. Often waist-deep and no fresh water.

Our landing ship was one of those used often in the Pacific in World War II. It was capable of running up to a beach and had a square bow that raised and lowered to allow easy access to land. There was room for a hundred odd soldiers in the hold and a couple of spare seats on a rear 'bridge deck' where two senior naval NCOs captained the vessel.

It was with great pleasure that I put my feet up and watched the coast go by. There was a small kitchen opening onto the bridge and one day I could not help noticing that a towel, containing half a dozen broken eggshells, was lying among the controls. The charts didn't seem all that good and the senior NCO at the helm was getting quite stressed about reefs and sandbanks and, started to perspire even more than normal in the humid conditions. His brow was wet, sweat dripping into his eyes and his glasses were fogging up. Swearing, he picked up the towel to wipe his face, forgetting about the eggshells, which he proceeded to smear from ear to ear. Much swearing from the helmsman and laughter from the army personnel on the bridge.

Seeking to preserve his dignity, I enquired how he managed to navigate at all with such poor charts, while surrounded by so many coral reefs.

'Oh', he replied, 'I just keep bumping into the bloody coast until we hit Port Moresby harbour, and hope we arrive there before we hit a bloody reef.'

More laughter all around, hoping he was really joking.

Anyway, it was all very pleasant. Sometimes we would drop a platoon off and rendezvous the next day, where another platoon would go ashore. Each night we managed to find a congenial place to stop. Sometimes near a village, or a patrol post or a plantation where we were always made welcome. One of our stopovers was near a light aircraft strip and Russ flew into see how things were going. He was quite surprised when I asked if he had brought a message from Ro or a photo of my new baby. He had the manners to look slightly embarrassed—not his thing.

...the love of my life ...looking remarkably svelte...

In due course we nudged into Port Moresby harbour before we struck a reef and were taken to Taurama Barracks before flying home. We arrived to find that it was in lockdown because of an outbreak of measles, and we would also be held in isolation.

'Sorry we didn't think to let you know.'

143

Much muttering from the soldiers and swearing from the officers. Eventually we got back to Wewak and I at last met my new baby princess, Georgina, darling Charlotte and the love of my life looking amazingly svelte and beautiful after Georgina's birth.

***

When we knew we were coming to Wewak we were told by a friend that we must look up a local businessman, Eric Tang and his wife, Eileen. We soon became great friends and we have caught up regularly over the years, including a couple of visits back to PNG. These days Sydney is their home and we see a lot of them. They are our daughters' oldest friends and often come sailing with us.

Eric likes golf and although not the mightiest hitter in the world, he can stay on the fairway most of the time, unlike me! It was Eric who organised a group of us on a golf trip to Rabaul, via Mount Hagen and back by Madang, for the PNG Golf Championships.

But to digress for a moment.

In later years, many of my golf-playing friends keep asking me why I do not waste my time belting a golf ball around a course with a collection of ill-designed sticks. It is an involved story, which I have never really had the chance to unburden myself of. It all started in Wagga, and well, here it is.

After Vietnam, and before our return to Papua New Guinea, we had been posted to the army training centre at Wagga Wagga, a prosperous town in southwestern New South Wales, a few hours west of Canberra. I was given a quite demanding major's position—and very importantly, a major's pay—which did not allow me much free time. But there was a nine-hole golf course near the married quarters, and on most Sunday afternoons I was able to steal a couple of hours for a round of golf with Ro. As a teenager I had had the occasional game of golf on the Manly Warringah Golf Course, which abutted Keith (Wacka) Walker's tennis courts. I enjoyed the game, but it was not something I was mad about.

But years later when I arrived at Wagga and I knew that a combination of the years lumping a heavy pack around the jungle, an imperfectly mended leg and the passage of time had turned me into a limping draft horse as far as rugby, tennis and squash were concerned. I needed another sport and wanted something Ro and I could do together.

Golf looked the thing, and I just knew I would be good at it! So, we began hitting a ball around the army course whenever we had the chance—together with Cha with her own ball and club, and our Doberman, Gunga Din on a leash. We generally had the course to ourselves.

However, as winter approached, I found myself being railroaded into taking on the extra-curricular job of 'Rugby Officer'. The CO at Wagga, Colonel Colin East was a great bloke, but like many senior officers of this era, he was a rugby fanatic. His adjutant was John Phippen, a friend who had been a couple of years behind me at Duntroon and famously was one of the winch grinders on *'Australia II'* when the America's Cup was won. John was also a keen rugby player but wanted to avoid the time-consuming job of Rugby Officer, and the odium if the unit's teams performed badly.

Now, some years previously, at the end of the rugby season in my last year at Duntroon, Ernie Johnson the rugby journalist for the Canberra Times—you still cannot trust much of what the paper writes—had anointed me as 'probably the most dangerous player' in the ACT competition— 'you're only dangerous to your bloody girl-friend'—was my friend, Peter Langford's response. This was quite a brave call as there were three Wallabies backs playing in the competition at the time. Ernie had also selected me in his end of year team ahead of the current Wallaby inside centre. So Phippen, remembering this and being a consummate military politician, sold me to his boss as the next best thing to having a Wallaby in the job, and really, I should be the playing coach of the firsts as well.

Nothing I could say could sway Colonel East. So reluctantly I was back into rugby and we did not have much time for golf. But in my second game as an awkward slow-moving inside centre I fractured my left arm above the elbow. We were able to continue chasing balls around the golf course on Sunday afternoons, but I played one-handed. The arm mended and two games of rugby later I broke the scaphoid bone in my left wrist.

I gave up playing rugby for good but couldn't get out of being rugby officer and coach.

My one-handed golf was still confined to the occasional Sunday afternoon. But by this time, I was pretty good, going around nine holes under fifty – in fact I became quite boastful about what I would be doing when I got my left arm back. Scaphoids take forever to heal, but eventually all was ready, and I took my first two-handed swing for many months. A debacle. Both arms thought they were in control and my left kept pulling the club head way over the top of the ball. Air swing after air swing, and no matter what my brain transmitted to the offending arm it was ignored once the swing began. I simply could not hit the ball.

The only ones enjoying the golf were Ro, Cha and the dog.

About this time, we were posted to Wewak. Between the stint at the outstation at Vanimo and the long patrol in the Milne Bay region, it was some time before I had the chance to have another go at golf. But eventually Ro and I got around to the odd game on a Sunday at the Wewak Golf Club. In those days, postings to the Pacific Islands Regiment came with servants, so we sometimes left the girls at home.

Finally, many months after getting the use of my left arm back I began to start connecting again. Gradually the power in my game came back, but unfortunately not my control, and my woods and long irons had hooks that most boomerangs would have been proud of. Some observers thought it would not be long before I could hook a long drive back to the tee. I spent much of each game negotiating the return of my golf balls from the local children who made a living from appropriating them if they found them before you did, even my occasional ones that stayed on the fairway.

But there was slow improvement and finally when Eric Tang proposed that a group charter a light plane and compete in the handicap division of the PNG Championships at Rabaul, Ro and I agreed to go along—leaving Charlotte and Georgie with friends.

It was supposed to be played over four rounds, but the first three rounds were washed out and it was not until the Sunday morning that there was a break in the weather and the exuberant partying that had replaced the golf. I started off badly and things got worse. By the thirteenth hole I was already an extreme embarrassment. My drive off the fourteenth was a truly awesome hook towards an out of bounds road on the other side of the neighbouring fairway.

'Don't worry mate, no one in the history of the game has ever hooked out of bounds there,' I was told as I set off in search.

But it was out of bounds. Back to the tee. Another monstrous hook and the ball unrecovered. Back to the tee. Yet another stupendous hook.

By this time there were three or four groups waiting to tee off behind us, including the visiting professionals Jack Newton and Ian Stanley who were the young up and comings of the golf world. I heard someone at the back muttering in an incredulous tone. 'This bloke won the PNG Squash Championship ?!?!?'

Totally humiliated I retired as gracefully as possible and, walked the remaining holes with my group.

Eric had already finished his round and was watching as we were walking up the eighteenth. He has only retold his recollections four or five times a year for the last forty or so years. 'I was, I was, I was' —he sometimes stutters a bit when excited and always has trouble getting it out because of hysterical laughter—'I was watching, watching everyone everyone, play, play, play their third shot'—more laughter— 'and when when, when you didn't didn't play, play'— more laughter—'I thought you must have been already on on on the green'—more laughter and spluttering— 'then then when you didn't putt putt putt I thought you must have been in the hole hole hole already for an eagle eagle two'. More laughter and starts to retell the story, adding that I was the only one in the history of the event with Did Not Finish beside my name.

It took a long while to get on a golf course again. But years later Ro insisted we have another go, in the course of which we played a round with her brother, Eugene, on the Royal Brisbane. This was a few months before I ended up having a heart operation.

I fainted on the sixteenth green and came to as one of Eugene's mates was asking in a loud voice. 'Come on, can't we pull him out of the way now, so I can putt-out'.

As you can see golf has not been kind to me.

Having got golf off my chest, back to Wagga Wagga again, for just a moment. I was in charge of training National Service conscripts on the first step along the road that led to war service in Vietnam. I had a large staff of captains, lieutenants, senior and junior NCOs and supervised a complex rotation of recruits through various training activities and assessment for fourteen hours a day, six days a week. There was a reward in seeing it all work as it was supposed to, but you could never describe it as exciting and stimulating and there are only a few lingering memories.

After all the years since, one memory still annoys me. It concerned our family living arrangements. The move to Kapooka

Barracks at Wagga would be Ro's tenth move in a just over three years of marriage. The married quarters were mainly small World War II era unloved prefab houses, that had been maintained on a shoestring budget for the last quarter of a century or so. There was no insulation between the iron roofs and the Masonite ceilings, no floor coverings over the unpolished timber floors, an empty fireplace in the small living room, no fans, no dining room, no curtains, bare gardens of grass and perhaps a stunted shrub or two. They were freezing in the arctic winters of Wagga and ovens in the summer. So, in short, most dogs would have turned their noses up. There were a few modern brick houses, but these were allocated from a 'waiting list' and there would be none available for a few months at least.

We arrived in town at the height of a dry hot summer, Charlotte was now only seventeen-months-old, just as the district was about to be invaded by a plague of mice. Soon there were mice everywhere; open a drawer and out would jump several, open a door or a cupboard and there would be a dozen more. Sit at a table, relax in a chair and you would be regarded by more of the rodents staring from some dark space or scuttling across the floor. The ceiling was alive with them and a strong smell invaded our space. The smell grew into a putrid aroma that no amount of scrubbing would dispel. We were worried about our health, but far more for Charlotte's. It was dreadful. I was out of the house from dawn until evening, so Ro had to cope mostly by herself. Our complaints fell on unsympathetic ears.

The climax came one evening when we were expecting some of Ro's old schoolfriends, mostly local landed gentry, to arrive for dinner. The house smelt like a barn and in exasperation Ro gave the sagging living room ceiling a prod with a broom handle. It burst open, showering us with twenty-five years of dust, dead mice and mouse excretion, just as there was a knock on the door.

Not a great start to our social life in Wagga.

But there is one memory that does still give me a tinge of pleasure, and perhaps a glimmer of what my life could have been if I had not been seduced by a recruiting officer and, had continued with a career at the (law) Bar. I had cause to refer one of my corporals to Colonel East over a disciplinary matter. So, in due course I appeared in front of the colonel with the offender and prosecuted the case that he should be punished. The colonel took an even dimmer view of the corporal's offence than I did and, decided to refer the man to a court martial in Sydney. In this situation the accused man can select an officer to act as his 'friend' and defence counsel. Although the corporal would have been entitled to feel some resentment for the man who had just prosecuted him, after a brief moment of indecision, he opted for myself.

Off we went to Hyde Park Barracks in Sydney, to a courtroom presided over by a bench of stern-faced, red-tabbed senior officers and the convincing prosecution's case was put by a legal officer. Now, I knew the man was guilty and deserved what he had coming. Unbeknown to the red-tabbed officers I was the reason the bastard was standing before them. But I owed him the best defence I could put up. I have never forgotten the look on Colonel East's face when back in Wagga I stood before him and admitted that the criminal, with my aid, had been found not guilty.

***

Anyway, back to Papua New Guinea. The Tangs lived on the tip of Wewak peninsula with breathtaking views over the Bismarck Sea. The best place in town, and in later years part of the extensive real estate portfolio of the 'father' of' PNG and the first Prime Minister of the country, Sir Michael Somare. Here great parties were held, with the rich aroma of 'muumuued' pig wafting in the warm tropical darkness amidst much laughter and the best of 70s music. In those days there was quite a large 'expat' community, mostly young Australians who worked and played with considerable gusto—so the Tang's parties were always hilarious fun. Looking back over the years I cannot remember how we used to get back to the barracks.

Eric and Eileen took over and greatly expanded Tang Mows, the business that was started by Eric's father and mother. It was always a family business with Eric's brothers involved and, when they eventually sold out it was easily the largest export/import, retail/wholesale business in the province, and one of the largest in PNG. The turnover was incredible and, they also fostered local businesses in villages all over the Sepik. Eric's face would be recognised by half the population in the far-flung province, and the family were liked and respected by everyone, from Michael Somare to schoolkids in the smallest village.

I tell the family's story to my grandchildren in the hope they will take something from it. Eric's father came from mainland China to Rabaul in New Britain as an indentured/apprentice carpenter in 1930. After a few years he was given permission to return to China to be married, but his wife would not be allowed to join him for six years. They were united before WWII and moved to Wewak where they started a small trade store. During the Japanese occupation they were held captive in one of the off-shore islands.

After the war they re-opened the trade store. At this stage Mr Tang could still neither read or write any language and, relied on his wife for all bookkeeping and correspondence. When Eric was a bare footed 10 year old, his father took him on a trade ship to Sydney, carrying a bag-full of trade store cash, and enrolled him in Trinity Grammar. In due course, by investing all the profits of the business, his brothers were able to follow. All went on to university paying their way with a variety of jobs.

...the Tangs... with breathtaking views over the Bismarck Sea ...

Eric drove a cab for many years, got an Economics Degree and a pilot's license and in due course returned to take over the business, with his very lovely young wife, Eileen. That an illiterate small trade store owner valued education so much and loved his children so dearly to make such sacrifices, still brings a tear to my eyes.

I had been away in Vanimo or on patrol for the best part of four months before I actually took up residence in Moem Barracks. By this time Ro had things pretty much organised. The girls were both well, they were comfortably ensconced in our new married quarter with a house-keeper/gardener, our personal luggage other than what we brought on the plane had arrived by ship, we had bought a small cheap second hand car, and new life-long friendships had been made. There were around forty members of the officer's mess - including padres, teaches, doctor and dentist - of whom probably thirty were married. The commanding officer was in his early forties, as were the padres, most of the rest were between twenty and thirty and off-hand I cannot think of anyone who didn't like a good time – well, Russ could be a bit stiff at times.

The rapid expansion of the army for the Vietnam war had resulted in quick promotions and the other company commanders were around the same age as me. It seemed I had gone from a carefree young lieutenant always whinging about the senior officers, to a stuffy old bugger myself, in no time at all.

The centre of social activity was the officers' mess, where almost every afternoon those officers who were in the barracks and not out in the bush somewhere, congregated for a drink after work. This was more or less compulsory. As the early tropical night settled over us, the single officers would wander into the dining room where they would be served by uniformed stewards. A little earlier most of the married officers would have strolled home to their bungalows, as the tropical night began to fall over the surrounding gardens and the views over the beach and the Bismarck Sea. Most nights we would entertain, perhaps one or two of the subalterns from the mess or another couple or, be entertained somewhere ourselves. Frequently we would play bridge—although card games and gambling in general was illegal in PNG at this time. Fridays there would be a party at someone's house, if there was not, it was because there was one in the mess or in town. Saturday nights could be spent at one of the clubs in Wewak or a restaurant like the popular, Windjammer, where years later we celebrated a milestone birth for Ro with the Tangs. There was a family movie night in the mess on Sundays with a buffet dinner.

You could never say that we did not enjoy ourselves.

One of the pillars of military society was the institution known as a 'Dining-in Night' and these were a feature of our lives for many years. They had been a tradition in the English military forever, certainly while the Romans were in charge and the Saxons, Vikings and Normans carried on the tradition. They were a feature during the Napoleonic period, probably reached their zenith during the times of the British Raj. The officers of old regiments, the mess awash with battle honours, their polished tables groaning under silver trophies and golden candelabra would drink fine wines and entertain royalty. And boast of their traditions and the glories of the past. Most of our military traditions came from the British, and 'Dining in Nights' is one that we took to enthusiastically. In the tropical environment of the Pacific Island Regiment we saw ourselves as upholding the fine traditions of the Raj in India, including toasts to the monarch and stirring music played by 'Pipes and Drums' of the battalion's band.

There were 'Dining-in Nights' and there were 'Mixed Dining-in Nights'. If it was the male-only version, we were seated in hierarchical order, the junior subaltern at the bottom and the President of the Mess Committee or his substitute at the head. We were dressed in 'tropical formal'—blue red-striped trousers, long sleeved white shirts with black tie and cummerbund. Attentive native waiters hovered, serving drinks and five traditional English courses. At the end, loyal toasts were drunk and, the subaltern's court was held. At first in Port Moresby things could be a bit staid early on, but as the year wound on, we all had a pretty good time most nights. After the loyal toast the Subaltern's Court was often a lot of fun. Any subaltern could prosecute a case against anyone—Major Jones for some imaginary rudeness, Colonel Smith visiting from Australia who was not in formal dress etc. Successful prosecutions were judged by acclaim – actually no one was ever found innocent—and punishments awarded in glasses of port to be sculled. More toasts and lots of shouting as discipline evaporated. Once, the soon to be Prime Minister, Malcom Fraser, was prosecuted, found guilty of something and fined seven ports. Announcing he would accept the punishment, provided we all drank along with him, we all cheered and sculled our ports.

After the court it would be time for the 'Mess Games.' Furniture was pushed to the walls and no rules 'carry the mail' a sort of rugby union with no rules, was played until exhaustion, bruised and battered limbs, and inebriation overtook us all. I'm not sure these rituals were all that good for us, and how we ever avoided all becoming alcoholics, I do not know. I suppose in hindsight we were mostly slogging it out in the bush with nothing to drink but heavily chlorinated water.

When, as newly-minted lieutenants, we arrived at Taurama Barracks in Port Moresby, and where Russ was the second-in-command at the time, we were obliged to dine 'in' every weekday night, with pre-dinner sherries, ports and 'toasts'—but not the other games. After a while, when Russ judged we had been 'polished-up' enough, this was relaxed and we had only one formal meal each week, but if we were 'eating in' on the other nights, long sleeves, trousers and ties were required. Initially women were taboo; there were no female officers at the time, but later, in a truly seismic shift, our wives and even girlfriends were made welcome.

Thankfully, by the time we arrived in Wewak, the all-male affairs were infrequent, but we had a 'mixed dining in night' perhaps once every couple of months, whenever there were enough of us around to get a reasonable crowd together. Beautifully coiffed wives, fiancées and girlfriends in long dresses with plunging décolletage graced the occasions. Looking through the candlelight gleaming on the long-polished tables, the fans rotating lazily overhead, the scent of the tropics through the open shutters, it would be hard to imagine a more glorious assemblage of stunning girls. Generally, the battalion band would assemble outside to serenade us before dinner and be there for God Save the Queen at the end. But later the LPs would come out and before long some gorgeous creatures would be dancing shoeless on the long tables. On one occasion they were led by the glamorous wife of the then Minister for the Army.

Writing this reminds me of a night some years before in Port Moresby. Often Ro and Di Battle, being the most beautiful of the girls, were seated near any visiting notable so that they would have no option but to look back on the dinner with rosy, and perhaps hazy memories. This night Di was seated next to a visiting British general whose name she had missed. Luckily, he was wearing a silver name tag which proclaimed, General D. Smith OBE—which stands for, of course, Order of the British Empire. The charmed general seemed happy to be called General Obee for the night, although Di, when it was pointed out to her, was a bit embarrassed by her mistake.

The nine-hole golf course was halfway into town, and although we didn't get a chance to play all that often—and my enthusiasm had waned again since the trip to Rabaul—we still had the occasional game and enjoyed a drink in the open-sided clubhouse. The Wewak club was on the waterfront at the edge of town and there was always an interesting group of long serving expats with interesting tales to tell of the old times. We made a number of firm friendships and still look back with joy on the fun we had.

Not so long ago, while Eric and Eileen were staying with us in Tasmania, we drove up to Launceston to catch up again with Graham and Bronwyn Walkem who we had met shortly after arriving in Wewak. We were finishing dinner in one of the fine restaurants on the Launceston waterfront, and naturally enough reminiscing about old times in Wewak, when the name of one of the lotharios of the old social scene came up. It turned out that Eric still had a phone number, and on the off chance that it was still current, it was given to Eileen to make a call.

Ring, ring. Answer. 'Please leave a message.'

Eileen - impersonating a young woman speaking in fluent pisin - *'Gude tudak Masta, mi kam long Wewak long PNG. Mi pikinini bilong yu, nau mi lik tok tok.'* Which translates to. 'Good evening sir, I come from Wewak. I am your daughter and would like to talk to you'.

Before leaving the restaurant, Eileen tried again. No answer. But over a night-cap, and before retiring she tried again. Ring, ring, ring. The other end picks up. Heavy breathing. 'Hello'. In a doubtful, quavering voice.

Eileen. 'Masta??'

Sound of call being disconnected. Much laughter in the Walkem's living room. The next morning, in a slightly less party mood, we were able to put the Lothario's mind at rest!

So, all in all the social life was great, but spoilt by the tedium of the barracks work routine. Marching, drilling, inspecting, range practices, weapons training, more marching, more inspections, more drill, more physical training, more weapons training, painting rocks white, more marching as the hot sun moved with infinite slowness across the oh so wide expanse of the sky.

***

So, despite the separation from Ro and the girls and the physical demands, the bush did have some compensation in that it was an escape from the drudgery of the barrack's work routine. Towards the end of the year the battalion was flown into the Western District of Papua to conduct operations along the border, which were designed to discourage crossings by soldiers of the Free Papua Movement (OPM) or of the Indonesian Army. It was not an area that I had been to before, other than having flown into Daru, a low-lying muddy island not far west of the estuary of the Fly, for a weekend with Ro during our first tour. It is not the most beautiful island in PNG, but the hospitality was warm and the fishing unbelievable—even I landed a good sized barramundi.

It was towards the end of the dry season when the battalion was flown in. The country was flat and covered with vast tracts of melaleuca and eucalyptus savannas. Battalion headquarters had flown in the day before and by the time my company had been unloaded they had established a comfortable camp for themselves, adjacent to a dusty airstrip about ten kilometres from the border. There were a couple of jeeps to cart the headquarters officers into the 'club' at the nearby patrol station, spacious tents with the sides rolled up, tables and chairs, duck-board floors, folding beds, showers, a tented cookhouse with a generator purring away to keep the beer cold.

We had already been allocated our area of operations and would be heading off almost immediately, but I reported to Russ at the 'operations centre', an airy tent with plenty of maps and comfortable canvas chairs, for a last-minute briefing. The operations officer, the intelligence officer and the adjutant, all good friends and dressed in clean jungle greens that looked as if they could have been starched and ironed, were there trying to look busy. Evidently there had been unconfirmed reports of 'activity' on the border. I was pretty certain the only 'activity' would have been locals fishing, and that these 'reports' were just Russ's idea off adding a bit of excitement. But as we were carrying weapons and live ammunition, I realised I would need to be bloody careful not to get some harmless fisherman shot.

Our route to the river was through an area that in the wet season would have been an extensive marsh, crisscrossed by a lattice work of small creeks. In some places there were still pools of muddy water and patches of glutinous mud in the creek-beds, but mostly they were dry. Tenacious trees, grass and vines clung to the banks. By PNG standards the going was not too bad. At least it was flat. But it was very hot and circuitous, winding in and out of creek beds, and as usual we found ourselves in a long single file moving slowly along like a giant caterpillar.

We saw no sign of anyone and camped near a creek with some small ponds of filthy muddy water, which was to be the staple for the next few weeks and needed to be laboriously filtered through canvas filters and chlorinated before use. I resolved to also boil it and add tea whenever possible and, managed to avoid poisoning myself. The next day we reached the Fly and camped on a high bank overlooking the broad sluggishly-flowing river. A pleasant, though by no means inspiring view to the far bank, lined with the same struggling copses and savanna as our own. The water quality was only marginally better than last night's muddy creek and it still took the best part of an hour to fill our bottles. We had seen several deer during the day and there had been a few large crocodiles sunning themselves on the bank when we had arrived, the arrogant buggers were actually a bit reluctant to let us near the water. It would have been a marvellous place for some 'survival training' but I thought that it would have certainly not have been appropriate with the reported 'activities' along the river.

It was an extraordinary night, not remotely like any that I had ever experienced. Once blackness settled the river seemed to become a noisy, macabre carnival, alive with splashes and grunts of hunting crocodiles and the thrashing of fish—the water was alive with them, particularly as it turned out, giant barramundi. I had claimed a spot at the very edge of the bank for my hutchie, which did have a fine view, but in the dark it seemed to be very close to the feeding crocs, and it was only the fear of loss of face that kept me there. In future I slept further back, views can be overrated at times.

The next day, we headed north before establishing a base and sending the platoons out searching independently for any signs of border crossings. Nothing, but plenty of wildlife, including wild pigs and cassowary. It came as no great surprise that one evening a couple of days later, I was served a very tasty fillet of barramundi. Thereafter, the Fly River was often lined with carefully concealed and alert fishermen. But those animals which could not be hunted silently, the deer, pigs and cassowary were left alone—as far as I know. The platoons were spread for some fifteen kilometres along the river, each with their own area in which to carry out patrols and establish look-out positions. My small company headquarters group was camped in the shade of a patch of melaleuca on a small peninsula that jutted into the river, and which seemed high enough to discourage any visits by crocs during the night. Soon, the nightly cacophony from the river became just part of the rhythm of life, and the days a gentle commune with the river. In the grey dawn animals would be drawn to the riverbank, nervous deer sipping and peering carefully over the water, birds would begin flocking to the trees along the bank. The warmth of the rising sun brought stillness, the slowly drifting water calm, no wind stirred the sparse trees or the reeds. Occasionally native canoes would come past and we would invite them for a chat and advertise the reasons we were there. The occasional squelch of the radios linked to the platoons and the battalion. The company sergeant major would idle off with a fishing line. Dusk, the flickering flames of our campfire, the aroma of cooking fish. How apt were the words of Luigi D'Albertis that he had recorded when he had passed this spot some eighty years earlier:

'The aspect of the country does not vary —always the same low lands, reeds and high grass... from time to time some forsaken huts reveal the presence of man, who finds not only food, but even a happy existence in these solitudes; where the European sees only squalor and death ... these, our fellow-beings, are perhaps happier than many millions of civilised white men'.

So, the border was secure, the soldiers well fed and in good spirits and there were three beautiful girls waiting for me (I hoped) in Wewak. When passing back through Battalion Headquarters on the way home, I had enjoyed myself so much, that I could hardly bring myself to make any derogatory jests about the comforts enjoyed by the pogos lolling around there. Few men could have ever enjoyed a fishing safari the equal to ours. And that was on top of the satisfaction of defending western democracy, of course.

In the new year it was our turn again for three months at the Vanimo outstation. This time however officer's wives were allowed to visit, and the Assistant District Commissioner at Vanimo, who had been a RAAF fighter pilot during the war and his gracious wife, offered us the old District Commissioners house on the hill for as long as we wanted it. It was agreed by all that a month's visit would be appropriate. It was one of the happiest months of our marriage. The old house was a quite elegant thatched roofed cottage with woven palm frond walls and wooden floors. Very short in modern amenities, we all bathed in a small steel tub, no electricity and candles were the only lights, but very long on charm. We mostly cooked on a fondue if at home but other nights we had drinks or played bridge with our hosts in the new more modern DC's residence by the beach or entertained in the mess. The normal routine went on during the days, while the girls amused themselves in the 'house wind' or swam and played on the beach.

...the Officers Mess, Vanimo...Georgie and Charlotte...

Friends came up from Wewak and we had many drives up to the

Indonesian border so that feet could be put over. Sadly, the girl's visit was over too soon, but it had broken the back of the three months.

On the way back to Wewak Ro's small plane had landed at Aitape to pick up a couple of passengers and drop a few off. I cannot blame blokes making a fuss of my wife—she is, after all, a gorgeous creature. The two blonde princesses were also usually entertained by fellow travellers, and this had been the case on the flight. A couple of patrol officers chatting up Ro, the girls being nursed by two friendly *merris* who carried them off the plane when it landed. After fifteen minutes or so farewells were made, the ongoing passengers reboarded. Before the plane took off, a new patrol officer took over where his mates had left off.

As the passengers were strapping in Ro was startled by Charlotte's anxious enquiry. 'Mummy, where's Georgie?' Still in the gentle arms of the *meri* who was now sitting in the rear of the plane. A month later Ro returned for the weekend of an organised function in the mess, partly financed by a jar on the bar put there by my fellow officers with the label. 'Bring Ro Back.'

When I was back in Wewak the usual routine continued. Officers arrived to begin their two-year tours; others flew home at the end of their stint. Mid-year, myself and the platoon commanders took a light plane to Bougainville to begin planning for patrols of the island. A very pleasant few days flying around the coast, sleeping in administration guest houses and talking to the District Commissioner and his staff at the various patrol stations. There was a cloudless sky on the way home. We had refuelled at Lae, then flew along the north edge of the Markham Valley. On our right lay the awe-inspiring sight of the Finisterre Range. And yes, down below us was the small village of Boana with its short grass airstrip. Four years ago, it had been the base camp for a patrol across the ranges and back via 'Shaggy Ridge' one of the famous battlegrounds of the New Guinea Campaign in WWII. It had left me with remarkable memories and some pride in the mountain crossing.

Many years later I was to come across a marvellous book, *Fear Drive My Feet* written by a remarkable man, Peter Ryan. During WWII, while he was only eighteen, he was sent behind Japanese lines to reconnoitre and gather intelligence in the Finisterre Range. For me there were two remarkable coincidences. His war-time route, a loop across the mountains and back, was as near as I can tell identical to my patrol route—only, of course done under far, far more difficult and dangerous circumstances than my hike. And he actually wrote his story in *'a narrow cell furnished with a bed, a table and a chair, all of monastic austerity. My window opened outwards towards Mount Pleasant ...'* I wondered if it was my old room at Duntroon.

However, his description of crossing the range did bring back many memories of my own. This is an excerpt, about the track a few miles north of Boana:

'As we pushed onwards the track became increasingly vague and faint, but there was no fear of losing our way, for travel in any direction except along the top of the ridge was impossible.

At ten o'clock, at an estimated height of ten and a half thousand feet, the moss forest stopped abruptly, giving place to a growth of short prickly grass, and small shrubs about two feet high. We felt freer and less oppressed. There was a little pale, week sunlight, which seemed to warm us up and lift our spirits. Far below, spread out like a map, was the Wain and Naba country and beyond, the flat country of the Markham. Lae and Salamua were both visible, and a huge stretch of coastline which we imagined must extend as far as Buna. Smoke was rising from the gardens of Naba, where men were clearing the bush. Down below us, infinitely remote, natives were working, white men and yellow men were fighting, people were being born and people were dying. But these mountains seemed to put the momentous battles and affairs of mortals into another perspective: it seemed as if they did not matter at all, and as the clouds blocked out our view we felt that other people and other lives were little more than an unsubstantial memory.

We still had several thousand feet to climb, and we set ourselves to do so before midday. Bare rock-faces, smooth and polished by the water that had trickled over them for countless ages, blocked our way every half-mile or so. To walk around them was like walking around the side of a brick wall. To enable us to negotiate them, not once but many times a native crawled around to the other side, and the others tossed lengths of vine over to him, to be made fast to the rocks, or, when convenient rocks could not be found, to himself. Then hardly daring to breathe, we crept over, feet on one rope and hands gripping the other. When we got there, we always found ourselves

160

sweating profusely, with a pain in the chest from tensed muscles and constricted breathing.

The top of the range was a semi-plateau some six or eight miles wide, a scene of utter desolation. A howling wind, with nothing to break its force, lashed us pitilessly as we struggled forward. The great limestone outcrops seemed like bones poking through the crust of the earth. When not struggling across the treacherous face of the range we were plodding painfully through a black, sodden bog of spongy earth that sucked at our feet as though it would pull us down forever. Walking, instead of being a natural rhythmic movement, became a matter of individual footsteps. Every time we lifted our feet we wondered if we had the strength, or the desire, to put them forward one more. Once—but only once— we made the near-fatal error of sitting down to rest. Intense lassitude caused by lack of oxygen in the atmosphere overcame us, and we wanted to sleep. As soon as we realised what was happening, we forced out protesting legs to resume our weight, and we stood for the remainder of our brief spells.

Headaches, faintness, giddiness, and attacks of nose-bleeding plagued us all. Then the carriers started to give us trouble. Kari (a native constable) ... in spite of his own heavy pack, rifle and ammunition, moved among them and, one by one, gave each carrier a spell for half a mile or so, shouldering their loads himself. We had no words to express our feelings, but we both looked at Kari and marvelled as he ran from one end of the line, bullying here, coaxing there, and sparing no one less then himself.

About half past four we began the descent of the north side. At first it consisted of a perfectly vertical cliff, down which we had to lower ourselves on the inevitable vine. This continued for the first three quarters of an hour or so, and thereafter it was still almost vertical until we left the grass behind and came to the forest level. About six o'clock darkness and heavy rain descended on us almost simultaneously.

(The next day) Kari sat by himself near the door ... looking out into the rain from time to time. I tried, some-what clumsily, to tell him how grateful I was for his magnificent work. He flashed me one of his rare, quick smiles. 'Something-nothing, sir. Me policeman – work belong me'. I realised that Kari, in his way, was a truly great person. The dangers, the difficulties, and the petty annoyances of our

precarious existence never troubled him: he thought only of his duty and the responsibility which command had put on his broad black shoulders ... Kari was, all the tribesmen realised, was someone who had earned respect'.

While I had been staring down at Boana and the mountains, I suddenly realised what had been worrying me. Did I want to waste my time sitting under a coconut tree beside a beach somewhere on Bougainville? I probably would never get another chance to go into the wild unknown, and there were still a couple of those in PNG.

***

The Star Mountains, sitting astride the PNG/Indonesian border, are part of the great range of mountains that runs down the spine of the whole island. They are 4,000 metres high, one of the wettest places on earth with an average rainfall of 10 metres a year, and for many months of the year, freezing. Across the border in West Papua some of the peaks are snow-covered for much of the year. The country surrounding the high mountains is some of the most difficult on earth: steep ridges, deep ravines, precipitous cliffs, sink holes, caves, roaring torrents and places where the solid ground lies twenty or thirty metres below a floor of suspended moss-covered fallen timber. Their southern flank is protected by the towering cliffs of the Hindenburg Wall. A series of almost vertical cliff faces rising precipitously to heights of 3300 metres, over 2000 metres above their jungle-clad feet. In the mountains lie the headwaters of two of the world's great rivers. The Sepik flowing north to the Bismarck Sea and the Fly south to the Coral Sea.

As I have already mentioned, the first European to approach within sight of these great massifs was the Italian explorer Luigi D'Albertis, and it was his account that first spiked my interested in this wonderful island. On his 1876 voyage up the Fly River in a tiny steamer he managed to reach a point some four hundred miles from the coast. Extracts from his account of his expedition make compelling reading.

'20 April 1876. Having obtained from the Governor of New South Wales a steam-launch for my projected cruise up the river Fly, I left Sydney ...

18 May. At 1 pm we weighed anchor, and came through the

Albany Passage, saluted by our Somerset friends with the usual waving of white handkerchiefs...The 'Neva' was a small steam-launch, her greatest length measuring fifty-two feet, and her greatest width seven feet. She was neither deck nor cabin...and was about six inches out of the water amidships ... Lord Byron Wrote, in 1810. 'Today in a palace, tomorrow in a stall with cows; today with a pasha, tomorrow with a shepherd'. These words of the poet occurred to me forcibly today as I looked to my surroundings. I have a tent for a house, with sand for a bed, and a stone for a pillow ... The wind is blowing fiercely, and the sea roars as it dashes on the shore. The noise of the wind rushing through my tent, through the grass, and leaves of a pandanus tree, is positively deafening'.

22 May. ...at half-past six we anchored (in the mouth of the Fly River).

26 May. The island is covered with beautiful vegetable growths, and its trees are very tall, and of a rich deep green. The muscatel-nut abounds. The shore is covered with tangled vines, and especially with a magnificent long-leafed rattan, which climbs to the top of the highest trees...the trunks and branches are covered with ferns and orchids. There is also a plant in flower which forms the most beautiful ornament of the forest I recognised the notes of two or three species of birds of paradise...flocks of pigeons...white and black cockatoos ... the shrill cry of several species of lories ... hoarse voiced horn-bills...many small insectivorous birds gave merciless chase to the insect...a solitary eagle-fisher...discovered a family of bats ...

28 May. We passed more islands, covered, like the former ones with magnificent forests, impenetrable to the eye.

30 May. In the afternoon we passed a village ... five natives were shouting and gesticulating like madmen ... they were armed with bows and arrows...wore large white shells on their breasts.

31 May...we found ourselves in a country which the white-man has not hitherto invaded. The river seemed to assume a more uniform appearance, its depth is from seven to nine fathoms ... the vegetation diminished as we proceeded...we were leaving the immense forests ... the left bank was almost barren...(but) a few feet from the water abounds a small tree, or shrub... thousands of large flying foxes, who pass the day on the trees, waiting for night, when they sometimes travel enormous distances in search of fruits ...

3 June ...we reached a small cocoa plantation...behind came a village, then dense forest and low hills.

4 June. The aspect of the country does not vary – always the same low lands, reeds and high grass...from time to time some forsaken huts reveal the presence of man, who finds not only food, but even a happy existence in these solitudes; where the European sees only squalor and death...these, our fellow-beings, are perhaps happier than many millions of civilised white men.

5 June. ...by their shouts, gestures, arms and adornments, I understood they had come to fight ... we steamed on until we came to some old dwellings...where we anchored...we had again reached thickly wooded country.

6 June. The banks of the river are high and covered with fine forests which obstruct the view across the country, but it is, I believe undulating.

7 June. Late ...another deserted village...there were many tobacco plants of great height, with long broad leaves, and seemingly of excellent quality.

10 June. The forest is more beautiful than can be imagined ... another plant covers the tops of the trees with leaves and masses of flowers. We continued to advance north. The banks are beautiful and richly wooded. The bed of the river...continues from three to five fathoms.

16 June. The river is very much narrower, and winds in and out between hills, which rise higher towards the interior...the man on the look-out shouted, 'House ahead, and people running away!' After having examined everything and taken possession of some of the more interesting curiosities, leaving in exchange knives, glass beads and cotton cloth...we resumed our voyage. The depth diminishes...we felt the grating of the keel. The great quantity of stones indicates the neighbourhood of mountains, which, however, are hidden from us by the dense forest, that forms ... two lofty walls along the bank of the stream...the variety of plants and animals is such as to make the heart of a naturalist beat with joy.

17 June. At last I have seen the lofty mountains of the interior of New Guinea! I have seen them, like giants of differing heights, towering one above the other, and extending from the principal chain down to the river. But we are still far from these Papuan Alps – forty or fifty miles or more. My mind is on the rack. I feel like

Moses, in sight of the Promised Land, destined never to enter it! Although each day we draw nearer the end of our voyage, our difficulties are increasing. Illness is wasting the strength of my people; each day we feel painfully the dearth of provisions, but we know not how to remedy it. Shortly after starting this morning we found ourselves in only three and a half of water, and Neva bumped violently...two more men were attacked with fever.

19 June. Our provisions...are almost at an end ... the current is strong...the river narrower and more shallow...we had the ill-luck to ground three times.

21 June. All the night heavy rain.

22 June. ...the engineer, the cook and two other men, are all ill with fever. The current is so powerful that we cannot attempt to breast it. We are holding by two anchors which occasionally drag along the bottom and make us afraid of being swept away at any moment. I noticed numerous footpaths and beaten tracks over the hills, so there is no doubt about its being inhabited.

28 June. ...the current is six or seven knots, the channel narrow, the eddies make the rudder useless ... we are without provisions.

With no hope of going any further D'Albertis gave the order to turn back, having reached a position some miles north of the junction of the Fly and Ok Tedi rivers. There were a number of skirmishes in which some local natives were killed, and he has been criticised for acts of theft and desecration as well as fishing with dynamite. He was born in 1841 in Voltri, Italy and began an adventurous life when at the age of eighteen he joined Garibaldi's army. In 1885 Captain Everill and in 1890 Sir William MacGregor also ascended the Fly to within sight of the mountains. The first European to actually reach the mountainous area around the headwaters of the mighty Sepik River near Telefomin was Richard Thurnwald, a member of a German exploratory expedition in 1912-13. Leo Austen, a PNG patrol officer was the first to reach the southern foothills of the Hindenburg Range in 1922.

The first recorded crossing of the Owen Stanleys from the Sepik River to the Fly was in 1942. Unwilling to risk a maritime escape from the approaching Japanese, a party of eight European men undertook an overland escape to the Papuan coast. Led by Jack Thurston, they departed Timbunki on the Sepik River on 14 April 1942 and proceeded up the May River by canoe. They commenced walking on 8 May and arrived in the Telefomin valley on 25 May. In late July they reached the Fly River where they were able to build canoes and paddled downstream arriving at Daru on 24 September.

But even twenty years later, by the early 1960s few people had lived or passed through this remote and rugged country. It was one of the least disturbed tropical landscapes on earth. It was not until 1963, three years before my first patrol in the Southern Highlands, that Des Fitzer a patrol officer stationed at Kiunga, led a mapping expedition through the Hindenburg Range to the Star Mountains.

The following are edited extracts from an article in the Journal of the Papua New Guinea Association of Australia, written by Judith Blogg 12 January 2017.

The 1963 Fitzer patrol to the Star Mountains, was the first of its kind into that high wild country. Three men and sixty carriers left Kiunga on the Fly River on 17 Jan 1963 aiming for the 'top pocket' near Mount Capella. Walking up to seven hours a day their route took them along barely identifiable tracks that led from the swampy, leech-plagued low country into the craggy, cloudy, precipitous mountains. They built bridges and contrived ladders to scale sheer bluffs. They were always wet and dirty and met villagers who almost certainly had never seen a white man. They had moments of sheer delight at the unfolding magnificence of the country they were struggling through, of jumping into crystal clear pools.

At several villages they were told there was no track to the 'top pocket' but Fitzer decided this was merely reluctance to guide them into difficult country and they struggled on. It was slow, slow going. But eventually, near the foot of Mount Capella they found a group who was willing to show them the way. They were critically short of food. The terrain was terrible, and it became necessary to hack their way through jungle, at times crawling on hands and knees and wading in icy streams. Finally, the terrain, the state of the carriers and the lack of food defeated them. They were forced to retrace their steps to the south side of the range and follow the Hindenburg Wall for some distance east before crossing the range to Telefomin, descending into the broad grassy valley on the eastern side of the 'Stars'. They were ordered to await the arrival and be presented to the Governor-General who 'seemed quite nice but of course very English'.

Two years later in 1965, an expedition into the Star Mountains by six Europeans with thirty odd Telefomin carriers was organised and led by the teacher and anthropologist Barry Craig. He had been living in Telefomin since 1962 and had done a number of surveys in the nearby valleys and an aerial survey of the Star Mountains and, was in touch with local patrol officers and missionaries. The object of the expedition was to begin topographical and geological surveys, explore the caves systems thought to be in the area, make a collection of flora and fauna, study evidence of glaciation, record anthropological and linguistic data, collect frogs and lizards for the South Australian Museum, together with the collection of botanical plants from above 9,000 feet. Also, to provide topographical information and track times for the military, who had provided 1963 maps.

One of the indigenes on the expedition was Nimisep, who had been jailed, along with another 31 Telefomin men, for killing two patrol officers and two policemen in 1953. He had been released in 1962 and proved to be an exceptionally reliable and thoughtful member of the expedition. Another was Dakamdapnok whose natural curiosity had taken him along some of the trade routes by which certain important artefacts came to Telefomin—including stone adze blades from West Papua and bow staves from the southern lowlands—to see new country and meet new ethno-linguistic groups.

There are several ethno-linguistic groups in the surrounding mountains. A distinguishing feature was the graded initiation rituals for young men that ensured skilled gardeners, fearless warriors and enlistment of ancestral spirits for the well-being of families and communities. Men, women and children all participated in gardening and gathering activities and the men specialised in hunting, most particularly in hunting feral pigs, an activity almost as dangerous as attacking humans. Domestic pigs were primarily the domain of women. Relationships with the locals in the region of the patrol were generally friendly and co-operative. We had glass beads and trinkets, salt and tobacco for trade (mostly for garden produce).

For Barry Craig, the most memorable incident of the expedition occurred at a place called Kawolabip, amongst the Wopkaimin tribe:

I came across a burnt-out men's house with a burnt shield in it. I asked about it and was told it had been an accident – a fire had broken out from an unattended hearth. That night a couple of our

167

Tifalmin carriers came to me with the suspicion that a relative who had gone to live among the Wopkaimin and had married a girl there, had been murdered in the hut—and the hut burnt down to conceal the evidence (it turned out that they had joined the expedition precisely to find out what had happened to the relative who had been reported missing). My reaction was, 'No body. No case.'

So, the next day they went and looked around the area of the burnt-out hut and located the body thrown in a nearby stream, with evidence of a mortal axe-blow to the neck and a length of rattan tied to one ankle. Suddenly this was a serious matter. I was on my own at the time (the rest of the team had gone ahead) and had a couple of the relatives of the dead man wanting justice, a nervous local population and a handful of Telefomin carriers who were sympathetic to the alleged victim's tribe.

My first action was to photograph the body as evidence for any future action by the Administration, I then conducted a careful investigation to identify the culprits and motivation. The Wopkaimin assumed, incorrectly, that I was part of the Administration and identified with the judicial process. Under local custom the resolution would have involved a pay-back killing. After a few hours I had identified the killer and the motivation and produced a report for future action. But by 1981 nothing had been done.

The main dangers were falling into a crevasse in the limestone karst up on the mountains, or off a makeshift sapling footbridge across a turbulent creek. I have notes in my diary for the track westward along the 11,000 foot ridge running between the headwaters of the Kwol River flowing south into the Digul River and the headwaters of the Din flowing north into the Sepik.

There were many small sink holes which were hidden beneath moss that were very dangerous. I fell into a couple and they were very difficult to get out off; some crevasses were 20 to 30 feet deep. Often, to, a step on harmless-looking moss precipitates one downward into large holes, also very dangerous.

There were rumours of Indonesian patrols immediately across the border and there was concern that we might cross the border and create an international incident. On the other hand, the Pacific Island Regiment at Wewak wanted to hear as much as possible about Indonesian movements near the border (nothing of significance emerged). They also wanted copies of photographs and to be able to obtain track-times from us to assist with any future army patrols through the area. During the 1960s, units of the Pacific Islands Regiment based at Wewak were active along the border, led by officers of the Australian Army.

The main things we achieved were the clarification of the geography of the region which had until 1963 been a 'blank space' on the maps. Our collections of flora and fauna extended the range of many previously known species. Anthropological and linguist data filled the gap between what is known of the Telefomin of PNG and the Sibil valley people of then Dutch New Guinea.

Somethings that I personally learnt from the experiences in the mountains. Having been trained as a social anthropologist, I began to see the irrationality of the Christian belief system and that I was no longer a Christian. I learnt other lessons—about understanding myself in relation to others, my anxiety about being 'alone'. Perhaps unsurprisingly fifty years later I no longer have this anxiety, nor the fear of death although, also unsurprisingly, I would prefer death to happen later than sooner. I have a quote from Umberto Eco posted at the entrance to my museum office: 'It is necessary to meditate early and often on the art of dying, to succeed later in doing it properly just once.'

At the time of the expedition, PNG was still under colonial rule and some people might suggest that the expedition and its goals were an extension, even indirect, of that rule over another people. But post-modernist and post-colonial trains of thought have no traction with me. We are what we are and act in the context of our times. We cannot be held individually for the currents of historical circumstances which shape us more than most us can ever shape them. As individuals, what matters is the nature and quality of our relationships with the 'other', whether in a colonial or post-colonial context. The men who came with us crazy Australians to climb the Star Mountains had their own agendas—adventure, to see the wider world beyond their valley, do some personal trading, to find out what had happened to a missing relative. They were fed and paid well, their health and welfare were maintained, they participated and made possible the success of our venture and were appreciated accordingly.

One of the expedition members was Doctor John Huon, who expressed the common attitude of Europeans towards carrying their own gear.

'Gentlemen, it is not that I do not wish to carry myself, but it is unseemly for my European dignity. There is nothing, we may say 'colonial' about it, no but the respect of a carrier is dangerously lowered. By all means take your carrier and rain cape or something of the sort. That is what I advise. I myself carry the tea thermos and camera in a shoulder bag. It is, so I call it, my 'prestige load'.'

As soon as I got back to Wewak from the aerial reconnaissance of Bougainville, I made an appointment with the CO and prevailed upon him to transfer the patrol to the Telefomin area. Apart from my personal desire, there were compelling reasons to have a good look at the border ranges from a security perspective in any case. Our patrols would be tasked with filling in some of the gaps not covered by the two earlier expeditions, that are described above.

In late 1972 my company was flown into Telefomin by Caribou transports. This small outpost was set in a beautiful high valley, ringed by the Victor Emmanuel Ranges, their great peaks beginning to disappear behind the shrouded afternoon clouds. Our planned patrol routes were for one platoon to follow the Sepik valley south to the lowlands. Company headquarters and two platoons would follow the Ilam River westward to its source, cross the Star Mountains plateau west of Mount Capella to the Hindenburg Wall and descend into the valley of the Ok Tedi. After patrolling the border in this area, we would follow the southern side of the Hindenburg Wall to the headwaters of the Fly River and cross back over the Hindenburg Range to Telefomin. In contrast to Doctor John Huon I had my familiar pack, weighing some thirty kilograms on my shoulders, rather than a team of thirty locals carrying all the comforts of home. My European dignity was somewhat impaired by my groans as I assimilated the weight and lurched off, leaving a small administrative group camped near the airstrip. Despite the groans, my spirits soon soared at the thought of the high mountains and unexplored mysteries that lay ahead.

A narrow well-formed track, slippery in places, led downhill from the western end of the airstrip to a footbridge over the rushing headwaters of the Sepik. After crossing the bridge, the track gradually rose ahead of us, following the contours around the ridges above the valley of the Ilam River. They were covered in waist-high kunai grass with copses of forest in the gullies, some scattered native gardens and the occasional thatched hut. Some groups of chattering 'meris' passed us, returning home with heavily laden billums.

Around midday we stopped beside the track for lunch, and before

...a bamboo bridge over the headwaters of the mighty Sepik...

long mugs of tea were simmering on our small hexamine stoves and I was savouring the brief relief from the burden of my pack. A wide blue sky stretched above us, framed by the green of the mountains, a light breeze drew down the valley, gently stirring the tall grass. During the afternoon, as we skirted around the kunai covered walls of the valley from where we could admire the majestic views surrounding us, dark clouds began to form on the mountain tops. But we were able to reach the small village of Ulapmin and had our hutchies up before the rain was heralded with a roll of thunder. It was cold as darkness fell and I was very thankful for the warm sleeping bags and warm waterproof jackets that we were carrying in our bulging packs. But I could not help wondering what it would be like when we were another six thousand feet up. Bloody freezing was the only possible conclusion.

The next day took us to Tifalmin, where there was a small light aircraft strip and a group of scattered huts around a small mission station, manned by a young couple with two small children. You could not help but admire them as they carried on their life surrounded by tribesman decorated with all the glory of highland warriors: body paint and tattoos, necklaces of shell and pigs task, pieced nosed and carrying bows and assorted arrows, some long and tipped with deadly barbs, others lighter with 'nobbed' ends that were for hunting birds. The Telefomin area is famous for its painted war-shields of shaped timber up to about five feet in length and elaborately carved and painted. I shared a cup of tea and exchanged gossip with the missionaries before thankfully crawling into my warm dry bed with the rain again drumming on the taunt roof of my hutchie.

We were still following the route of Barry Craig's expedition, but by the fourth day we were close to the headwaters of the Ilam where we planned to turn southwest and, follow a spur line to the high plateau east of the walls of the Star Mountains. We camped early, on the edge of the open kunai, with a view back down the valley we had been labouring in, to the mountains behind distant Telefomin. We needed to take a resupply by helicopter. Our next stage would be in the high country with no chance of either finding local food or because of the perpetual cloud cover, taking a resupply. I estimated that we were now close to 2600 metres and it was another wet and cold night; I slept in my pullover and padded waterproof jacket just to get a sense of whether I was going to freeze to death or not in the high mountains that were now getting very close. A faint trail led upwards into the rainforest.

Off early the next morning, while the first pink flush of dawn was framing the eastern peaks. The shadows and the chill of the night still lingered once we were under the thick canopy of the rainforest, there was only the hint of a track leading steeply upwards through the fallen leaves and tangled vines. It was slippery underfoot and shortly we were struggling along a narrow ledge, with a drop to our right that disappeared into the undergrowth.

By the time the sun had penetrated the canopy the cold of the night was forgotten and before long we were our normal sweat-soaked selves. The track soon petered out and the trees pressed in on us, becoming more and more choked with fallen and decaying trunks and branches that became harder and harder to find a way through. The trees and the detritus of the jungle floor grew ever more covered with mosses of every size, shape and colour, and we sensed that we were approaching one of the fabled 'moss forests.'

...soaking, muddy and exhausted...on the edge of the moss forest...darkness had just started to creep through the mist and drizzle ... how quickly a patch of wet jungle can become a welcome haven... camp site above the Hindenburg Wall at around 3,400m...

Progress was slow as we scrambled through the fallen undergrowth, and when we stopped for something to eat at midday it was so thick that it was almost impossible to find a seat amongst the tangled timber. We crawled, as much as walked on, and found that we were now on a false floor of fallen moss-choked timber some distance off the ground. Through the shadows we could not even see where it lay. In the early afternoon a mist drifted down through the jungle, the cold returned and it started to rain. It was impossible to know how far we had come or what height we had reached.

Darkness had just started to creep through the mist and drizzle when a shout from ahead announced we had reached firm ground again. When I got there, I found a narrow ridge top with a distant view obscured by mist and cloud. But there was enough room to camp on the ground, and before long hutchies were up, and in their shelter hexamine fires were casting a small glow amid the muted sounds of camp. How quickly a patch of wet jungle can become a welcome haven. After checking on things, I retired to my hutchie, stripped off my soaking 'jungle greens' and pulled on an air force flying suit which I was experimenting with instead of spare jungle greens, because it was much lighter and easier to carry, and my warm jacket and wondered where the hell we were. My ordnance map was useless, showing no detail other than the cryptic comment 'obscured by cloud'.

It rained for much of the night but in the morning some weak sunlight was struggling through the greenery and I was delighted to find that there was an open view to the west and south. And, there on our western horizon were the massive walls of the Star Mountains, and perhaps, peeping through some distant cloud was Mount Capella (3960 metres) which had been climbed for the first time a few years earlier by Barry Craig's expedition. We were probably at something around 3400 metres and the high plateau stretched before us.

Tui, my batman, brought me a coffee as I admired the grandeur of the view, standing where I was pretty sure no European had stood before me. Back into my wet greens, breakfast of curried bully beef and rice, and off into the plateau, which from where we stood looked benign enough.

We spent the next two days winding our way carefully westward. At times through low grass broken by hillocks and tarns, swamps and patches of moss-forest crammed into narrow valleys. We warily skirted sink holes, some large ones that looked like mighty meteor craters, and smaller ones a metre or two across; the tarns and bogs reminded me a bit of some of the peat lands on the west coast of Ireland. Mostly it was slow, rather than tortuous, and at times the sky cleared for a while and we were granted dramatic views of the range ahead, and of probably, Mount Alyang back to the east. But mostly we walked in drizzle and mist, it was freezing and, we were very thankful for our waterproof padded coats.

The first night we camped beside an enchanting tarn and Tui conjured up a small smoky wood fire, the second on a rocky ledge on the lip of the Hindenburg Wall, overlooking the valley of the Ok Tedi. Both nights had a special ambience that has stayed with me; the perfection of the tarn from the bank on which my hutchie stood, the smell of the fire, the intimacy of the dark. The second, the height of the sheer drop of the Hindenburg Wall, the mighty mountains, seemingly endless jungle below stretching away to the horizon. Perhaps I could see, but not identify the hill from which Luigi D'Albertis first laid eyes on these great mountains, not so many years ago.

We were close to the Indonesian border now; it lay just beyond the eastern ridgeline of the Ok Tedi, but there had been no sign of either the West Papuan rebels or of the Indonesian military. To be sure we were missing nothing we camped for a day and I sent the platoons to scout further to the north and west, but there was no sign that any human being had ever set foot in the area. It took us the best part of the next day to get down to the level of the bottom of the wall, climbing down some steep rock faces, clambering along the rocky banks of the river with some detours along ridgelines. At the bottom we met the first tribesman from the south of the range. He was an amiable warrior, and although we had no common language, he seemed to be saying that it was nice to meet us, and his village was some way downstream. It was a pleasant spot where we met, and by the time we had finished chatting we decided we may as well make camp.

The next morning was a relatively pleasant stroll to the village and we were there by mid-morning. It was sitting on a knoll over-looking the junction of the Ok Tedi and another stream, about on the same level as where the notorious Ok Tedi mine was to be located some years later. A stroll up the hill would have put me on top of some hundreds of tonnes of gold and nine million tonnes of copper, which would have set me up nicely for life. Unfortunately, the friendly villagers neglected to tell me, although I did negotiate the purchase of three exquisite wooden shields, which I backloaded to our base camp on the resupply helicopter. Fifty years later they

... some of the girls of Tabubil...

remain treasured possessions, of infinitely finer quality than the dross adorning the national gallery. Do I feel guilty having purchased items of such cultural value? Sometimes. But think more that they have been saved. They would have long since vanished or rotted in the damp smoke-filled gloom of the '*haus* man' where they were stored.

The '*haus* man' was actually in a great spot, dominating the village and with a panoramic view eastward along the face of the Hindenburg Wall. Definitely a good place to smoke twist tobacco, tell lies and solve the problems of the world with your mates. Sergeant Suku, the police constable and I spent quite a few hours here chatting to the men of the village, and our oblique enquiries did not discover any knowledge of across border activity.

Our track continued south, still following the course of the Ok Tedi—sometimes along the rocky edges, sometimes cutting through the thick bush. It was another easy day to the village of Tabubil, where I spent more time talking with the men about what was happening across the border. We camped close to the edge of the village for four nights so that the platoons could have a look along an old trade route that ran west into West Papua and another south along the river. There were no signs on either of any cross-border activity. After they returned, we had a rest day then packed our hutchies and turned our faces homeward. We were about halfway.

At the edge of the village, where the main track continued south along the river, a less used one headed eastward. We were told would take us to the '*big pella warra tu mus,*' which we presumed was the Fly River. Which in due course it did, and there were even some native bridges over some of the gushing torrents that we crossed on the way. But it was across the grain of the country and we toiled up dozens of ridgelines, all steep and muddy, some higher than others and over dozens of streams, mostly wading knee deep across slippery rocks. It was hard, hard work. Sometimes the clouds and the forest would open up and we were rewarded with the sight of the immense sheer rock faces of the Hindenburg Wall. But mostly it drizzled, or sometimes eased to a thick wet mist. The dense foliage and the jungle floor were always wet, and to take a seat on the ground or on a fallen tree would invite a plague of leeches—I could literally watch the blood-sucking little bastards propelling themselves towards me, over the sodden mud like small snakes.

After three days we took another resupply at the light aircraft strip at Olsobip. Camping on open ground adjacent to the strip we had a fine view over the headwaters of the Fly and the mountains that wrapped all around us. We luxuriated through a sunny afternoon, a rare chance to get things dry as we repacked our gear and tried to eat and drink what we did not want to haul back over the range. Our mostly useless ordnance map showed just one range, the Hindenburg, along with a number of blank patches with the familiar captions 'obscured by cloud'. You can imagine my disgust that after hauling ourselves to the top of the Hindenburg we were confronted with another unmarked monster.

But we did not know about this as we set off northward along the ridges on the western side of the river. The sun had left us, a misty rain fell from a leaden sky. There was a footpad for the first few hours, but it was only a memory by the time we made camp, cold

...when I finally staggered to the top, after God knows how many false crests...from close to our camp we could see Telefomin in the valley ahead...

and wet, on a high ridge. Sunrise the next morning revealed that we were on the rim of a huge crater, covered in jungle and kunai, which was the cup that held the headwaters of the Fly. The last of the Hindenburg wall wrapped around its northern face, and from where we looked it seemed as close to the mythical 'Shangri-La' as is likely to be found in this world.

I admired it over a cup of coffee and took a compass bearing to what looked the most likely place on the far side for us to climb out. It may well actually have been Shangri-La, there was no rain, only blue skies as we followed interlocking patches of kunai down to the river, crossed without any problems and found a reasonable easy climb out. The jungle was thick at the top, but there was a spot to camp with a fine view back over where we had come the last couple of days, so we camped while the sun was still with us. We were probably back at around 3200 metres. The rain returned in the night, but I was ensconced in my finely built hutchie, its roof as tight as a drum-skin, I was dry, under an impenetrable mosquito net, wrapped up in my warm jacket and sleeping bag and soundly asleep.

But the gods had not finished playing with us. So far, we had spent several days dragging ourselves through some very thick moss forests, often several metres off the ground.

But nothing as bad as where we now found ourselves, and just as we thought it couldn't get any worse the rain turned to sleet and we did literally slow to an actual crawl, as we climbed, crawled and wriggled through the maze of moss-covered rotting timber. At the time I didn't appreciate that this little bit of hell in which we were imprisoned, was the actual watershed of PNG's two greatest rivers. Behind us, rainfall drained to the Fly, ahead to the Sepik.

Late in the day we finally reached the far edge of the broad mountain top we had traversed. There was a place with enough room to camp, so we dropped our packs and started to get organised. While this was in hand, I traipsed off a bit to see what lay ahead. I was assuming that we had climbed our last mountain before Telefomin. But, imagine my disgust, when I did find a vantage point and saw ahead another bloody range about as high as where I now stood.

A hot curry restored my morale and after another freezing night we slid down probably fifteen hundred metres into a swampy valley with dozens of small meandering water courses, which turned out to be tributaries of the Sepik. Then up one of the longest kunai-covered ridges that I have ever seen, to the top of what I had thought was a separate range. But when I finally staggered to the top, after God knows how many false crests, and could have a good look around I realised that it was actually a spur of the same range. If our bloody map had a bit of detail on it, we could have crossed a few miles to the west and avoided most of the day's hard labour. Oh well, it didn't matter now! From close to our camp we could see Telefomin in the valley ahead.

That patrol was the last time I spent any length of time in the PNG jungle. Towards the end of the year Ro, Charlotte, Georgie and I boarded a plane for home, and that chapter of our lives was closed. But the memories have stayed with me. The excitement and challenge of exploring remote places and sharing so much of it with Ro, and the pride we took in helping to create a new nation.

***

There was another aspect also. During our five years in PNG, World War II was never far away. I had visited all the battlefields where Australians fought. Most have been reclaimed by rainforests, jungle and tall grasses and it was easy to appreciate the conditions the soldiers endured, while the numbers killed and wounded testify to their bravery, and the bitterness of the fighting. The experience left me feelings of both pride and sorrow. During my first posting to 1PIR in Port Moresby we spent a lot of time training along the Kokoda Trail or in the areas adjacent to it. I lost count of the number of times our week started with a long climb down from Ower's Corner to the crossing at Goldie River and ended on Friday afternoon with the long slog back up. It was only twenty-five years since the battles along the trail had been fought, and there were still reminders hidden everywhere in the undergrowth: trenches, helmets, weapons, ammunition and the other detritus of war. I had of course, studied the campaign at Duntroon and was familiar with the details, and I now became intimate with the battlegrounds: Imita Ridge, Ioribiwa, Menari, Brigade Hill, Efogi, Templeton's Crossing. But the more I walked among the fading reminders, the more I asked myself, was the whole bloody tragedy, the cost in killed and wounded really what had to be paid to win this brave victory, fought in ghastly circumstances. Have we been critical enough of the unnecessary lives lost here, and in the later battles along the north coast? Lives lost by poor planning and preparation before the war and sacrificed by their high command. I realised that among the tragic white crosses at the Bomana War Cemetery, that there were many that should not have been there.

Three years later, when we arrived in Wewak, the reminders of the World War II battles were still there. Within a kilometre of the officers' mess, the remains of a Japanese headquarters position were rotting in the thick jungle. Strangely, among the ruins was a swimming pool built from thousands of glass bottles embedded in cement. The Battle for Wewak was the last battle of the PNG campaign, and probably should never have been fought. The

Japanese 18th Army, numbering around thirty-five thousand men,

...we had flown back to Wewak to celebrate one of Ro's important birthdays with Eileen and Eric Tang...

was spread along the coast and mountains between Aitape and Wewak. They were effectively cut off from Japan, short of ammunition and supplies and could have been left to either starve or surrender. But in the name of being seen to be doing something in support of the US forces fighting elsewhere, a campaign was launched by the Australian Sixth Division. The Australians suffered 587 dead and 1,141 wounded. The Japanese losses were absolutely horrific. Only two hundred and sixty-nine of the thirty-five thousand survived to be taken prisoners. There were perhaps nine thousand battle deaths and the remainder died of starvation or disease in the jungle.

In 2006 when we had flown back to Wewak to celebrate one of Ro's important birthdays with the Tangs, the horror of this campaign was rammed home to us by a chance meeting. We had driven up to the Moem War Cemetery, a visit which in itself is a very, very humbling and sorrowful thing.

The white crosses marking more unnecessary deaths of so many brave young Australians, and stark reminders of the pain and emptiness their deaths left behind.

While we were standing there a bus pulled up and a number of grey-haired Japanese climbed out. In due course we got to talking to two charming ladies who were about our age. It turned out they were on a pilgrimage to the area where their fathers, whom neither lady had met, had been among the thirty-five thousand soldiers whose bodies had been left to rot in the jungle sixty years before. That encounter was one of the most mournful moments of my life.

It had been over three decades since we had walked the streets of Wewak. Now we were the only white faces among the throng in the main street. The locals seemed the same, plenty of smiles and greetings as we wandered around the market full of the tropical produce that we remembered so well. But a lot had changed. There was an unloved aura about the buildings, rusty roofs and broken glass, and the bitumen of the roads was potholed with broken edges. The once manicured gardens had been replaced by overgrown grass and barbed wire fences. The garden of the Tang's home was surrounded by high barbed wire, with a locked gate manned by a sentry. Guards patrolled the grounds after dark and Eric slept with a pistol under his pillow.

Although it was not as dangerous as Port Moresby had become, which at this time was one of the most dangerous cities in the world, you certainly wouldn't stroll the streets after dark, and six months after we left one of Eric's brothers was seriously wounded and almost killed by a machete-wielding robber. The once charming Sepik club, where we had spent so many fun evenings was a sad memory of what it had been, still standing beside the sea but nearly deserted at sundown. There was still the yacht club and a functioning golf course, but it was impossible to run any competitions due to the prevailing attitudes towards counting the number of strokes and other irritating rules such as not improving your lie!

We visited Moem Barracks and found it in a sorry unkempt state. A sad mouldy ruin of what it had once been, peeling paint, broken roofs, boarded-up windows. But we were welcomed by the young Pacific Island commanding officer who would have not been born when Russ sat in his seat, and we had a cup of coffee and a chat. He was disgusted by the endemic political corruption which left wages unpaid and little money to run the army.

What was otherwise a wonderful couple of weeks with Eric and Eileen, including visits to the offshore islands, and some of the villages along the Sepik and the coast, was dampened by the obvious failings of government and widespread crime and corruption. A decade later the Tangs organised a cruise to PNG and we visited Milne Bay, Madang, Rabaul and the Trobiand Islands and sadly we could not help feeling that perhaps the efforts of our younger years had been wasted. But we were reminded of the many vast beauties of the country and the tenacious industry of the villagers, who still support themselves by their own labour and pay for their children's education with very little government assistance. But the signs of government corruption and incompetence were everywhere, and I despair for the future of the country. We had suggested that Don and Sue Clark, our friends from Koonya, might also like to come along, for as well as being great sailing companions, we were united by a remarkable coincidence. Not long after meeting them on our arrival in Tasmania in 1980, we discovered that we had both honeymooned at a remote and obscure guest house in the village of Tapini, in the highlands of PNG in 1966. Quite possibly, the only two couples in the history of the world to have done so.

~ THE LOWLANDS 2017 ~

Back onboard *Sea Dreams* anchored in Poros in 2015, those far off days in Wewak seemed a lifetime ago. Over dinner on the quay Ro and I reminisced of our last visit to this beautiful island and had a few laughs with the same gregarious proprietor we had befriended the previous time. That also seemed a long time ago.

Two days later we passed through the Corinth Canal and then had a while in Trizonia. It was still enchanting, still with the masts of the sunken ketch leaning drunkenly in the marina. Then onto the Ionian Sea, where we finally anchored in Ormos Vliko, still in our eyes, one of the most pleasant anchorages in the Med. Along the way I had read that Odysseus may actually have had his palace in the overlooking mountains here. If this was so, I could not fault his choice.

There are three tavernas on the eastern shore of the bay that enjoy a wonderful golden ambience as the sun drops below the mountains. They are shrouded with vines and greenery, so that although the light is surreal the heat of the late sun is no bother. We were anchored a few hundred metres off the Apotabepna Gialos restaurant and used to row in late each afternoon to enjoy the light and watch dusk fall, and the lights begin to glimmer across the water. It was a great spot to dream and to make plans. So, it was while there we made the decision to leave the Mediterranean and begin exploring the inland waterways of Europe.

Why give up something we were enjoying so much? Europe has around 53,000 kilometres of navigable waterway; its only 40,000 to go around the world. Following rivers, lakes and canals it is possible to sail from deep inside Poland, not far from the old village of Peterswald, through Germany, the Czech Republic, the Netherlands, Belgium, through France to the Mediterranean coast or along the Rhine and Danube to the Black Sea. In addition, with the right yacht you can cross the English Channel to Britain and on to Ireland or

Ro, a great spot to dream and to make plans...

cruise the shores of the Baltic and North Sea, the Atlantic and the Mediterranean. The numbers of alluring destinations are countless. Great cities such as Berlin, Hamburg, Prague, Copenhagen, Amsterdam, Rotterdam, Paris, Lyon, Dijon, Marseilles, London and Dublin. Small towns and villages nestled astride the canals and rivers, peaceful banks shaded by overhanging trees, or lost in fen lands, or overlooked by steep valleys terraced with vines, or beside pastures dotted with cattle and horses.

With great reluctance, and feeling very disloyal, we took Sea Dreams to nearby Cleopatra Marina and put her on the market, surrounded by the shades of Cleopatra's long defeated army. Our marvellous nine years Mediterranean odyssey was over. And we started looking for a yacht more suitable for what we had in mind. *Sea Dreams* had been a majestic chariot and selling her was akin to selling a daughter, well...perhaps giving one away in marriage! Thankfully she passed into deserving hands, a New Zealand couple, Lee and Larry Deverick who seem to love her almost as much as we did and planned to sail her home. We followed their progress and the sight of her anchored in some familiar or unknown bay always sent a pang through our hearts. She was back in New Zealand in 2018 and in December, after a class of 1965 RMC reunion in the Bay of Islands, we called into say hello to her and Larry and Lee. She was still as beautiful as ever, and it only felt like yesterday when we had first fallen in love.

***

When we started looking for our new yacht, we had no idea where to begin. It needed to have a shallow draft and be able to fit beneath low bridges and through narrow locks. Of course, *Sea Dreams* was French, so that seemed the obvious place to start. But friends of ours from Tasmania, Ric and Helva Murdoch, had a beautiful Italian motor cruiser they had sailed in the Med for some years, which would have been suitable. While we were investigating Italian boats, we came across some makes of Dutch boats that captured our interest. The Dutch make some great steel sailing yachts that are designed to go anywhere in the world in any conditions, but in terms of numbers of yachts suitable for the Med and warm weather sailing, they are off the radar a bit.

Once we started looking at Dutch boats, we realised we had stumbled across a boating wonderland, which really, we should have been aware of. The Dutch have been a pre-eminent maritime nation for centuries. Their early navigators discovered much of the world, including Tasmania of course, and they inspired Tasmania's marvellous wooden boat festival. But we were not prepared for the magic we found. We searched through the internet for boats for sale in the Netherlands, made a shortlist, and a boatyard itinerary and flew to Amsterdam in April 2017. The two top contenders were in a boatyard at Sneek, a provincial town in the north. They did not suit, but on the morning of the second day Ro could hear a beautiful Boarn Cruiser calling, *'Ro, Ro, look at me, look at me'*. A quick glance and she was in love again and within five minutes we had decided on *Linna*. Some hard bargaining—even Dutch traders were unprepared for what lurks beneath Ro's sweet exterior—a survey and she was ours.

... 'Ro, Ro, look at me, look at me'... Linna

Linna was a 12.4 metre steel cruiser built in 2004, designed to last a hundred years and go anywhere in the inland waterways of Europe. She had a spacious aft deck with an exterior steering position. Downstairs to a sunny saloon amidst ship. Down a couple more steps forward to a galley, dining alcove, forward cabin with two berths and a bathroom. At the stern, was a stateroom, with bathroom and laundry. All finished with beautiful solid wood joinery and powered by 135hp diesel and bow and stern thrusters. She had been built in a shipyard in Jirnsum, only a few miles away.

It took a few days to complete the formalities and transfer the money, but by the following weekend we were tied up alongside the canal at the edge of the ancient town of Sneek. I had been encouraged to have a 'test drive' on one of the quiet canals outside town and had done just enough to realise that there was a world of difference between steering a deep keeled yacht on the wide ocean to an almost flat bottomed power boat in the tight waters of a canal. We were used to dropping the anchor in a harbour rather than squeezing into a jetty, we had not really worried much about how you make a boat go sideways, or reverse long distances down narrow canals. So, even getting into town was a bit of a test and I couldn't have done it without someone to shout at me. Over the next few years Ro often came close to losing her voice. The apogee of 'shouting' came a few years later while we were navigating the French canals, some of which had narrow tunnels up to four kilometres in length. They had been dug around the middle of the 19th century when most barges were drawn by horses—although wives were a not uncommon alternative—and a pathway about a metre wide was left just above water level on one side of the canal for the horse - or woman - to trudge along. In the age of the combustion engine the French have not seen fit to upgrade the architecture, so in a boat of the dimensions of *Linna* this protruding ledge cannot be seen by the helmsman. Which means your hull is only a foot or so away from a rock ledge, which you could not see even if the dark canal was actually well lit. Our passage through these canals was accompanied by much shouting, but we did come through unscathed.

But that was all in the future. Meanwhile we were happily preparing to explore Sneek and equip *Linna* with all we needed for travelling the waterways of Europe. We had given ourselves a seven-year time frame, but at the time of writing we still have not yet heard back if this is okay with the gods. The correct name for what is commonly called 'Holland' is the Netherlands (the Lowlands). There are twelve provinces in the Netherlands (NL). The northern province of Friesland, bordering the North Sea, and where we now found ourselves. Then there are North Holland in which is Amsterdam and South Holland where Rotterdam is located. The other provinces are Groningen, Drenthe, OverIJssel, Flevoland, Gelderland, Utrecht, Nourd Brabant, Limburg and Zeeland.

The story of the Netherlands is an inspiring one. Of a group of seafaring peoples, comprising Frisians, Saxons and Franks coalescing and overcoming the hardships and privations of living in the exposed fen lands of a cold river delta. All the while being continually subject to the invasions from the Vikings, German peoples pushing westward, and the great empires of southern Europe pushing north. During the middle ages there was no unified equivalent of today's Netherlands. It was not until the Dutch revolt in 1568-1648 against the rule of Habsburg Spain that the modern Netherlands came into being.

Sneek like most cities in the Netherlands, started life as a small settlement on the banks of an ancient waterway. In Sneek's case it was called the Magna Fossa, and it happened sometime in the 10th century. By the 13th century it had grown into a thriving small city enjoying 'city rights' and the freedoms of self-government that this allowed, and by late in the 15th century it was encircled by a moat and stout city walls. Today these same moats enclose a charming 'old town' and are a haven for watercraft of all shapes and sizes: ancient lee boarded steel sailing boats still beautiful after over a hundred years of use, modern sailing and motor yachts, dinghies and charming launches.

There are many exciting aspects of the history of the Netherlands that sets them apart from the rest of the world. One of the most important is the story of their 'Free Cities.' Because there was almost no comparative development in England they have been neglected in our histories. But they were one of the truly great achievements in the march of societies from the domination of the feudal aristocracy to democratic self-government. In many aspects they mirrored the democratic growth of Venice, but there are not many other examples. They existed from around the late 10th century until they were abolished after the Batavian Revolution in 1795, when it was recognised that they were probably incompatible with the self-rule of a united democratic nation. During the medieval period there were over two hundred 'Free Cities' in the Netherlands who had bought, fought and negotiated their freedoms from the old feudal landlords. They had the right to build city walls to protect themselves from the invasion of foreigners, and the possible future depredations of the feudal lords themselves. They could hold their own markets and receive the financial benefits, charge tolls to pass into or through the city, mint coinage and levy taxes. They governed themselves, made their own laws and the citizens had freedom of movement, and they contributed towards the abolition of serfdom in most parts of the country by 1500. Serfdom was little better than slavery, and they were hundreds of years ahead of their neighbours in Europe. Austria, the seat of the Habsburgs and the Holy Roman Empire kept their people enslaved until 1781, Poland 1791, France 1789 and Prussia 1807. In England it was abolished by 1574, helped along by the Peasants Revolt and the power that the long bow had given them. The creation of Free Cities was a great transfer of power from the aristocracy to the bourgeoisie and a great development in the creation of wealth for the working class.

Another transfer of power came from the arming of the peasantry. England armed its archers with the deadly longbow to fight the French and Scots and in time it gave them political leverage. Later, soldiers armed with firearms transferred further military power away from the mounted knights of the aristocracy. The topography of the low countries, like that of Venice, made the independence of free cities possible. The waterways and canals, the fens and the bogs enabled cities to defend themselves by force of arms, which was not possible in most other places where some aggressive lord with a large army could wheel up to the city gate with bigger cannons and the machinery of war.

Once securely tied up in Sneek we began getting ourselves and *Linna* ready for whatever lay ahead. We were moored below the canopy of a row of plane trees a short stroll through a narrow brick alleyway to the brick paved town square of the *old town*. It was surrounded by characteristic two and three-storey Dutch buildings, with intricately laid brick patterns, red and grey tiled roofs and arched windows overlooking the square. There was seating beneath shady trees and outside the many inviting restaurants. The whole of the old town was surrounded by canals, most of which were still navigable and, it was also crisscrossed by a pattern of smaller ones. In olden times entrance to the town was through guarded gates in the canals and fortified city walls, and today the old towered 'water gate' still stands, looking much the same as it would have done four or five hundred years ago.

Each afternoon we used to stroll around the encircling canals. It took us around an hour and the walk became a daily ritual where-ever we were. Along canals, through the winding brick roads of the towns, along trails through the thickly canopied forests and luxuriant parks and gardens. We often comment that we may well have covered more distance on foot than at the helm of *Linna*. The walk in Sneek took us past a few hundred metres of itinerant yachts like ourselves, where the roads on each side of the canal were lined with neat brick cottages with attic bedrooms, once worker's cottages now becoming gentrified. A few with small neat gardens in front. Then past a number of big old barges, around thirty metres in length, which were converted to homes and permanently hooked up to the shore. They all had flower gardens. A patch on shore with more on the fore and aft decks, some with a roof garden also. Often the owners would be enjoying a drink in deck chairs ashore amongst their flowering pots. Nods and hellos as we passed. Ducks would be fossicking along the shore or 'on manoeuvres' with a stately mother duck leading a line of chicks. On through the ancient water-gate, where we would pause to survey more passing yachts and the late reflections of the sun on the basin. Plenty of bikes heading west out of town. On again where the canal passed through a section of gardens and lawns, with willows drooping over the water and some permanently moored launches. More busy ducks and snooks. Then past a section of restaurants and pubs on one side and some grand old homes on the other. Past more brick cottages interspersed with a bit of commercial, lots of bikes, mainly students but the occasional granny heading west and south, until we found ourselves back at our own stretch of canal. Right turn, past a pub and the chandlery, under the canopy of the plane trees and the muted cooing of pigeons and, there was *Linna,* waiting patiently for drinks.

It took us a few days to get organised, but we were loving the town and in no great hurry to be off. We lingered for a while, but eventually one day shortly after the bridge keeper came on duty at nine, we threw off our mooring lines. Not without a few trepidations we motored through the raised bridge, tossed the keeper a cheery wave and vowed to ourselves that we would be back. It was still a bit of a shock having to pay such careful attention to steering and to the multitude of canal-side signs commanding you to: pause, stop, keep to the centre or the right or, not come within ten metres or five. To keep below 10kph or 5 kph or 15kph, or the clearance of the next bridge was 4m or 4.5m, or there was no passing or no overtaking. Not like the ocean, where we just put on the autopilot, lay back and relaxed and let the wind waft us onwards.

We were only going a few miles to the Sneekersmeer (Sneeker's Lake) a nearby lake where we moored against a wooden jetty in a canal between two islands. We planned on doing a bit of training in backing and filling and give all the mechanicals a good working while we were close to help. Delightful community stopovers, like the jetty we had just tied up to, have been created all over Friesland. In canals, lakes and wildernesses they are available free for three-night stays, provided you have paid a small annual fee and fly the flag that says so.

The weather so far had been beguiling. Clear skies and a warm sun, gentle breezes teasing the green countryside dressed in its fresh spring growth. While exploring Sneek, I had been very attracted to a range of heavy Norse woollen pullovers and cardigans that were semi-waterproof and were heavily reduced in price. But I was forced to agree with my wife, that with summer almost with us, when would I ever get a chance to where one? They would just take up space, they weighed a tonne and I would have to lug them around everywhere. So, I settled for a light windcheater, although after dark I did think that the Norse pullover would have been better when winding our way home through the narrow cobblestone streets. And, on our first night on the road I did detect a slight chill in the breeze and, sort of wondered, if I would regret not snapping up one of the warmer pullovers.

Ah well. Happy wife, happy life.

***

We had a plan of sorts. Go south a bit, before looping around to the north, first following the canals and rivers that run behind the coast of the inland sea known as the Ijsselmeer and, then behind the North Sea. Follow those to the German border, then turn south for some distance before swinging westward back to the Ijsselmeer and, then head south through the heart of the Netherlands.

After a couple of nights tied up at our jetty, we were happy that both *Linna* and ourselves were ready to go, and we set off south through the Sneekermeer to a canal leading to a smaller lake, the Langwarder, and another canal to Echtenerbrug on the southern shore of the Tjeukemeer.

Arriving at Echtenerbrug, we were about to learn a couple of lessons. The first one was about stopping. When we were turning *Linna* around in the narrow confines of the canal, in preparation to mooring between two boats, the motor without any warning, stopped. On a sailing yacht in the ocean, being able to stop the boat going forward, or backwards, was never a thing that gave me the slightest concern. If you were under sail you simply swung into the wind and the boat stopped. If the motor did stop, there was always plenty of room to pull the sails up, or ghost to a stop and anchor.

But!

On a motorboat in a canal, the only way you can stop is by putting the boat in reverse. So, if the motor stops, you have no brakes. If you are in a river or a broad canal you do have some options, but in close manoeuvres in docks there is nothing to save you. If the motor stops, the boat will only stop by running into something. Luckily, we ran into the muddy bank of the canal, no damage to us or anyone else. But it was a salutary lesson and gave rise to my guiding principle when manoeuvring in close quarters. In crowded city canals, or when entering a lock or passing under a narrow bridge or entering a tunnel or docking—go slower, and slower and yet slower.

What caused the 135hp John Deere Diesel to stop? We had spent a small fortune on servicing everything that could be serviced, and had been guaranteed by the finely spoken, multi-lingual, now wealthy boss of the workshop that did the work, that not even God himself could make things more perfect. We thought that, the double-dutch speaking mechanic, whom we could not understand one word of, who the boss sent to take the rap, said, that the 'idling' had been adjusted too low. Or that the diesel was too hot, which sounded a terrible excuse to use while the now freezing north-sea breeze was whistling around our ears.

That night I did some research on turning boats through 180 degrees in narrow canals. Even with *Linna's* bow and stern thrusters I had had trouble rotating in a channel that was about two meters wider than the length of the boat. Again, this is not a problem that is encountered on the high seas, but it is in narrow canals. It turns out it is quite simple. You must rotate in the same direction as the rotation of the propeller. In most yachts, including *Linna*, this is clockwise. So, you turn the wheel as far as it will go to the right. Push the throttle forward gently and count, one (short pause) two. There must not be enough throttle to move the boat forward. Leaving the wheel turned to the right, pull the throttle back gently (short pause in neutral) into reverse. Again, there must not be enough throttle to move the boat backwards. Count, one (short pause) two. Move the throttle forward and, keep repeating. It comes as a great relief to know that you can spin the boat in its own length without thrusters. Similarly, you can move the boat sideways using the same manipulation of the throttle and the rudder turned in the opposite direction to the way you wish to move. Again, great relief that you are not completely reliant on thrusters which are often not powerful enough in windy conditions and, can be a bit temperamental in any case.

My newly discovered expertise was handy for showing off from time to time, and on some occasions was actually quite handy.

Our evening's walk had taken us past a wonderful garden created by an old sea captain to keep himself amused. We had been leaning over his front fence admiring it, when he noticed us, opened the gate and invited us in. Describing it as a garden, in no way does justice to what he had created. It was a wonderland of miniature lakes connected by streams and waterfalls with schools of many-coloured fish hovering under the water lilies. Colourful garden beds and banks of shrubs, here and there half hidden in the greenery, delightful whimsies to bring a smile to your face. An aviary, as much like a natural forest as man's ingenuity could conjure, with happy, brightly-coloured birds. We thanked him from our hearts and, continued to stroll down the canal to where it joined the broad grey expanse of the lake, and watched a yacht come carefully up the channel markers.

After leaving Echtenerbrug we continued south and into the Linde river, where we were confronted with our first operating lock. Something we had been feeling a bit apprehensive about ever since we had stepped aboard *Linna*, and there is no doubt that locks can be, at times, daunting. But they are an immensely important pieces of infrastructure. Without them the Netherlands could not have become what it is, so I must try to tell their story. Water evaporates over the sea, the vapour condenses into layers of air, rains down over the land, is swept along rivers and ends up in the sea. A cycle of nature that keeps the fields green, the rivers running, and the skies varied. But in the Netherlands the plenitude of rain creates a substantial problem. The country is situated on the delta of the three largest European rivers and a significant part of it is below sea level. This creates two contradicting and existential problems for the Dutch. They must keep the sea out, but also discharge the rainwater that falls in great abundance over the country and the vast amount of fresh water that drains from the Rhine and Moselle rivers. These problems have been solved by canals. locks and windmills. The windmills have enabled them to drain their land and the locks regulate the flows of the canals and rivers. And at the same time create great pathways for waterborne trade and movement. Locks not only regulate and preserve the flow of water, they effortlessly raise and lower the weight, no matter how immense, of any craft that can fit inside the lock.

Locks were first used in China around the 6th century BCE. The most common locks in the Netherlands are the 'miter lock', which uses the weight of the water to jam together two angled gates to form a waterproof seal. The invention of the miter lock is commonly attributed to Leonardo da Vinci. But once again it seems a bit of a coincidence that his design came at a time when contact between Europe and the East began to flourish, and China had been transporting huge quantities of goods over its canal system for two thousand years or so. Perhaps intellectual theft was already a problem a few hundred years ago during the renaissance, and these days China is just getting its own back.

The lock we were approaching was a miter lock, which may or may not have been invented by Leonardo di Vinci. It had been built here so that the river water would not all run out to sea and leave the river unnavigable and, to lift boats up the 2.6 metre or so to the next stretch of river. A lift of around two metres is most common but can vary from this to up to twenty-seven metres for one lock in France. This lock was 60 metres long and 8 metres wide, so in theory it would take four boats our size, but the large commercial locks are quite gigantic, around 325 metres x 24 metres.

When you arrive at a lock there is almost invariably a wait. This can sometimes be quite lengthy as the lock keeper may be waiting to get enough of a load to justify operating the lock—although they are generally pretty good about this. There will almost invariably be an awkward wind to contend with and there may or may not be a place to tie up while waiting. You must protect your place in the line, or you might find some Frenchman rushing in ahead of you and, in some places, you must pray that no commercial boat arrives and takes precedence ahead of you.

Once you eventually get to enter the lock the first thing you must do is to get your mooring lines over a bollard, so that the rush of water filling the lock does not crash you into a neighbour or onto the wall of the lock. If you are only going up a couple of metres bollards are not too hard to find and get your rope over, but even then, their location might not work for the length of your boat. There can be a bit of shouting and swearing while this is going on—particularly if it is a high lock with bollards sunk into the lock wall that are hard to get lines over and have to be refixed as the water rises.

Once you are tied on the lockkeeper will start to release water into the lock and the water level rises. There will normally be quite a lot of pressure forcing the boat backwards. But you cannot tie your lines off because as the water rises, they must be continuously adjusted and if tied off they will probably jam. After a few minutes the water in the lock will rise to the same level as the upstream river. The gates will be opened and, you motor slowly out waving thanks to the keeper as you go. Most gates are operated by electric motors, but there are plenty of old ones in the back canals where the keeper must laboriously push them open and shut with long wooden handles, or toil over an ancient steel flywheel. Entering and leaving locks and passing through bridges is run by a system of lights, not much different to normal traffic lights, with a few foibles that I will complain about later.

Pushing on we wound our way through more beautiful countryside to the small village of Ossenzijl where we were able to tie up in front of a petite general store. It was a quiet stretch, and the canal was lined with a scattering of lovely homes, until it disappeared into the Weerribben National Park. Many of the homes were actually quite grand; some had very expensive looking thatched roofs and sat in lovely gardens, some with their own small canals leading into the main one. It was all very picturesque and very peaceful. Perhaps, we thought, this might be nicer than an island in the Med. There were a few small 'installations' along the path beside the canal to amuse the passers bye. A herb garden in an old wooden dinghy, a small decorated mobile shop mounted on a bicycle, an arrangement of clogs. All very pleasant. We were expecting Hubie, who was travelling through Europe after finishing his final exams at the French school in Sydney and it was a charming place to wait. Charlotte and the family had now moved back from France. The reflections in the water in the mornings and around dusk were entrancing. Here, and no matter where we were on the waterways, the chatter of birdlife was always with us. The rear window of our cabin is only a foot or so above water level, and most nights we left it open a bit. Nearly every morning I was to be woken by a Mrs Duck quacking at her children or picking on her unfortunate husband, carelessly disregarding the fact my head was only inches from her busy beak. Whenever we stopped, we would soon be visited by a family of ducks, or snooks, and nearby, a flock of geese would probably be picking over a patch of field while glaring at any transgressors. Often, we would be overlooked by egrets or storks nested on high branches or even chimney tops. The cooing of pigeons was always with us, particularly in the dawn and dusk.

We grew to really love swans. Mostly when we would tie alongside for the night, there would be a husband and wife, sometimes with their chicks or sometimes with none, jealously fending off any other swan who ventured onto their territory. Of course, the swans do not chatter away as do their more-humble brethren but fix you with a steely-eyed stare as they glide past. It was only while we were here that I became aware of the origin of the saying, 'swansong'. White swans are known as 'mute' swans, because they don't chatter or sing that much – except at the moment of their death. Then they launch into a beautiful song. Hence singers, musicians etc doing a 'swansong' before fading away. This led me to the obvious, when you think about it, connection with the saying, 'swanning around'. Swans are always 'swanning around' in regal fashion. No other waterbirds 'swan around', the ducks and snooks fossick, herons stand one-legged and occasionally stab an incautious fish, geese are just a gaggle on a bank and many others just sit on a nest and watch the passing world. Unless you are a bird of prey, circling ominously above.

Most mornings as we set off through the calm water, we would come across a large grey heron standing on a branch or muddy bank, who would check all was well as we glided past. Sometimes the heron would see us coming and fly ahead, wings beating the water before soaring aloft and beckoning us to follow. We liked to amuse ourselves with the thought that it was the same loyal fellow we saw almost every morning, for three years and counting. Perhaps it was.

Hubie arrived, and we motored gently into the beauty of the Weerribben National Park and tied up to the canal bank at the first opportunity. There were a couple of lovely walks around and through the park, running for a while along the canal bank. A number of storks nested on platforms, built for their convenience in clearings, some six metres or so off the ground. Eyeing passers-by with a slightly hostile indifference. After a couple of nights we followed the canal through the park and found another delightful anchorage on the edge of the next collection of charming homes; some with a few horses, some miniature ones, another with a few sheep, a hot tub or two, and of course all with an appealing launch moored in front, or in a boat shed off the canal. More with thatched roofs, all with manicured gardens. We were all getting plenty of steps in on our late afternoon patrols, and it was a wonderful place to wander through, something beautiful to catch your eyes every few paces. The canal beside *Linna* captured the blue of the sky, edged with the silvery blossoms of the reeds on the far bank. Towards the sunset the water was a glistening path of silver.

Onwards to another village straight out of a fairy story. Blokzijl has quite a large basin, lined with two and three storied brick buildings, some dating back to the 16th century and enough restaurants to give ample dining choice after our days roughing it in the wilderness. In the late afternoon the church steeple, surmounted by a silvery spire, was set against a pale blue sky, washed with filmy brush strokes of white.

We had now entered a region called the Noordoostpolder, so we must talk about Polders. Another of the true marvels of the Netherlands. A Polder is an area reclaimed from the sea, a lake or a fen and began to come into being in the 14th century. Windmills were first used to pump water from low lying lands to create farmland. Some polders are above sea level and surplus water is mainly returned to the Ijsselmeer through locks. But many are below sea level and the water must be pumped up into the canals. These days this is accomplished by a combination of traditional Dutch windmills, some modern windmills, and diesel and motor-driven pumps. More about Polders here.

Lots of tulips are grown in this region so perhaps we should have a quick look at the Dutch Tulip Mania. This could have been history's first financial mania. Certainly, since times began, there have been lots and lots of financial crises brought on by plague, or war or the threat of war, or economic turmoil or just shortages or oversupplies of commodities. But they have not been accompanied by the complete abandonment of rationality. Of course, there have been plenty of non-financial manias, mainly of a religious nature. There have also been plenty of political manias such as socialism, and we are enjoying one of the quite frequent climate manias at present.

In 1554 the first tulip bulbs were sent from Turkey, where they were already a prized flower, to Vienna. Soon it had been established that the conditions in the Lowlands were suitable for their cultivation and the tulip began to grow in popularity. They were different to all other flowers in Europe and with more intense colours. They became a status symbol at the time the newly independent Netherlands was entering its *Golden Age*, where merchants were beginning to make fortunes in the East Indies trade. Tulips rapidly became a coveted luxury item, and a profusion of varieties were developed. More and more exotic varieties, of greater and greater beauty, were developed and given exalted titles. As popularity grew, growers were paid higher and higher prices for the hard to develop bulbs. By 1634 speculators had entered the market and prices continued to rise, and soon bulbs could fetch hundreds of guilders. A futures market was established, and tulips were the nation's fourth leading export earner. Prices skyrocketed and men made, and lost fortunes overnight. Mania reached its height in the winter of 1636-37 where some bulbs were bought and sold ten times in a day. A 'lot' of bulbs sold at auction for the equivalent of 1.2 million Euros. A single bulb for the equivalent of 30,000 euros when a tonne of butter was worth 1200 euros, and a skilled labourer might earn 1200 euros for a year's work. Everyone was buying and selling and trading anything that could be traded. A bulb could be swapped for 12 acres of land. The market index was 10 on 12 November 1636, soared to 200 on 3 February 1637, and had crashed to 10 on 1 May. Fortunes were lost and confidence destroyed.

Onwards along the Lemstervaat Kanal to the seaport of Lemmer, which first appears on the historical record in the early 13th century. It was in a desirable, but vulnerable position on the shores of the North Sea and has had a rather brutal history, before things settled down and it became an important fishing port. By the time we arrived it was windy and quite chilly again, and we were happy to find a snug berth close to the town harbour. Although it was still early in the season there was plenty going on and we could not get over the variety and numbers of boats already berthed around the quay. In the afternoon the sky had become a leaden grey and there was a wind howling in from the North Sea. We could tell where it was coming from, because it was bloody freezing. I again cursed having left my old warm wet weather gear on *Sea Dreams* and not being allowed to buy one of those fine Norwegian pullovers in Sneek. When I saw a medium weight red waterproof yachting jacket for sale at a reduced price in a nearby chandlery, I realised that if I was to survive, I needed it. Although while wearing it as we strolled back to the boat, I started to wonder if it would keep me as warm as I would really have liked.

These days Lemmer is no longer on the shore of the North Sea, it is on the shore of a large freshwater lake known as the IJsselmeer. The creation of the IJsselmeer is another of the 'wonders' of the Netherlands and in many ways defines both the country and its people. Along with the 'Polders' it is emblematic of how the country was created and the special qualities of the Dutch people, their creativeness, tenacity and their capacity for hard work.

The area was first mentioned as a complex of lakes in Roman times. Over the years the lakes were expanded by rising sea waters, flooding and wave action from the North Sea. By the early middle ages, it had become a large shallow bay open to the North Sea and was known as the Zuiderzee. It covered some five thousand square kilometres, with the shoreline protected in places by dykes, or sea walls. Over time it was the scene of many disasters, caused by storms, floods and broken seawalls, and many thousands were killed. I do not know how to get across the scope of the continued tragedies without actually listing some. They included; around 60,000 killed in 1212, 36,000 in 1219, 10,000 in 1421, 50-80,000 in 1287, 10,000 in 1421, 100,000 in 1530, 20,000 in 1570, 15,000 in1703, 14,000 in 1717. To modern eyes these numbers are almost incomprehensible and certainly makes you realise the tenuous nature of life in olden times.

With all these deaths and tragedies most people on earth would have packed their bags and headed off somewhere else. But not the Dutch. They were not going to let a small thing like the freezing, stormy North Sea beat them.

In 1932 the Zuiderzee was closed off by a 32 kilometre dyke connecting North Holland to Friesland, creating the Ijsselmeer. Over time the sea water was flushed out by fresh water flowing from the Rhine river via the Ijssel river, giving the country a huge reservoir of fresh water. By 1967 over half the Ijsselmeer was drained, creating two thousand square kilometres of farmland. In 1975 the lake was split in half by a second dyke and eventually a third dyke enclosed the portion adjacent to Amsterdam. Most of the farmland in the Netherlands has been reclaimed from the sea, or from fresh and saltwater swamps, and it is a wonderful thing to have achieved.

After dinner we decided to amble into the very picturesque 'old town' to have a look around. We had almost completed a circuit when we came across an 'Irish Pub'. Yes, they are just about everywhere, but we always have trouble walking past one and we decided to have a stout each, while overlooking the canal and an array of interesting boats. We went inside to order, a pint for me and a ladylike size for Ro. The bill was rung up. 10.00 Euros. The barman proffered his card reader, I inserted my card.

'Enter your pin and press OK,' he instructed.

I complied. But just as I pressed the OK, I realised that the bill was now reading 10,003.47 Euros. It turned out my pin number had been added to the bill because the bartender had not 'locked-in' the purchase price.

Immediate panic. The owner tried to reverse the transaction but, could not as it was well beyond his credit limit. But, within minutes we were speaking to a very helpful representative of the Australian and New Zealand Banking Corporation (ANZ), who we have been banking with for forty years or so. He assured us not to worry, the transaction would not, under any circumstances, be processed. We all relaxed, the owner apologised, the barman apologised and, fresh drinks were brought to us at our window seats overlooking the quay. In due course we wandered back to *Linna* and the next day we continued on our way. A couple of days later, I thought I had best check all was okay with our credit card account, and almost fainted when I saw that A$16,497.23 had been deducted for our two stouts at the Irish pub. It took us over three weeks for the transaction to be reversed. During that time, we spoke to many representatives of the ANZ bank, most of whom spoke heavily-accented English and seemed only vaguely aware of the location of Australia. The helpful representative we first spoke to seemed to be the only helpful person employed by the bank. We certainly didn't come across another during our continued calls to the bank in the wee small hours of the mornings. It was not until we sent the hierarchy a copy of an article, we were about to have published, describing their complicity in defrauding old customers $16,497.23 for two drinks, that we got action. '$16,497.23 for two drinks' is not a bad headline. Anyway, it was all quite stressful, and remined me again of the outrageous price of the dinner in the Maddalena Archipelago with our friends, Helen and Lenny a number of years before.

It was only a short distance further on to the ancient town of Sloten which was founded in the 13th century and attained free city rights in 1426. It was once an important gateway and its old defences and moat works are still largely intact, providing remarkable landscaping for the beautiful old town. Our arrival at Woudsend, only a few miles north coincided with a tugboat festival—and I'm not sure what adjective would best describe the weekend. Certainly the boats were beautiful and interesting, many were over one hundred years old, the owners were friendly and by sunsets most were quite boisterous, they were fiercely proud of their boats and the competition between them was ferocious, but you could tell they all loved each other and their boats. We enjoyed ourselves greatly, became familiar with a wide range of Dutch beers, but thought it best if we left them to it while we headed north before the finale on the Sunday night.

We had a couple of nights at Heeg moored on a grassy bank an easy twenty minutes stroll to the centre of town. But there was a collection of lovely traditional wooden boats along the way, their rich golden woodwork glowing in the late afternoon sun. It took us the best part of an hour to admire them on the way to town, and longer coming home when we were in a more mellow mood. We enjoyed sashimi and mussels at a table on the town quay where we had a view across the rounded blunt bows of a lovely old barge, to steeply-gabled brick cottages framed by trees and flowering shrubs on the far bank. There was a passing parade of townsfolk in small yachts and launches. Children and fathers coming home from a day on the water, a smartly dressed couple in an immaculate launch off to somewhere quite formal, grandfather giving his much-loved boat a run, courting couples, wind-blown and radiant. There were glimpses of patches of blue sky behind large fluffy grey and white clouds, more chill than warmth in the air as the sun set and greyness crept across the water. I was glad of my warmest red jacket.

Then onwards again, the canal banks lined with neat brick homes and carefully tended gardens, the sky and water a sullen grey but the colours somehow clear and strong. Workum is another charming port city on the shore of the IJsselmeer and we followed the canal past Heek; the flat green paddocks stretched away to a distant tree lined horizon. White clouds, some with shadowed undersides, drifted across a blue sky. The pasture was dotted with dairy cattle, blacks, whites, browns and piebalds feeding busily in the succulent pasture. Not one munching head was lifted as we passed them by. Plenty of geese, looking bold and aggressive along the banks, and as always families of ducks and snooks busy in the tall green reeds.

The wind was up, driving scurrying grey clouds and flurries of showers eastward as we wound our way to Bolsward. On the outskirt of the town we had the misfortune to be confronted with a bridge keeper who did not seem to give much importance to our lonely selves as he let streams of vehicles cross his bridge, while keeping it firmly closed to us. The wind was howling across the canal, there was no jetty to tie up to, and it was hard keeping ourselves out of the reeds. It gave me plenty of practice of pushing the boat sideways using the propeller and rudder. However, he eventually acknowledged us, naturally let the boats coming the other way through first, then allowed us to scamper past. Once into the village we found a lovely bank, shaded—not that we needed shade as it was still drizzling—by plane trees and lined with a profusion of brightly-flowering shrubs, close to the *old town*. That evening all the visiting yachts were serenaded by a couple of boatloads of choristers, all robed in padded red jackets. There has been a village on this site, built on man-made mounds, from around the 1st century and it achieved Free City status in 1445. Unfortunately, the same bridge keeper seemed to be on duty on the way out, the same wind was blowing, and I had even more practice in going sideways. I was getting pretty good at it, actually.

After Hubie left us to continue his travels we indulged ourselves a few days later, with a short stay back in Sneek, moored in the basin in front of the ancient water-gate, its brick towers golden in the last of the sun, and framed by the dark blue clouds, which became an ominous black as night fell. There were still a few things we needed for *Linna*.

Some of the lovely Norwegian pullovers, still at greatly reduced prices remained on sale. But I could only look at them longingly. Surely summer was not far off now, and I already had two sailing jackets.

... moored in the basin in front of the ancient water-gate, its brick towers golden in the last of the sun...

We visited a couple of our favourite restaurants, patrolled the canals along our usual route and got more Internet cards and cash. It is much more of a cash economy in Holland, that's what the restaurants liked and very few markets would even take our visas.

***

When we finally managed to get going again, we returned to our jetty in the Sneekersmeer for a peaceful night. Then, off east the next morning towards distant Germany, along the Princess Margriet Kanal, part of the main canal network that runs from the North Sea adjacent to Germany to the Ijsselmeer. It is wide and deep enough for the two thousand tonne commercial barges to pass, and with a bit of courage as there is not really room for three abreast, to overtake while travelling at 10 knots or so. We found the first few times we were overtaken by one of these behemoths a little unsettling, as we edged as close to the bank as we dared and were thrown about by the wakes as they lumbered past. We exited the Sneekersmeer through a monstrous double lock, with two chambers each 260 metres x 16 metres, which is generally kept open at this time of year, into the canal itself. In places it was separated from the surrounding flat green farmland by low grassy banks. There were plenty of large German and Dutch commercial barges, and even an Irish one—the *Shamrock,* of course. These barges are the travelling homes of the skippers/owners and they all carry a car on the aft deck with a crane to lift it ashore, as well as a dinghy, as there are plenty of places where they cannot unload the car. There were also a couple of beautiful restored traditional barges heading towards the first of the season's races, which are fiercely contested events programmed at different venues right through summer.

We spent a few days at Grou as there were still a couple of things on *Linna* that needed attention. Ro's brother. Eugene and his wife, Jenni. arrived and we dined in the local pub on battered cod and fries served in witch's hats with fresh salads, before we crossed over the busy Princess Margriet Kanal. Then into the maze of narrow winding canals of the De Alde Feanen national park, a large tract of fen lands. We tied up to one of the wooden jetties built alongside the high reed-covered banks of a small island and later in the day we were joined by a couple of other boats. There were walking tracks cut through the reeds that led to other jetties and the occasional clearing where crews had set up barbecues. The birdlife was prolific amongst the reeds and small copses of trees: swans, ducks, egrets, herons, snooks, all busy with life and their families, the occasional circling kite and, all overlooked by imperious black and white storks from high spacious nests. In the late afternoon sky, there was a glimmering strip of silver above the dark treelined horizon, and flat sombre clouds overhead. The far bank of the canal was in shadowed blackness, the water a dull ruffled grey. The balmy days of the false summer that we had enjoyed when we first arrived had still not returned. Although I didn't wear my new red jacket to bed, I had it on the rest of the time, and still mourned for the lovely Norwegian pullovers.

It is accepted wisdom that everyone in the Netherlands owns a boat, and it is not far from the truth. There is a rich design history of traditional Dutch boats and many well over a hundred years old, are common sights. The families of past and present owners often meet to pay homage to the craft that may have been in the family generations ago. There are societies of every imaginable type of boat which have annual festivals in honour of their craft, and boats from near and far will spend days and weeks wending their way there. This proclivity is not limited to watercraft; we have witnessed a couple of dozen John Deere tractors of every size, old and ancient, following in close single file along a country lane. Acres of classic cars in hotel forecourts, mobs of men with large moustaches etc etc.

After our allowed three days at the jetty we wound our way out of the watery wilderness, crossed over the Princess Margriet Kanal again and entered the Warten to Leeuwaarden canal - draft 1.9 metres and mostly about 20 metres wide. We were just approaching Warten when we came across our first opening bridge where a toll was charged. When the bridge keeper finally decides you have waited long enough, he/she will change the red light to red/green, which means you are to get ready. The bridge is then raised. But wait, the keeper has yet to decide which side will come through first. Almost always this will be the boats on the other side and, you will have to cringe into the reeds and possibly go aground, to allow them to pass. Eventually the lights change to double green, meaning you can proceed. Most of the passages through the bridges are narrow, allowing us only a foot or so on either side and most have a projection somewhere which may catch the unwary. So, you can see there will be a little shouting required as we eventually motor through. At this stage the bridge keeper may—but not always— dangle a wooden clog hanging from a fishing rod in front of your face, which means you are required to pay a euro or two for your passage.

At our first paying bridge we were caught unprepared with no money handy and, were out the other side enduring black looks from the woman with the clog before we knew what had happened.

'I'll come back.' Ro called, making confusing gestures at the same time. After a short distance we came to the town square, but we were not sure if mooring was allowed, then we were out of the town and heading into the country. Not going back was not an option. We imagined not paying a toll in Holland was probably considered grand larceny and *Linna's* reputation would be ruined forever. No bridge keeper would ever let us pass again. The canal had also narrowed to about the length of the boat and turning was difficult, but we eventually got back to Warten and tied up to some iron rings in the town square. Ro hotfooted it back to the bridge, paid the friendly girl, and all was well. Nearby there was a small restaurant overlooking the canal, and we treated ourselves again to some lovely cod and salad. I think it was here that I realised I had become infatuated with Dutch beers.

In the morning the distant horizon was lightly smudged with white, giving way to a cloudless pale-blue overhead. The still water captured flawlessly inverted images of the barges, yachts and emerald green trees along the wooden quay, and the three-storied brick dwelling that sat on the bank at the edge of town. Further along waterlilies lined the water's edge and bluebells, water mint and purple loosestrife grew along the canal bank, along with patches of unruly reeds and grasses and small dense copses of willow. Further on, the canal widened again, running between well-tended fields, dotted with small woods, gabled roofs and church spires, and by late morning had become a winding blue mirror of the windless sky.

At Leeuwarden there were moorings beside a large wooded park on the edge of the town. There was a university not far away and it was a popular place with the students who came to loll around and chat. It was quite crowded on the Saturday afternoon we arrived. Female students were protesting against not being allowed to go around topless, by going around topless. Needless to say, there were lots of boys there to support them and some police to keep an eye on things. Being a well-known feminist, I was happy to sign their petition as we passed through on the way to the shops, but Ro politely declined their invitation to join in the protest. What was the weather like, you ask? It was a beautiful warm summer day, finally. Made me wonder what god was in charge of the weather this far north? I don't think the old Roman and Greek gods ran things up here, and I realised I had better get a handle on the Norse gods.

The beginning of mankind's search for an explanation of the unknown is lost far back in the mists of time. Certainly, it predates the rise of the earliest civilisations, although it is these that provide the only indications of the gods their predecessors worshipped in much earlier times. Perhaps around 50,000 years ago mankind developed the intellectual ability to wonder about the sun, the moon and the stars, the cycles of the seasons, and to relate them to their lives. Eventually they sought an understanding of these things that controlled their lives and, on which their very existence depended.

As they could see no rational explanation of these wonders, they turned to supernatural ones. The first object of their worship was the mighty sun, whose daily and annual progressions brought comfort or hardship, life or death.

Much later, some of our early ancestors began to ritualise this worship and the first religions were created. Later there were further momentous developments. Firstly, the concept that the natural world was actually controlled by supernatural gods, on whose orders the heavens rotated, and the winds blew. And secondly, communication with these gods required a priesthood. And also, that there must be a supernatural explanation for human passions: love, hate, desire, greed and lust. This, of course, makes priesthood the world's oldest profession. Preceding the other contender to this claim by many, many millennia, and who probably could not be regarded as professional until the age of towns and coinage.

One theory believes the Greek and Norse languages are related to an ancient mother tongue known as 'Proto-Indo-European', spoken by nomadic tribes from the southwest steppes of Russia during the 3rd or 4th millennium BCE. The chief deities of the Greeks and Norse/Germanic beliefs have also been derived from the gods of these nomadic tribes and, has been carried along with the spread of their languages into Asia and Europe. There are many parallels attesting they are branches of the same tree. Multiple gods linked to the vast natural forces of the earth and the natures of man and using the supernatural to explain events and passions. The major gods of each, Zeus and Odin head up similar hierarchies of lesser gods, although overall it is not hard to see that Zeus ran a hedonistic Greek organisation and that Odin led a Viking gang. Which included, Thor the storm god, Njoror who helped calm the seas and fires, and granted wealth and land. And Freyr, whose interests included weather and farming, and bringing pleasure and prosperity.

There was a Norse/Germanic mythology from the 2nd millennium at roughly the same period as the Greek—scattered runic inscriptions dating from late antiquity attest to the existence of the deities—but the first written testimony is much later. The Prose Edda, authored by Snorri Sturison and the Poetic Edda, an anonymous collection of old Norse poems, were both written around the 12th century CE.

So, who should be blamed or praised for the weather? Around this area, probably the Viking gang. But we were getting close to the lands of the Romans. Just outside the park we walked past the tall Oldehove church tower, which was commenced in 1529. In 1532 it was noticed that it was leaning to one side and building work was halted. Today it still stands unfinished, its intricate brickwork a joy to behold, and leaning at a greater angle than the famous leaning tower of Pisa.

There is a memorial in nearby Terschelling to of one of the early great Dutch seafarers, Willem Barentsz (1550–1597) who was born there. He carried out three expeditions to the Arctic and made several attempts to find a northeast passage across the top of Russia to China. He died while on the third voyage. He was possibly the first of the great Dutch explorers and, perhaps no country contributed more than the Dutch to the maritime exploration of the world. Their sailors discovered the Falkland Islands in 1600, Northern Australia in 1606, charted Manhattan in 1609, charted the Brouwer Route to Java 1610. They discovered Long Island Sound, the Connecticut River in 1614, Cape Horn, Tonga, New Ireland 1615-16. Papua New Guinea in 1616, the Gulf of Carpentaria in 1623, the Southern Australian Coast in 1627. West Australia in 1629, Tasmania and New Zealand in 1642, Easter Island and Samoa 1722. They were the first to carry out systematic celestial mapping of the Southern Hemisphere between 1595 and 1597, and the first to conduct a major scientific expedition to Brazil between 1637 and 1644.

Our route beyond Leeuwarden was along the gentle waters of the Dokkumer River, running through rich dairying country with large herds of cattle gazing intently at nothing at all — a sure sign of happy cows. Tubular straw bird nests were built on stakes in the water close to the riverbanks, and as always snooks and ducks pottered around among the reeds. Dokkum was one of the early 'free cities' and stands on the edge of the Frisian forests. It retains many of the old ramparts and still holds its ancient charm. As well as being defended by a surrounding moat, it was divided by interior canals which meant that it would have to have been conquered sector by sector, as well as allowing the citizens to park their boats in front of their homes. There were comfortable moorings beside a high bank which was once part of the town's perimeter defences and, are now decorated with two charming old windmills, which in more troubled times were cannoned bastions.

Despite having a reputation for dourness, the Dutch actually have a delightfully wry sense of humour. It is widely manifested in their gardens and how they present their homes to the world. For the rest of the world, a window is something you look out of, then draw the curtain. For the Dutch, it is a window into the soul of your home, which presents the passer-by with something for his appreciation or amusement—a beautiful vase of flowers, a suspended fish that transforms the room into a fish bowl, an oil painting looking outwards, an endless supply of personal 'installations'. There can be no greater race of gardeners than the Dutch. Every home has a well-tended garden of taste and colour, generally with a subtle, or not too subtle statement hidden in the profusion.

The river widened quite a bit after we left Dokkum still running through rich farming land with numerous prosperous brick farmsteads and small copses. Here and there were a few yachts moored to the riverbank and the occasional one passing us with a cheery wave. In due course we came to the fen lands of the delta of the Dokkumer and then we were in the open waters of the Lauwersmeer National Park, a large bay cut off from the North Sea by a barrier of dykes. A small breeze pushed away the last of some puffy white clouds, leaving a wide pale blue sky and there was some warmth in the sun.

Life was perfect. Channel markers guided us into the mouth of the Reitdiep River connecting the provincial centre of Groningen with the sea. We were soon once again surrounded by rich farmlands, some a vivid green, or sprinkled with the pale golden heads of ripening rye, and others the gentle honey coloured stubble of a harvested crop. The warmth of the afternoon had bestirred some herds of long horned cattle into the cooling water of the river, where they stood gazing disinterestedly at us as we went past. Past Zoutkamp, a small harbour town of picturesque two-storied steeply gabled cottages painted in ochres, blues and yellows that looked more Scandinavian than Dutch. Their fishing boats, looking as well loved as the houses, were neatly displayed in front. We sailed past a marina, almost turned around to go back, and were pleased we had not, when shortly after we came to a narrow inlet off the river with a small jetty, with space for just one more boat. It was delightful. A tall stand of trees to windward and a field of waist high corn on the other, with a vineyard on a slight rise—not quite a hill—behind.

We had not expected to find a vineyard so close to the North Sea, so we had to have a stroll up to investigate. Past a communal vegetable garden, through a small village of three or four houses, along a quiet country lane past an 1828 brick farmhouse with a beautiful sunroom and a large attached barn, and then we came to the gates of the vineyard. No cellar door, but there was a small produce stand selling some veggies, herbs, duck eggs, jams and a few bottles of wine. Naturally, like all good 'hunter gatherers' I was carrying a small rucksack, so we returned home well-laden, enjoyed the wine with dinner and great duck-egg and herb omelettes in the morning.

At nearby Lutjegast, the Abel Tasman Museum commemorates his voyages in the Pacific in 1642 and 1644, two of the world's epic voyages of discovery. The voyages of Willem Janszoom (1570 – 1630) who was the first European to see the coast of Australia, Dirk Hartog (1580 – 1621) who in 1616 was the second to see Australia and first to leave something behind, a pewter plate secured to a post, and Francois Thijssen who mapped 1500 kms of the south coast of Australia in 1627, all testify to the part played by the Dutch in the exploration of the last great unknown.

We continued up the Reitdiep, crossed over the main arterial canal, which was now called the Van Starkenbourhkannal and not long afterwards we were into the suburbs of the grand old city of Groningen. It is encircled by canals, lined by many magnificent old buildings that attest to the wealth of the city when it was a prominent trading hub during the days of the Dutch East India Company. These days its prosperity rests more on education—there are over 45,000 university students—and on administration. It is the provincial capital and the largest city in the north of the Netherlands, with some modern architecture mixed with the classics of old. Particularly the museum with a large collection of modern art, but also an interesting capsule of the past.

We were absolutely fascinated by the great array of old barges. In some places they lined both side of the canals, sometime two-deep. Many were converted to permanent residences of amazing panache, large windows and skylights, decorated outdoor settings and rooftop gardens. The homes of wealthy professionals, writers and artists. Others are slowly decaying hulks, a gallery of things past painted in a thousand hues of rust, a brutal record of what were once lords of the waterways of Europe. Perhaps, now homes to vagrants, lost cats or drug addicts.

The grandness and beauty of Dutch churches often took our breath away. As in all Europe every village is graced by at least one, but because of the flatness of the land their spires are more visible than in the hills and mountains of the south. Like everything else, grand castles to modest homes, they are built of brick made from their sandy soil. Our visit coincided with some occasion the university students were celebrating and, we sat on the fringe of an old courtyard garden watching the merry confusion, while picking at a lovely prawn and vegetable salad with a side dish of freshly picked asparagus.

We left Groningen on the Winschoterdiep Kanal heading south east towards the German border. The sky was covered with dark clouds, the wind boisterous. The canal was advertised as having a minimum depth of 3.50 metre, giving us plenty of water between our keel and the muddy bottom and it was broad with plenty of room for passing. But there were lots of low bridges which had to be raised to let us through. After some 20 kilometres we turned south on the AG Wildervanckkanal and passed through the village of Veendam then onto the Oosterdiep Kanal. We were now well away from the bustle of the arterial and tourist canals and into the heart of rural Netherlands. From the first day the beauty of the countryside had far surpassed our expectations. Its charm was mesmerising. The waterways dense with birdlife, the villages of captivating design, built in creatively laid and patterned coloured brick. Even the roads were brick—there was no stone and not enough timber in the country so, the Dutch had to manufacture everything. Large farmsteadswith attached barns dotted the manicured pastures of green and gold fields holding large herds of cattle. We learned that this small country, with so much of it reclaimed from the ocean and much of it still below sea-level is the largest rural exporter in the EU.

The Oosterdiep was narrower and shallower, we now only had 40 centimetres under our keel, and there were opening bridges almost every kilometre or so. They were operated by a bridge keeper riding a motor bike, who scooted ahead of us to each bridge and opened it manually with lots of muscle and using a long pole, as we came to it. After five or so bridges he waved us goodbye and he was replaced by another genial man. Great service, and by the end of the day we had been through about fifteen narrow bridges and locks with only a few centimetres clearance on each side. Ro could hardly speak because of all the shouting she had to do to keep me on track, and it took a few wines that night to get her voice back. But the hard work was far from over. We only had a few centimetres to spare passing under a fixed bridge into the even narrower Musselkanaal with a depth of just 1.20 metres which gave us a bare 10 centimetres under the keel, and even more opening bridges before we found a welcoming canal bank at the village of Stadskanaal

Rural Holland can make you think of a huge retirement village, where the healthy residents drive around in much loved boats and peddle their bikes along the canals from village to village. The elegantly-dressed madams riding with rosy cheeks, high heels, carefully coiffed hair, and handbags in a basket up front. Younger riders wend their way with an amazing number of adaptions to their bikes, some with infants front and back, some with grannies on side-by-side armchairs in front of the peddler, others with large plastic crates carrying numerous children and dogs of all shapes and size. We were amazed by the popularity of fishing in the canals. Not just by grandads—don't think we ever saw a grandmother—but plenty of men of all ages, some dressed in camouflage hunting outfits, wielding long fishing rods that in many cases reached halfway across the canal. Most sat comfortably on folding chairs close to the water or on short fishing jetties. Many had a small tent close-by—where sometimes a girl friend or a new bride could be seen reading a book, surreptitiously yawning and glancing at her watch—to escape to if the passing showers became too wet. Along some stretches of canal there could be a fisherman every twenty metres or so for a kilometre or two and on wet cold days there seemed to be more. We didn't actually see many fish caught but most anglers had funnelled nets to release their catch. Which wouldn't be a bad idea, as the poo of some millions of dairy cattle drains from paddock to canal all over Holland, apart from the usual contaminants. We initially thought that boats would have right of way over the long rods and floats cast well into the centre of the canals, but the steely eyed stare of the fishermen soon disabused us of this notion.

...were now well away from the bustle of the arterial and tourist canals and into the heart of rural Netherlands...

We overnighted at the village of Ter Apel and then passed through the Rutenbrokkanaal and onto the Veenvaart/Veenarkkanaal and we were now heading west back towards the Ijsselmeer. The canal was wider, with lines of beech and oaks behind each bank, but it was still raw, with grey skies and enough wind to ruffle the leaden water. Still red coat weather through the village of Hoogeveen and on to Meppel. Choosing a place to tie up can often be quite stressful. As you approach a village there may be a number of options. There could be a marina on the outskirts, but we generally prefer the *old town* close to restaurants and surrounded by architectural gems. But what if there are no spots available there, and perhaps the marina could well be closer to a supermarket. But if we stop and have a look in the marina the two boats behind us will dive ahead and take the last two spots in town. Frantic discussion and no conclusion reached until it's too late for the marina. Onwards to a fork—left or right. Again, vigorous discussion but no unanimity, although the branch chosen will generally be the wrong one, necessitating a difficult retreat through a very narrow passage, and the following boats are now ahead of you. A spot appears, quite close to town but has no shore power—if we go past will someone else take it? But wait on, is that a spot under the large tree thirty metres ahead. Can you see if there is shore power? God, there is another boat coming up behind us! This indecision dogged us all the way into Meppel and, we thought we were doomed when we arrived at a small basin at the end of the canal, and there seemed to be no place for us. But at the very last moment we spotted one just large enough—the best one in town without a doubt. Jubilation. Ro claims all credit for the find.

A couple of days later Hubie arrived again, bringing a brief burst of late summer before a cold wind came back, with clouds and a few showers. Later on, the still water of the basin took on the colours of the overcast sky, but a patch of late afternoon sun brought out vivid reflections of the red-roofed houses and the blues and whites of the boats moored along the quay. We caught up on all our eldest grandchild's news. Afterwards we wandered into town, discovered a Chinese restaurant where you could eat all you liked for a very reasonable sum, which is always a popular option for teenagers. The next morning, we were able to restock our larder and depleted cellar at a bustling vegetable and flower market before setting off westward on the Meppelerdiep canal and then north back to Sneek. We were planning on leaving *Linna* undercover in one of the large, 'aircraft-hanger' style sheds that are common there, while having a few improvements made over winter. The warm weather resumed, a clear blue sky, sunny reflections of the profusions of flowers along the canal banks, as we motored into Sneek. There was a celebration of all things nautical scheduled. Parades of every kind of boat known to man over the weekend and, we were lucky enough to get our old spot, where everything would pass us by. It was a wonderful few days, although the nights were definitely chilly. There were still a few of those lovely Norse cardigans for sale, but you know who reminded me that it would be silly to buy one when we would be heading home soon.

***

In early May the following year Ro and I were back in Sneek, and a week later we had retraced our steps to Meppel. I had been talked out of the Norse cardigans again—it would be summer soon—and we were on our way to explore the heart of the Netherlands. Following the Meppelerdiep west we soon entered the broad expanse of the Zwarte Meer and then into the Ketelmeer another tongue of the IJsselmeer. We found ourselves amongst a maze of channel markers leading us across the shallow waters to the passage between the southern shore of the IJsselmeer and the island of Flevoland, which had been reclaimed from the waters after the inland lake had been created. We found a peaceful haven for the night in a broad stretch of calm silvery water. The colours as the sun set were rich and clear, a lovely amber light on the water, merging with the darker reflections of the scattered clouds. The sun, a golden orb sinking below a tall woodland on the island. In the morning we had a chat with a passing canoeist, a pretty Dutch girl in a red lifejacket, with her black cat looking equally smart in a smaller matching jacket. She was planning a trip of a week or so back to Amsterdam.

Onward to the ancient village of Elburg, which was once a saltwater seaport before the shore of the North Sea had been tamed by the construction of the IJsselmeer. It is possible there may have been a Roman army camp here in the 1st century BCE and it has a written record dating from 796 CE and, it gained city rights from the 14th century. We found a charming mooring beside a leafy bank a short distance from town and strolled in for dinner in a narrow lane behind the old brick fortifications. The town basin, its banks secured by wide steel planks driven deeply into the muddy bottom, was full of small sailing yachts and many traditional wooden craft, glowing a golden brown as the sunset. All very beautiful, neat brick houses with steep-pitched black-tiled roofs, old brickwork, the canal banks lined with a mass of colourful hydrangeas: mauves, whites, pinks and rich roses. The hedges, perfectly trimmed, the lawns, closely mown. And, it was warm enough to enjoy a tasty fish and pate salad, and a couple of large Dutch beers, dressed only in shorts and a cotton T. It was all so good we did the same next night, except I went for the battered cod—no fries of course.

We were tempted to linger longer. Lingering is what cruising is all about—although curiosity about what lies ahead is the other side of the coin. The sky was a serene blue with only a few wispy white clouds above the dark green of distant woodlands. Beside the canal four horses were picking over the scattered remains of a bale of hay, still hungry enough to look questioningly at us, as we went by.

It was quite difficult getting into the old medieval, and at one time Hanseatic League, city of Harderwijk, as recent alterations to the canals had not made their way onto our chart. But eventually, in the late afternoon, we found a handy spot. Drinks as usual on the aft deck before setting out to explore the city. Cool again, the water mirroring the steely-grey sky, while a glimmering sun peaked briefly through fleeting gaps in the dark scudding clouds. An old windmill at the edge of town was forlornly silhouetted against a greyness.

The Hanseatic League was something I can remember reading about when I was much younger, I think it may have been the nemesis of some English or Scottish sailors at some time or other. But if I had once known anything about it, I had long since forgotten.

It turns out that it was another institution that played a vital role in the growth of democracy in these northern lands. From almost nothing it grew into a powerful trading federation of cities along the north coasts of the Baltic and North Seas from 1356 to 1862.

It was an extension of the medieval guilds that were formed to strengthen the position of merchants and craftsmen in their relationships with the nobles and the Church. The guilds were an essential step in the growth of modern society. They helped prevent extortion and intimidation by the ruling class and transferred some power to the merchants, tradesmen and the peasantry. The medieval guilds protected both their members and the wider community. For example, the bakers' guild protected its members interests as well as setting standards and monitoring prices. Building guilds set standards of construction and helped assure payment from both the nobles and churches who enjoyed immense negotiating advantages against individual craftsmen.

The Hanseatic League gave an increasingly powerful voice to merchants and sailors, who became the most important wealth creators, and it was of immense value to the wider society. As well as protection from rapacious nobles it gave safety to its members from robbery on land and sea, during a period when crime was endemic. The league became so powerful that it was able to successfully wage war against the combined forces of the kings of Denmark and Norway to obtain free trade throughout Scandinavia.

It was also powerful enough to fight trading opponents and lock them out of markets they regarded as their own.

Its power eventually waned for many reasons. The growth of the naval and trading power of the Atlantic nations, jealousy between members, the Black Death which killed almost half the population of Europe, and the Little Ice Age all contributed.

We continued on our way along the broad channel between Flevoland and the mainland until we came to the Eem river, which leads south to the ancient fortress city of Amersfoort. It was a peaceful stretch of water, running between broad green fields, broken here and there by plantings of camellias, magnolias and rhododendrons. There were drifts of snowdrops under patches of chestnuts and the green domes of maples. There were quite a few bridges to get through on the way into town and by the time we reached the narrow quay our patience was wearing a bit thin, and there were very few moorings.

We were about to dive into the last one, when we noticed a canal-side instruction that all boats were to turn around before tying up. Another boat was just behind us. Although it was flying a Dutch flag, I suspected the skipper could be a Frenchman, which would mean he would ignore the instruction about turning around before docking without a second thought. If he took our spot it was four or five bridges back to the last mooring and a long walk to town. Oh, the agony of being a law-abiding Australian when faced by the possibility of French perfidy. Perhaps, instead of going forward to the turning spot, we could back up a little where it may, just may, be possible to turn around and protect our spot at the same time. Black looks from the Frenchman as we put our plan into action, and after a little longer than I really would have liked, manage to rotate *Linna* with barely a centimetre between the stone wall and a boat on the other bank. More black looks from the Frenchman as he went past, fruitlessly searched for another spot and eventually headed back to the remote mooring in the outer suburbs. Ah, it can be a dog eat dog world at times, but we did have a very fine view along the tree-lined banks to the walls of the imposing brick water-gate guarding the entrance to town, while the Frenchman was muddling around in the sticks.

It was well worth the trouble, Amersfoort was wonderful. There are remains of settlements that were established around the end of the 2nd millennium BCE and the city itself dates from the 11th century CE and gained its city rights in 1259. Today it is a charming place to visit. To stroll along the twisting brick-paved streets that wind their way from the cathedral's great tower and, to dine in the canal side restaurants canopied with luxuriant greenery and decorated with brightly coloured beds of flowers and shrubs, is wonderful. There were two or three squares full of life, laughter and music and lots of people eating outside and enjoying the warm ambience.

On the edge of the old city one of the three-storied brick houses, probably three hundred and something years old, was having some work done on its below ground foundations. In most places in the world you would just need to dig a hole and get on with changing the blocks of stone. But here they had needed to build a waterproof retaining wall to keep the canal at bay, and keep pumps going to keep out below ground seepage. Goodness knows where the old builders got the stone from. Even with the steps the Dutch are willing to go to protect their ancient cities, there are still lots, perhaps even most, of buildings with quite alarming leans.

It was quite hard dragging ourselves away, but eventually we retraced our route back along the river and through the southern end of the IJsselmeer to the Sixhaven Marina at Amsterdam, capital of the Netherlands. At one time only a small fishing village, later one of the great cities of the world and the financial centre of capitalism for two centuries. It attained city rights around 1300 and flourished as a trading port within the Hanseatic League. It was home port to a large and active commercial fleet and was an important shipbuilding centre.

In 1602, when its population was around sixty thousand—London was some two hundred thousand—an event occurred that was to propel the Netherlands into its golden age. And change forever the way the world's economy operated, bring great wealth to the Dutch, and in time to the world. The Dutch East India Company (VOC) was established as a chartered company, which meant it was granted certain rights by the government to trade with Mughal India. At this time half of the textiles and most of the silks coming from the far east were imported from India, most from the region of Bengal Subah. By issuing bonds and shares to the public it became the world's first formally listed public company, and its listing on an official stock exchange was a milestone in the rise of early corporate globalisation. In many ways all modern corporations are direct descendants of the VOC including the British East India Company. The VOC also began trading with other Southeast Asian countries and was granted a monopoly on the Dutch spice trade.

As well as the immense wealth that was generated by the purchase and sale of exotic goods—each shipload was worth a fortune - it spurred investment in a number of ways. Shipbuilding to create the large merchant fleet needed to meet demand and a navy capable of protecting the sea routes and its trading centres. It fostered the actual production of spices in the east, and South African wine and sugar cane. It enabled investment in infrastructure at home and spurred the products of the Golden Age in art, literature and architecture. Before long, it was not just a commercial operation but also an instrument of war in the Dutch Republics global conflict with the Spanish and Portuguese Empires. *'We cannot trade without war nor war without trade'.* It commanded almost five thousand ships and, a ship could return a profit of 40 percent on a single voyage.

Its overseas headquarters was in the Javanese city of Jayakarta, which it renamed Batavia and in the modern era became Jakarta. Over the next two centuries it acquired other ports and trading bases as well as investing in many countries. In its foreign colonies the VOC wielded many governmental powers—the right to wage war, the justice system including imprisonment and execution, negotiating treaties, issuing currency and establishing colonies. It funded exploration that resulted in discoveries of immense global importance and its navigators and cartographers were vital in amassing modern geographical knowledge of the world. At the height of its power it had some 25,000 employees in Asia and another 11,000 enroute, but it was dissolved in 1799 after the disastrous Fourth Anglo-Dutch War (1780-1784).

The VOC management consisted of delegates from the port cities of Amsterdam, Delft, Rotterdam, Enkhuizen, Middleburg, Hoorn and convened periodically as the *Lords Seventeen* - in effect the Board of Directors. They determined general policy, issued directives and coordinated chart making. The initial capital was 6,424,588 guilders raised from 358 shareholders with a minimum investment of 3,000 guilders.

The courtyard in Amsterdam in which a few Dutchman haggled over the exchange of shares in the company became the world's first important stock exchange. Although coordinated by the *Lords Seventeen* the ports managed their own operations. They built and crewed the ships, built and operated warehouses and bought and sold the merchandise.

Because of its pioneering institutional and powerful roles in world history the VOC is considered by many to be the first major, first modern, first global, most valuable and most influential corporation ever seen. Perhaps the first historical model of the megacorporation.

...Jenni, Ro and Eugene...

It was the driving force behind the rise of Amsterdam as a financial powerhouse and the financial centre of capitalism for two centuries. Perhaps the richest company of all time—richer than Apple, Google, Facebook, Microsoft, Amazon, Berkshire Hathaway, Exon Mobile, Johnson and Johnson, Walmart, Visa, Bank of America, Alibaba combined. Its present-day value was some $7.9 trillion in 1637.

The VOC was certainly one of the crowning achievements of the citizens of this great country, alongside the physical construction of the land they actually live in by draining the sea and the waterways to create their verdant, productive and prosperous country.

The charter of the VOC stipulated that only Dutch citizens could buy shares in the company. Many grasped the opportunity, and they were not only the wealthy. Among the first shareholders were corn dealers, grocers, bakers, tailors, seamstresses, sail makers, carpenters, cobblers and servants. Grietje Dirksdochter, a maid of the mayor of Amsterdam saw this new opening provided a chance for ordinary people to not only buy shares in a trading company, but to become a shareholder in the Dutch Golden Age. A period roughly spanning the 17th century when Dutch trade, science and military power rivalled all the nations of the world.

There are some that consider the Dutch to be a dour conservative nation, but they could not be further from the truth. Yes, they value their privacy, but without doubt they are liberal, adventurous, hard-working risk takers.

The peace of Westphalia in 1648 ended the Eighty Years War between the Dutch Republic and Spain, and the Thirty Years War, between the other European nations. It also brought the Dutch Republic formal recognition and independence from the Spanish Crown. In the preceding half century there had been a large immigration of Protestant merchants and financiers from the Catholic controlled centres in France and Portugal and, centres such as Bruges, Ghent and Antwerp north to Amsterdam. By 1630 it was one of the most important commercial centres in the world. Many argue that this contributed to the development of the Protestant work ethic, which in turn brought the lowest interest rates and highest literacy rates in Europe. Enhanced by cheap sources of energy from windmills and peat, trade flourished. Wealth and a massive fleet, enhanced trade opportunities and the projection of military power. The internal canal system provided cheap internal transport and distribution. Their situation between the Baltic and the trading ports in France and England, the links through Europe provided by the Rhine and Danube rivers, further enhanced trading opportunities. In 1640 monopoly trade with Japan was established.

Something in the Dutch psyche, perhaps living with the manifest dangers of the North Sea, made them natural traders and risk takers. Social status became to be determined largely by wealth, with the ancient aristocracy and clergy less important. Families and homes were the cornerstone of society, where women played an important role and enjoyed important social freedoms. Calvinism was the religion of the republic but there was a variety of sects, which were accepted with tolerance, which was also extended to atheists and agnostics.

This tolerance attracted scientists and intellectuals from all over Europe. The University of Leiden, established in 1575, became a centre of intellectualism. The Dutch were leaders in physics, science, astronomy, mathematics, microbiology, optics, engineering. Art and literature flourished. Many of the buildings of the period are still landmarks to this day. In the mid-17th century the Dutch navy was the largest in the world and, at the Raid on the Medway in 1667 inflicted the worst naval defeat in British history. For a period, the Dutch were the wealthiest people on earth, with an average personal income roughly double that of any other Europeans.

Amsterdam is a wonderful city to explore. Particularly if you love the sea, it is never far away, linked to the city by the miles of canals that wind their way through the streets and squares and are a constant reminder and carry memories of its nautical history. But, of course, it was not just commerce that made it great. We could not wait to visit the Rijksmuseum where much of the work of the Dutch masters is held, particularly Rembrandt, the artist most associated with Amsterdam, and Vermeer. Van Gogh lived here for a period and there is a museum dedicated to his work.

Walking the canals was a never-ending source of pleasure. Every few steps there is a scene that must be captured, a grand or quaint old brick building, a canal-side display of flora, a charming restaurant shaded by lush trees, a converted barge with an exquisite rooftop garden, a charming inward-looking window, a window displaying a beautiful girl for hire, a shop of entrancing antiques, the aroma of coffee and fine food, galleries of art and fashion, the passing parade of the bicycle-born, the beautiful, the old, the young, the elegant, the three or four to a bike, and salted liquorice.

It was warm, an early summer while we were there and, it was a joy to end the days exploration lolling at a table—under a canopy of oaks, beeches or limes—with a chilled wine or a pint of freezing

Dutch beer and, watch the passing throng and listen to the babble of many happy tongues. While anticipating plates of North Sea fish, fine Dutch Cheese and sumptuous salads from the not so far off green fields of the countryside.

While idling away our evenings and reflecting on things, we could not avoid talking about the Dutch settlements in North America, particularly what was to become New York, the capital of the modern world. What a great influence on the world they were, and how easily things could have been much different. By early in the 17th century the Dutch East India Company (VOC) had developed a lucrative trade in the furs of the beaver, a native animal of North America. It established a settlement and a fort, New Amsterdam, on the southern tip of Manhattan island, to control access to the interior via the North River—the Hudson River—to facilitate and protect their lucrative trade. In 1624 it was designated as the capital of the province of the Dutch Republic of New Netherlands. By 1643 the province had a population of 9,000.

In 1664, while England and the Netherlands were at peace, a squadron of the British Navy entered New Amsterdam and demanded its surrender. The city's surrender was followed by the Second Anglo-Dutch War and New Amsterdam passed to the British and was renamed New York. Although the Dutch had the opportunity of reasserting their claim when the war ended, they opted instead for control of sugar plantations on the coast of South America. The rest, as they say, is history.

However, perhaps not entirely. Some modern theories argue that the settlement of New Amsterdam by the Dutch has had a much greater influence than previously thought. The cultural diversity and mindset behind the ideals of the American dream, had already been established by the Dutch settlers. Looking at modern day Amsterdam, who could argue against that. And, when you think about it, the American revolution was much more of a Dutch or French thing. They were always revolting. The English, not so much at all.

Reluctantly, again, we thought we best press on. For a couple who do like wandering, there are still many times when we wonder why on earth we are leaving somewhere. But we were off to cruise the length of the Vecht river, which many consider the most beautiful river in Europe. Retracing our route through the IJmeer for a few miles we turned into the river at Muiden and, at the sight of the fairy-tale like castle standing proudly in its manicured gardens, we were immediately in love again. There was a marina on the opposite shore just past the castle and we were tempted but thought we would press our luck and try for the delights of the town centre. There were no places, and a number of boats waiting to go through the large two-chambered lock. There were several restaurants overlooking the scene, and the throng were being entertained by whatever was going on behind the closed lock gates. There was just enough room for us at a waiting spot on the right bank, so we thought we would tie up while things sorted themselves out. Eventually the lock gate ahead of us opened. In normal circumstances we would have been confronted with the bow of a boat proceeding downstream. But it was not a bow, it was a stern. It seemed vaguely familiar. Yes, it was. It was the stern of the *Avesol* the marvellous vintage barge belonging to our friends, a lovely Irish couple John and Win Eakins.

They had broken down, and by the time they were extricated it was closing time and the officials let us tie up together on the bank adjacent to the lock. With normal Irish priorities the misfortune of a broken down motor was forgotten while our unexpected reunion was enthusiastically celebrated. Spare parts are a problem for the old barges, some are available but more often they will need to be fabricated, and John and Win were to spend quite some time here. And were still waiting when we came back by car to celebrate an important birthday two weeks later. But if you had a choice of where to break down, this was a great spot.

The next day the lockkeepers helped us on our way, after we had arranged with our sore-headed Irish friends to go slowly and, catch up down the road a bit. The placid waters of the river wound through the emerald countryside, the bank sometimes hidden under canopies of oak, beech, lime and conifer. Grand residences, many built by wealthy merchants during the Golden Age, were scattered here and there. Among sumptuous gardens of lenten roses, bluebells and dicentras, euphorbias and azaleas. We glided past patchworks of azalea, rhododendron, and stands of maple and crab apple. Here and there were slight rises, some almost wooded hillsides. It was an enchanted stretch of water, and we travelled slowly, even for us. Stopping two or three nights at the first place we found each morning —sometimes we only went around the next bend in the river. We eventually came to the delightful village of Breukelen where we tied beside a luxuriant woodland an easy stroll from town and were joined in the afternoon by Win and John.

...the Avesol on the Vecht River.

There are many mansions along this stretch of the river and, we spent a lot of time admiring them as we ambled along the canal banks —some were most probably built from the profits of the north American fur trade. Brooklyn in America began life as New Breukelen, a Dutch settlement founded on the East River shore of Long Island around 1646. This was the site of the first and largest battle of the American revolution, of which General Washington quoted, 'What brave men I must this day lose'. You would have to think that among those brave men, there were some whose ancestors hailed not far from where *Linna* was moored.

We dawdled slowly along, getting as close to Utrecht as we could get without taking down our canvas bimini to navigate low bridges, and tied up a short distance from a multi-ethnic enclave with lots of spicy eating. The city has an ancient history, probably to the early 3rd century BCE, and a Roman fortress was built here around 50 CE after Emperor Claudius decided that this should be the northern limit of the Empire. We were getting into country where I would have to be careful who I prayed to, probably still Odin, but I would have to keep my wits about me. A series of forts were built along the line of the Rhine river, which in those days was somewhat north of its current position, each housing some 500 legionnaires. The Romans were forced to abandon the area around 275 CE by the invasion of German tribes and, there was little to mark the area until a Frankish Christian church was built inside the old fort in the 7th century and in due course it became a powerful centre of the Catholic church.

Ro had almost finished work on her novel *The Homestead on the River* which was to be published by Harper Collins early the next year, and we wanted to spend some time in Ireland to make sure she was happy she had captured the essence of the area it was set in. We had booked a lovely cottage on the Ring of Kerry for a few weeks, and shorter stays around Lough Derg in Tipperary and Glendalough in County Wicklow. At the end of June, we left *Linna* in a small boatyard just outside Utrecht and flew to the west coast of Ireland to sample more of the irresistible charm of the country and its people. Naturally, the first few days were wet and freezing and while we were driving around Lough Derg, where Ro grew up and still has close ties, we drove past the *Avoca Weavers,* who we have previously visited from time to time. They are famous for their heavy warm woollen pullovers and cardigans, and I think Ro must have been a bit regretful about her attitude to the Norse cardigans in Sneek. She didn't actually suggest that I buy an Arran wool cardigan, but she did help me select one from the 'specials' rack. And a fine thing it was—heavy and warm in the freezing rain of mid-summer in Ireland. It was great for the next two days. But then the unheard of happened. A hot summer arrived. There was not a drop of rain, not a cloud in the sky for the rest of our stay. It's hard to believe, but on some days the temperature approached forty degrees Celsius—but it did, and the newspapers declared we were now in *Desert Ireland.*

We had a lovely time around the dramatic coastline of County Kerry and lots of walks along the tracks weaving through the mountains and around the rocky coastline. But my heavy warm cardigan remained unworn at the bottom of my suitcase the whole time. And it was just as hot when we got back to the Netherlands.

I have been a little hard on some of the roads in the Mediterranean countries. So, in the interests of fairness I should mention Irish roads. There are four categories. There are some freeways, which are much the same as freeways the world over, except they are only ever two, somewhat narrow, lanes each way. Then there are national roads. These cover most of the country and are two lanes. But you can never be confident of two cars passing without one pulling over. If it's a bus you are passing you will almost certainly have to pull off the road and stop. The next category are district roads, and these are all single lane, but two cars can mostly pass if one edges off the bitumen. The last category are local roads, along which many people in the country live. There is no chance of two cars passing unless one car backs up to a passing spot, usually around five hundred yards behind you. Fortunately, the views generally make up for the stress of driving on the minor roads, even knowing an Irishmen may be coming the other way. The local roads tend to be about as relaxing as going through a narrow French tunnel on *Linna*.

After spending a delightful week in a restored barn in Wicklow, where Ro's sister, Viv, joined us from Wales, we arrived back at Utrecht to find that somehow the shore power had been disconnected while we had been away, and the three large 300 amp hour batteries were ruined and would not hold a charge. Utrecht is one of the major Dutch towns, but to our chagrin there were no battery dealers. The closest one was thirty miles away, but all the staff were on summer holidays and they could not deliver. They could supply if we came to them. We got the motor going and motored across, praying the motor didn't stop on the way. The battery dealer was some distance from the marina we tied up in, but there was still only the owner and he couldn't deliver or install. The batteries weigh about eighty kilos each and there was no way I could possibly get them into the engine room and install them myself. Thankfully we were rescued by our neighbour in the marina and his son. And that tends to be summer all over Europe. If something goes wrong, it is very, very difficult to find someone who is not on holidays.

Pressing on, we passed under an alarmingly low bridge with only a centimetre or so to spare, crossed over the busy Amsterdam-Rijnkanaal and on to the Hollandse IJssel canal. Late afternoon found us at Oudewater, tied to a brick wall shaded by the light green leaves of a row of plane trees, and overlooked by a large brick church adorned by a noble tower with high arched windows. Walking back to the boat as the sun was slipping behind curtains of white cloud, it cast a long reflection along the mirror like water of the canal. Another short day brought us to Gouda which was founded around 1100 in a swampy area of peat forest. In due course it became a port on the inland shipping route between France, Flanders, Holland and the Baltic Sea and enjoyed a period of prosperity. But it suffered badly from Plague epidemics in 1574, 1625, 1636, and in 1673 when it lost twenty percent of its population. Imagine if the COVID 19 pandemic had caused this magnitude of death.

There followed many bleak years, where the name of the town became synonymous with begging. These days it is famous for its cheeses, and we were lucky enough to arrive the day before the Gouda Cheese and Craft Market, held every Thursday. We both have a weakness for a good cheese, so we had fun shopping, and celebrated at a fine table overlooking the square and the impressively-towered church. We had tied up to the canal bank, overlooked by an old watermill peeking through the foliage of some elm trees, which caste soft green reflections on the still water. We had some old barges for company, with beautiful paint work, wooden masts and bowsprits, which we stopped to admire on the way home.

We kept heading west, following the old border of the Roman Empire. Casting off once we were sure the bridge keepers would be on duty and stopping before lunch or whenever the inclination overtook us. The city of Leiden_was built at the confluence of the Old and New Rhine rivers and in Roman times marked the edge of the Empire. It received city rights in 1266 and has been a prominent centre of the arts and sciences for over four centuries. Today it is very much a university town, with a vibrant bustle and plenty of places to be able to reflect on the great issues of the past and present, while chatting to the most beautiful girl in the world.

Moored in the large basin close to the centre of the old town we were only a short walk to anywhere. There were boats of all ages and all kinds, big and small, and the foreshore and the storied buildings behind, were decorated with colourful displays of flowers and shrubs. It was here that I first came across the title of 'The Hook and

Cod Wars' fought between 1350 and 1490. Being an old soldier, and intrigued by the name, I could not help delving further—was this an early struggle between the Green movement and consumers or fishermen, or between two factions of fishermen or just a good old trade war? No, it was a long and bloody conflict, which conflated a number of murderous themes. It was certainly fought over who was entitled to be the Count of Holland and, rule and collect the taxes from this wealthy part of the world. It could have been a power struggle between the bourgeois and the nobles, and who was going to collect God's share of the booty. There are lots of possible explanations for the use of the terms *Cod* and *Hook* to describe the warring factions, but no one but a Dutchman, could understand. However, after a long and bloody struggle the House of Burgundy were the winners. These days we associate the term Burgundy with fine French red wine, forgetting they started life as a fierce German tribe that played its part in evicting the Romans from France.

This city also has a close connection with the United States of America and the spread of the Protestant faiths. For a while, from 1608, it was home to the group of English exiles who had fled the religious persecutions in England for the tolerance of 17th century Holland and, who were to become known as the Pilgrim Fathers. Although finding safety here they found the Dutch morals much too libertine and were worried how that would affect their children. I think I would still have the same worries about our grandkids today! Eventually they decided to establish a settlement in the New World, and that was to be the Plymouth Colony in 1620.

We loitered around the city for a few days than began following the Delftse Schie south. It was a broad canal, deep blue under the morning sun, the sky an azure dome with a paler horizon. The green pastures were sprinkled with stands of trees, villages and church spires. We bypassed Delft, which was founded sometime around 1075, then past a group of old brick cottages with sunny verandas overlooking the canal, one with a covered dinghy suspended on davits over its own small quay, others behind hedges of flowering shrubs. Past a row of gardens protected by a hedge of yews, another row along a bicycle path, some scattered woodlands.

Arriving at Rotterdam_we found the many opening bridges and the volume and sizes of the commercial traffic a bit intimidating but managed to creep into moorings at the Veerhaven without damaging anything. We were close to the city restaurants and museums and after tying up we looked for somewhere to recover our nerves. It is a bustling waterfront, the largest port in Europe, and has been completely rebuilt since being flattened by German bombing in World War II. The modern architecture is very impressive, lots of spectacular and innovative high-rise buildings, which strangely enough brought memories of Shanghai. By the time we finished a fine seafood dinner, with ample wine, we had started to feel at home.

But, sitting at our fine restaurant, in this great port city, we could not help but wonder how this marvellous country, once the richest nation on earth, with the greatest trading empire, the largest trading fleet and the most powerful navy, had slipped from its pinnacle. It is still amongst the most prosperous nations in Europe—per capita income is only slightly less than some small special cases, including Luxemburg, Switzerland and Norway. Looking back, it is easy to say that the country was just too small. But the Spanish Empire had withered, and the borders of Europe were far from set. Germany and Italy were only a collection of minor states, England and Scotland were mortal enemies on the same small island and, France was riven by domestic rivalries, fluid borders and was on the path to revolution and military catastrophe.

The short answer is the perfidy of the powerful Dutch Stadt holder William of Orange, who became King of England, and the four wars that were fought between England and the Netherlands. The Dutch, facilitated by the Dutch East India Company (VOC) were first to exploit the great trading opportunities, and establish trading hubs, in Asia and North America. They amassed such wealth that they were able to create the greatest mercantile and naval forces in the world. Their Golden Age dawned. But at the same time, they still had to fight for their survival against Habsburg Spain, whose objectives in the new world centred on conquest, loot and the export of their religion. In 1628 the Dutch Admiral Piet Heyn captured a large Spanish treasure fleet. In 1639 at the Battle of the Downs they mauled a large Spanish fleet carrying soldiers who were intended for fighting in the low countries.

The Dutch ascendency continued. By the mid-17th century they had largely replaced the Portuguese in Asia and also dominated the Baltic. They had the largest mercantile fleet, more than all other nations combined. The end of the Thirty Years War in 1648 led to decommissioning of much of the navy and military, but soon after the Dutch and English were in conflict on the north eastern seaboard of America. Once Cromwell had taken charge in England the navy was revamped, more ships were built, officers were promoted on merit and he clamped down on dockyard corruption. He positioned England as a genuine challenger of the Dutch navy and mercantile trade competition fermented an anti-Dutch mood in England. It was exacerbated by the general belief that Holland was growing stronger than England, who had been her protector from the Spanish, and that the Dutch were exploiting the English herring fishery. That the overseas possessions of Spain and Portugal were up for grabs and the Dutch would steal them, also stirred up the English.

The English parliament decided on confrontation, and Cromwell's building had by this stage given them naval superiority, although the Dutch mercantile marine was still superior. In 1651 in a blow aimed at the Dutch, the English Navigation Acts mandated that all imports must be carried by English ships or the ships of the exporting country. This tended to be enforced by English piracy. The First Anglo-Dutch War started in 1652 when Dutch ships refused to lower their colours in honour of the Royal Navy, and a number of naval battles were fought before it was declared a draw and peace restored. But the Dutch were still the dominant trading nation, and immediately commissioned sixty more warships.

In 1665 the Second Anglo-Dutch War was precipitated by English anti-Dutch measures and by growing privateering and Royal Navy action. A number of Dutch ships were captured or crippled. But Odin must have been looking after his Norse cousins. England was attacked by the plague, the Great Fire of London nearly destroyed the city and, at the Battle of Medway in 1667 the Dutch inflicted the most humiliating defeat in English history. King Charles II, in fear of losing his throne, sued for peace. The third war was fought between 1672-1674 after the English navy had been rebuilt. With England allied with France, the French army invaded, but could not get past the Hollandic Water Line. At sea, the Dutch enjoyed four naval victories over combined Anglo-French fleets. On paper, a clear win for the Dutch, but it had put the country through a lot of pain and expense.

But, now for the perfidy.

The powerful Dutch prince, William of Orange, was the grandson of Charles I—the beheaded Stuart—King of England and married to Mary, the daughter of James—the Stuart—Duke of York. So, when he was crowned King of England in 1688 both he and his wife came with strong connections to the Stuarts and to England. But he was also the most powerful man in the Netherlands—Stadholder of the Dutch provinces of Holland, Zeeland, Utrecht, Guelders and Overijssel. Unfortunately, for Holland, William's loyalty to his new role as king of England—and Scotland and Ireland—and perhaps fear of losing his head, outweighed his loyalties to Holland. To safeguard his kingship, he granted the Royal Navy many privileges to guarantee their loyalty to him. And disastrously for Holland, mandated that the Dutch fleet could only be sixty percent of the size of the Royal Navy. This, and when the Dutch mercantile fleet started to use London as home port, was a blow from which they would never recover. From 1720 Dutch wealth ceased to grow, and in 1780 for the first time the gross national product of Great Britain surpassed that of Holland. The Dutch fleet was reduced to only twenty ships of the line, and although they did build a further ninety-five, the Royal Navy and the British economy remained dominant. There were no large engagements, but much harassment during the Fourth War 1780-1784 and by the end Holland was in eclipse.

Later, in 1797 at Battle of Camperdown the British Fleet decisively defeated the Dutch and, the French Revolutionary Wars and Napoleonic Wars between 1739 and 1815 saw it incorporated into the French Empire from 1810 until Napoleon's defeat. It became independent again, but its place in the first division was gone.

That night we walked back to *Linna* with mixed feelings. History again—not many happy endings. But, past glories aside, and forgetting about the weather, it is hard to think of a better place to be a citizen of—except Australia of course. We had almost reached the starting point for our journey up the Meuse River into the heart of France. We had loved every mile of our trip so far and perhaps in time, we will have the chance to do it again. There was plenty we had missed along the way. But, being the wanderers, we are, our minds were set on the next bend in the river. From here we were heading south east, and a few hours would take us into the Meuse.

~ THE GREAT RIVERS ~

...Linna - the Vosges Mountains - France

In the late morning we turned south into the maze of rivers and creeks winding their way through the densely forested islands of the Biesbosch National Park. The brown waters were calm, the reed-covered shorelines seemed like home to every known variety of European waterbird going busily about their day. Some foraging amongst the reeds, others patrolling with squadrons of chicks in tow, or coming and going from high nests while long-legged waders hunted on the shallow mudbanks.

Waters of two of the greatest European rivers, the Waal—(known as the Rhine everywhere else) and the Maas—the Meuse in France—formed the north and south borders of the national park, before merging a few kilometres westward to form the Hollands Diep, then flowing through dykes into the North Sea. Our plan for the remainder of the next two seasons was to explore these two great rivers, which for over two thousand years have been the arteries linking the nations of northern Europe.

First, we would follow the Meuse south to its headwaters in France, then cross eastward by canal to the headwaters of the Moselle river and then on again by canal to the headwaters of the Rhine. We would then follow that mighty river north, taking in some more of the beautiful Moselle on the way.

There were a number of small public jetties scattered here and there among the islands and, we claimed an isolated one for ourselves to enjoy the warm afternoon and a quiet night in the wilderness. A few families of ducks and snooks called in to say hello during the afternoon and towards dusk a pair of regal white swans approached, fixing us with steely eyes as they glided by. A beautiful sunset, a pink flush on the horizon, a star-filled night.

The next day we turned into the Maas river. It was some seven or eight hundred metres wide, the right bank lined by dense woodlands through which ran a myriad of small waterways that were home to a wide variety of birdlife. A procession of huge barges plodded upstream towards the heartlands of Europe or downstream to the North Sea. Before long the fen lands gave way to pasture. The sky was cloudless, a gentle breeze ruffling the water. The fields were sprinkled with dairy cattle—some munching contentedly while others contemplated the meaning of life. A squadron of black and grey geese had laid claim to a section of the bank and eyed us suspiciously, while demanding, with arched necks and ruffled feathers, what the bloody hell we thought we were doing. A little further on there was a small wood protected by a bank of tall reeds with bird nests concealed within shadowy tunnels and amongst the branches of fallen trees. Flotillas of ducks were on manoeuvres, determined that they had right of way over all but the mightiest of barges.

After an hour or so we turned north onto Heusdens canal, a short waterway connecting the Maas to the Rhine. By late morning, having passed through one medium-sized lock, we arrived at Woudrichem on the southern bank at the junction with the Rhine. Here there was a beautiful basin with moorings overlooked by the old ramparts of the town and the lovely gardens that surrounded it. The basin was protected by high banks, with thick rushes and willows trailing green tendrils into the calm water, all overlooked by an old brick windmill. In the distance the majestic square brick tower of a large church peeked over the greenery. We had a few days to fill in before we met Don and Sue Clark who were joining us from Tasmania and there was plenty to explore close by, as well as some well thought of restaurants to investigate. We moored at the end of a pier with a fine view all around and where we could enjoy the ghost of a breeze that cooled the now very warm afternoon. As the sun was setting, we strolled around to a restaurant on a large converted barge, chose a shaded table on the deck with a long view, ordered some cool drinks and enjoyed lovely cod and salad.

The next day, it was only a short ferry ride and a stroll along the south bank of the Rhine to the most impressive Kasteel Loevesteen. The castle was in, what was in the days of the seemingly endless wars of the middle ages, a very strategic location at a junction of the waters of the Rhine and Meuse. It still has excellent all-around water protection, which was complemented by very well-designed earthworks, which made it virtually immune to any cannon that could be deployed against it before the 18th century. By 1372 it was under the control of the Counts of Holland and eventually became part of the Hollandic Water Line, the area where the land was flooded as a strategic barrier to invasion. We spent an enjoyable few hours wandering about the labyrinthine interior and gardens and were amused by the tale of an important prisoner, who was smuggled out in a chest by his wife and went on to enjoy a long career as an eminent statesman.

The next day another ferry ride, across the Rhine, took us to Gorinchem which was probably founded by farmers and fishermen taking advantage of an area of slightly elevated land at the junction of the Linge river with the Rhine. By the beginning of the 14th century the city's defensive walls and ramparts had been built, incorporated with the usual extensive water defences, and it had become another cog in the labyrinth of fortified cities surrounded by lakes, rivers, canals and fen lands with cannon bigger than anything an army could haul along with them. All making the conquest of these northern lands situated in the Dutch Water Line such a nearly impossible task. But the city was for a time held by the Spanish until its capture by Dutch rebels in 1572. Amongst the prisoners were nineteen Catholic priests and monks, who when they refused to renounce their faith, were hanged and became known as the Martyrs of Gorkum. Famous citizens of Gorinchem were the classical artists Van Der Neer, Cornelis Saftleven, and Hendrick Verschuring. Also, the navigator Hendrik Hamel who was shipwrecked off Korea and held prisoner from 1653 to 1666 only a few years after Tasman's voyages around the South Pacific.

'Hamel's Journal and a Description of the Kingdom of Korea', provided the western world with the first accounts of that land in 1668. While he was there, he met another Dutchmen who was still held prisoner after he had been wrecked twenty-seven years before. Evidently Korea's penchant for locking people up for long periods of time, is not something that was just invented by Kim Jong-un and his family.

We spent a few more days exploring Woudrichem and stocking up with supplies, before returning along the connecting waterway to the main branch of the Meuse and the beautiful city of Heusden. The marina was in a protected basin overlooked by the city walls. In centuries gone by it would have been crowded with commercial traders from all over Europe—today the patrons were just idle yacht owners, like ourselves. The sun was a molten disc as it dropped behind a stand of maples on the far bank, colouring the horizon with strips of amber and mauve. The water became a still mirror and for a few moments held exquisite images of the darkest blue, until shadows washed everything in somnolent grey. On the eastern shore, behind the city's earthen ramparts, stood an ever-present outline of an old windmill.

There was a stronghold here from the earliest times, but the city dates from around 1202 when it was captured by the Duke of Brabant. The Duke expanded the fortifications, built a castle keep and began the extensive water defences, which have been rebuilt in recent times and are now an amazingly beautiful memory of what, in its day, was an equally amazing fortress. Until the advent of explosive artillery shells the earthen and rock ramparts were virtually immune to cannon fire and were surmounted by bigger cannons than could be brought against them. The intricate geometric design meant that attackers were always exposed to enfiladed fire while trying to cross the deep waterways protecting the walls and island strongholds.

The Eighty Years War or the Dutch War of Independence, from 1566 to 1648 is historically the most important event in Dutch history – it led to the creation of the nation. In 1566 the seventeen provinces of what are today the Netherlands, Belgium and Luxembourg, but at that time were part of the empire of Phillip II of Spain, revolted. At the outset Phillip sent in his armies and regained control of most of the rebelling provinces. But under the leadership of William the Silent the resistance continued and eventually the Habsburg armies were driven out and, in 1581 the United Provinces of the Netherlands was created.

At the beginning of the war, Heusden had been captured by the Spanish forces, but it was retaken, with its citizens fighting alongside the army of William, Prince of Orange. The revolt was not just about throwing off the rule of Spain, but also being forced to be part of the Holy Roman Empire and worship in the Catholic tradition. During this period the Spanish Empire, funded by the vast flow of treasure from its colonies in the New World, was the superpower of Europe. But in the Netherlands, there was nothing that would quell the desire for self-rule and, with the spread of Protestantism, the demand for religious freedom. 1300 Dutch were executed for heresy between 1523 and 1566. The long war saw another 100,000 Dutch killed in fighting and many more in the massacres common in captured towns.

The war continued in other areas, including the Dutch attacking Portugal's overseas empire, but the heartland of the new republic remained safe and it was recognised by the major European powers in 1609. But 1619 saw the beginning of the Thirty Years War, initially between Protestant and Catholic nations, which raged until 1648 when the Dutch Republic was recognised as part of the Peace of Westphalia.

It was great to see Don and Sue Clark, our oldest shipmates, climb out of a taxi from Brussels. After unpacking and a snooze we took them for a tour of the town and at the appropriate hour we were ensconced at a shady table overlooking the square. We were all amazed by the collection of cars, some driven here by our fellow diners, others belonging to the owners of the many beautifully restored residences along the winding brick roads within the town. There were Ferraris, Bentleys, BMWs, Lamborghinis, Paganis, Aston Martins, Bugattis, even a few relatively humble Jags and Mercs. Then we realised. We were within easy drive of Brussels and the rivers of gold that flow to the bureaucrats who reside there in idle splendour—the new princes of this age.

In the lingering dusk we enjoyed a lovely walk around the top of the ramparts back to *Linna* and a bit of philosophising on the aft deck. In the morning we slowly nosed out of our basin, carefully looking left and right for any lumbering behemoths that might run over us and headed upstream. The sun rose higher in a cloudless sky, the broad river, edged with noble trees ran through miles of verdant farmlands dotted with herds of cattle. There was a steady stream of large barges heading in both directions, but there was plenty of room for everyone and before long, we felt as comfortable as we would normally feel strolling through a park at home. In due course we arrived at the large lock at Lith_and experienced a whiff of apprehension at the thought of sharing it with a couple of monsters. But everyone was friendly and courteous, and we were through and on our way with hardly a raised voice on board. Before lunch we turned into the waterways around Massbommel_and secured ourselves a nice outside berth at a small marina.

A small bright yellow ferry, the *Pontje Ham,* licensed to carry twelve people—and an unspecified number of bicycles—operated a service across the Maas river from our basin. The passengers stood on a tray-like deck at the rear and the ship's captain occupied a small wheelhouse, large enough for only one person, perched on the bow.

I was rather startled, then a bit alarmed to see the captain was a widely grinning six-year old boy, who seemed more interested in waving to his admirers than steering. The Dutch have a liberal attitude about who is and isn't allowed to steer boats, but this did seem a bit extreme even if there were no passengers on board. I was relieved when grandfather appeared from the far side of the wheelhouse and told his charge to concentrate. Before dinner we had a long walk through the neat gardened village and around the nearby countryside. We were nearly caught out by a brief thunderstorm but managed to beat it back to the boat.

The next day we continued along the noble river and by late morning had made it to another small marina near the village of Gennep. It was a delightful spot in a quiet basin off the river and guarded by a few pairs of swans, who spent much of the afternoon quarrelling about who was boss. The marina owners had created a splendid garden display, including an old white dinghy on the shore overlooking the boats. It was planted with a profusion of flowers, presenting a riotous display of colour surmounted by the fluttering red, white and blue stripes of the national flag.

As the sun dropped behind the woodlands along the western horizon, our small bay was as still as glass and reflected a few patches of the last of the golden sky, mingled among the dark shadows of the trees lining the shore. A pure white swan, her beauty perfectly framed against the black mirror, glided past with no trace of a ripple. Her noble features an inscrutable mask, giving no hint of what she felt about our intrusion on her domain.

Onwards.

A cloudless summer sky, the water a glittering silver, the far bank a ridge of golden-brown. A sombre brick church tower peaking over a dark green copse. We moored in a small quay at Venlo. After eating in one of the restaurants overlooking the boats, we wandered the bustling streets of the old town. The market square, dominated by the imposing town hall that dates from 1597, was lined with bistros and bars full of people enjoying themselves in the warm ambience of the late summer night.

When we arrived at Maasbracht we were delighted to find that the outside jetty of the small marina close to the *old town* was empty. But, but, after we tied up found there was no power or water. This meant moving. Bit of cursing and some dark looks from you know who. The next day we went through a large double lock, and into a narrower stretch of canal. There was a lot of dredging going on, and there were stretches which were only one way, which meant lots of giving way to the big commercial barges. We were thankful when we eventually got to the striking old city of Maastrich and found a mooring next to a great stone wall that runs for some hundreds of metres in the centre of the river between two bridges. The age of the upstream bridge says a lot about building techniques. It had been built in 1275—so say 745 years or so old. It replaced a Roman bridge that had finally collapsed when it was around 1200 years old, spilling a church procession into the water. It is recounted that a new bridge was financed by the sale of papal indulgences, which does seem particularly public spirited of the clergy, who normally spent the profits on their own accommodation. But perhaps they charged a toll to cross the bridge for several centuries. On reflection, I'm sure they did.

In ancient times the river was crossable here for much of the year and there were settlements from the earliest times. Later, a Roman fortification was built, along with the first bridge, in the 1st century CE and the city is first mentioned in documents in 575. It was an important centre of trade and manufacturing in the Middle Ages and since at least around the 12th century an important religious centre, with wealthy churches replete with relics, sculptures, silverwork and paintings. It was home to the ancient 'Legend of Saint Servatius' by Henric van Veldeke. There is the best part of two thousand national heritage buildings in the city, which would make it a marvel to wander around even if it wasn't full of great places to enjoy yourself, in the company of hordes of merry—perhaps hallucinating—students. As with all the cities and villages along the rivers it suffered during the Eighty Years War and the Franco-Dutch War when it was occupied by the French from 1673 to 1678. It became part of the United Kingdom of the Netherlands in 1815.

When Donald was a young orchardist in Koonya in the 1960s and 70s, they employed a number of young Dutch men and women as casual pickers during the apple season. One of the young men, who was known as Johnny Red Cap, because of the cap he wore everywhere, stayed on rent free in the picker's quarters for some months afterwards. He was popular with the locals, even most of the blokes liked him, and was a talented artist and photographer. When he eventually went on his way, he left some of his paintings behind as gifts, which are still hung in the Clark's farmhouse. When Donald knew he was going to join us in the Netherlands he managed to locate his old friend, and an arrangement was made to meet at Maastrich. So, a reunion after nearly fifty years and we were lucky enough to be in on it. Johnny brought along his red cap, a portfolio of his current art, and his collection of his photos of what he still thinks of as 'the trip of his life.' Some of his paintings were of the wetlands and the bird life, and one of three eiders about to touch down on an isolated waterway, so captured the essence of the remote canals, that we could not resist it. It fills me with nostalgia every time I pass it. The reunion could not be accomplished in only one night, so it spilled into a second, and we were very sorry to wave Johnny and his charming partner, off.

We had hoped that we might have been able to catch up with one of the city's great musicians, Andre Rieu, while we were passing through. But unfortunately, we had left it too late for him to fly back from the USA in time to catch us. *Linna* was berthed at Maastrich over winter, and in May the following year we were back on board. Both well, Ro recovered totally from a hip replacement, and anxious to be on our way to France.

For most of the distance from the coast, the Meuse had been a scenic pathway through the green pastures and forests of the southern Netherlands. There had been the occasional industrial blemish, but they were forgotten by the next turn in the river. But things changed once we crossed the Belgium border, and got worse the closer we got to Liege. The first independent Belgium state was created in 1830 after centuries of rule by the Holy Roman Empire, followed by French and Dutch occupation. We had no idea that it was the first country in continental Europe to experience the industrial revolution and, was the most intensively industrialised country in the world for most of the period.

This development had been sparked by two British industrialists, William and John Cockerill who moved to Liege in 1807 and formed a company producing industrial machinery and iron. By the 1840s Cockerill was the largest steel manufacturer in the world. One stretch of railway between Brussels and Mechelen was one of the first in Europe, and Belgium was one of the foremost industrial powers in the world. By 1914, it had extensive railway networks, factories and mines along the Sambre-Meuse river valleys.

From the back deck of *Linna* it looked as if nothing that had been built in the last two hundred years or so of the country's industrialisation had ever been removed but had just been left to rot and decay along the bank of the river. The only redeeming thing about the day was that we were doing it by ourselves, and not inflicting it on some poor soul who had flown halfway around the world to enjoy the beauty of Europe. When we did make it to Liege it was not as bad, thank goodness, as we had feared. We found a berth in a small quay securely set behind insurmountable fences, which made us wonder about law and order, near the centre of town.

There is no such person as a Belgian. There are either Walloons, who live in the south around the valleys of the Meuse and the Sambre, are economically depressed, speak French and hate the other half of the population who are Flemish, live mainly in the north and speak Dutch. The Flemings benefit most from the flood of EU money around Brussels and the prosperity of the Netherlands – which makes the Walloons even surlier. Liege is the largest Walloon city and its outskirts are the most heavily scarred by industrialisation. We needed to spend a couple of days there to stock up on a few things and were happy to get going again. Gradually the Meuse reclaimed its beauty, it was still a grand river, six or seven hundred meters wide, and once we left the city, we found ourselves winding through a green valley lined with steep ridges and rocky bluffs, with only the occasional patch of dirty industry. There were many stunning chateaus set in leafy grounds, some of which looked as though they were not a spin-off of the 19th century industrialisation, and we wondered about them. Who had built them and were had the wealth come from?

It did not take long to develop a theory. The theory was the Belgium Congo. King Leopold II of Belgium acquired the rights to territory in the African Congo at the Conference of Berlin in 1885. He made it his personal property and called it, with a degree of hypocrisy that would have even embarrassed Stalin, or Hitler or Mao Ze Dong or any other of the blood thirsty tyrants of our recent history, *the Congo Free State*. It marked two decades of perhaps the cruellest rule ever inflicted on a colonised people, well, if you don't count the Spanish depredations in the Americas.

He established an administration that answered directly to him and set about building infrastructure, including a railway line from the interior to the coast, that facilitated the ruthless exploitation of the country's resources—mainly rubber and ivory. He decreed his ownership of all land throughout the territory, although he promised the Congolese the right to continue to occupy existing villages and farms at his discretion.

...fed the King immense wealth, including enough to build palaces and villas for his teenage mistress...was one built on the banks of the Meuse in southern Belgian, we wondered?

He created his own army, the Force Publique (FP) which was used to enforce these arrangements and to ensure Arab slave traders in the Upper Congo did not encroach on his labour supply. The FP officers were entirely European, either Belgians or mercenaries from other nations, while the rank and file were initially from other regions of Africa - including slaves supplied by the Arab traders. The FP's primary function was the coercion of the native population into facilitating the economic rape of their own country. Armed with modern weapons and bull whips they routinely tortured hostages, slaughtered the families of rebels, and flogged and raped the Congolese people, cut off the hands of those they interrogated and burnt their villages.

Between 1885 and 1908 millions of Congolese died through hideous exploitation and disease. Some estimates suggest that the population was cut in half. The atrocities committed by the Force Public in meeting the economic targets set by the administration were almost beyond belief. In the words of one junior European officer. *'The baskets of severed hands, set down at the feet of European post commanders, became the symbol of the Congo Free State ... The collection of hands became the end in itself. Force Publique soldiers brought them to the stations in place of rubber, they went out to harvest them instead of rubber ... They became a sort of currency. They came to be used to make up for the shortfalls in rubber quotas, to replace ...the people who were demanded for the forced labour gangs; and the Force Publique soldiers were paid their bonuses on the basis of how many hands they collected.'*

In 1889 Joseph Conrad published *'Heart of Darkness'* in which he exposed the horrors of the Congo. Under British pressure, Leopold sold the Congo to the nation of Belgium in 1908. He had never visited the country which had fed him immense wealth, including enough to build palaces and villas for his teenage mistress. Was one built on the banks of the Meuse in southern Belgian, we wondered? The Belgium government continued developing the Congo and its natural and mineral riches for the benefit of the Belgium economy. It remained an important source of wealth for Belgium, although gradually some emphasis was placed on health care and basic education of the native population.

Despite reflections on the Belgium Congo, after a pleasant day's run, we found a small picturesque harbour in the countryside south of the village of Huy and tied up before having a stroll around. We arrived back in good spirits to find a small neat man sitting on a bench overlooking *Linna*, with a brief case on the seat beside him. We nodded politely and he introduced himself as a Belgium boat inspector. Could he come on board to check our papers and equipment.

'Of course, can we offer you a coffee.' A strange place to be apprehended by a boat inspector, we wondered, miles from anywhere and we were the only visitor in the otherwise deserted harbour. He must have a quota of one boat a week if this was where he hunted. Anyway, *Linna* was equipped with everything that anyone, even the most pedantic Belgium inspector, could possibly require. After snooping through lifejackets, flares, smoke detectors, extinguishes, alarms, etc he could not find fault, but brightened up when he discovered we only had one 135 hp diesel motor. 'No auxiliary motor?' he snapped, his hand slipping towards his handcuffs and revolver, an arrest imminent. Very few boats our size in Europe have two motors, and an outboard motor on a fifteen tonne boat was ridiculous.

We were bemused.

'No other means of propulsion?' he asked with great satisfaction. 'Ah, only bow and stern thrusters.' I answered doubtfully, as they would not move us far if the motor failed. He thumbed through more paper; his smugness faltered when he found thrusters did suffice. But shortly after he did get us. All the boat's paperwork was in Dutch and my licenses were in English, so being a Walloon who was limited to French, he had some trouble following what was what. Now, in the Netherlands very few yachts are actually registered, as Dutch owners rightly see this as just another government tool for raising money, and boats are only registered so that a boat can be mortgaged if needs be. The only requirement is proof of ownership. We had an official looking page of paper assuring all that *Linna* was not registered and therefore not incumbered with debt. He had previously mistakenly taken the bit of paper as proof of registration, when in fact it was proof of non-registration.

Have I lost you, here?

He broke into a delighted chuckle and again reached for his revolver. 'It might be okay to sail a non-registered Dutch boat in the Netherlands but, it was not okay to sail it in Belgium'.

After contemplation, and after Ro mentioning we were planning to visit her great uncle's grave in Bruges—the truth—he changed his mind and settled instead on an official warning. But there would be a hefty fine if we were found in Belgium waters after one month. It was well and truly dark by the time he had packed his papers and headed off, having spent over an hour tormenting us.

It was only while we were having a simple dinner in the almost deserted dockside café, that I wondered if I should have enquired if the inspector's grandfather had been employed in the *Force Publique* in the Congo Free State, during the time of King Leopold II, and if he had any photos of him with a basket full of chopped off hands. When we had been puttering around the Netherlands earlier in the year, an old Dutch skipper had warned us about Belgium boat inspectors, but we thought he was just trying to put the wind up a pair if naïve Australians. Well, we now knew better, and they certainly wouldn't find us in their country in three days, let alone in a month.

In the morning we had put it all behind us as we carefully squeezed out of the small harbour. The sun was up in a pale blue sky, splashed with thin white clouds. Imposing stone towers capped by high gabled roofs and spires peaked out of the forest on the far bank. There was still the odd commercial barge about, but soon we be out of their territory.

Namur_the capital of Wallonia is located on the junction of the Meuse and Sambre rivers, overlooked by another mighty fortress on a steep crag. It has been an important trading settlement since Celtic times, straddling the east-west and north south trade routes through the Ardennes. The Romans established themselves after Julius Caesar defeated the Belgae at the nearby Battle of Sambre in July 57 BCE.

A large Belgae army surprised Caesar's army of some eight legions, say 40,000 men, as it was making camp adjacent to the Sambre River. Despite this, they were crushed by the Romans. This left only one Belgae tribe, the Atuatuci still in the field against Caesar. They retreated to their fortified city, which was protected on all sides by high rocks and cliffs - probably Mont Falise to the north of Huy. The Romans laid siege to the town by encircling it with a wall twelve feet high and fifteen miles long. When the Romans began to approach the town walls with a large siege tower the Atuatuci realised they had no hope, agreed to hand over their weapons and place themselves under Caesar's protection. But that night, after making their surrender the Atuatuci changed their minds, and tried to escape through the Roman lines fighting with weapons they had concealed. The attempt failed, some 4,000 were killed and 53,000 sold into slavery.

Caesar had been elected as a consul for the year of 59 BCE at the age of forty-one. At the end of his year, with the help of his political allies, he secured the governorship of three provinces of the Empire —northern Italy, south-eastern Europe and southern France, for a period of five years. He had four legions under his command, and two of his provinces bordered unconquered lands, which offered him the chance of military glory as well as accumulating enough booty to pay off his debts. Also, there was concern in Rome over the danger of Germanic tribes heading towards Italy, and Caesar raised two more legions and defeated them. This prompted other tribes in the north east to arm. Caesar treated this as an aggressive move and began a piecemeal campaign that was to take him as far north as Namur. There were later campaigns. In 55BC he built a bridge across the Rhine near Koblenz and made a show of force east of the river. In the same and following years, he invaded England but was forced to retreat. The conquest of Gaul was essentially completed in 51 BCE. According to Plutarch the Romans killed a million Gallic warriors, enslaved a million men, women and children, subjugated 300 tribes and destroyed 800 cities. This does seem to make Caesar something of a monster.

But it is easy to make the case that the German tribes had been intent on conquering Italy for most of the previous century and kept at it until they finally succeeded in 476.

During the early Middle Ages, the Frankish kings built a castle on the high rocky spur at the junction of the rivers and overlooking the jetty we had tied up to. It became part of the Spanish Netherlands in the 1640s and was taken by France in 1692. Then the Dutch captured the castle in 1709. The Treaty of Utrecht in 1713 handed rule to the Austrians although the castle remained in Dutch hands.

Confused? I shouldn't have brought it up. After more to and fro it became part of Belgium following the Belgian revolution in 1830.

The city has also been prominent in the great wars of the 20th century. Namur was the first major target of the German invasion in 1914, as they sought to use the Meuse and Sambre rivers as routes into France. The impregnable fortress fell after three days fighting. But the ruler of Belgium, King Albert I, had no hesitation in throwing away the lives of forty thousand soldiers and many of his people in a futile attempt to stop the German advance. They had no hope of stopping the Germans, but they did delay them enough to prevent the capture of Paris and possibly a different outcome from the war. Perhaps it could have had a negotiated settlement more in line with the 1871 war, and perhaps saved the forty million killed and wounded. When his son faced the same quandary in World War II, he opted to save his soldier's lives.

In that war Namur was central to the Battle of the Ardennes as the Germans drove through into France, and again later in the war during the Battle of the Bulge when the Germans sought to repulse the American forces pushing towards Germany. These days it is still an important commercial and industrial centre, producing machinery, leather goods, metals and porcelain.

There was still not much recreational traffic on the river. And we had no trouble getting a good berth on the right bank, with a dramatic view over the river and the grey arched bridge to the solemn walls of the fortress, astride the spur running down to the junction of the two rivers. We strolled up to the top on the way to finding somewhere for dinner, and it was not hard to imagine a still youthful Julius Caesar looking things over from this very spot.

In the morning we pressed on. A low grey sky weeping a misty shroud over the forested hills. The riverbank lined with stately trees – rich dark greens of oaks and elms, paler hues of maples and birch broken by sweeping green lawns and noble mansions. The water an unruffled sombre grey, winding its way from the south. Past a five-story chateau strait from the pages of 'Sleeping Beauty,' built of red and white bricks, edged by circular towers, large stately windows overlooking a noble stretch of the river. Certainly, good enough for the teenage mistress of the king. Through a village of old brick dwellings, some multi-storied conjoined, others two or three storied freestanding homes, strung out along a narrow bank between the river and the steep wooded hills and rocky bluffs.

Later, a line of tall birches ran along the foreshore, perfectly reflected in the motionless water. Overhead, lumpy white clouds with dark undersides. Past a grand old brick castle set amidst formal gardens. By midday the clouds had gone, revealing a pale blue sky. The colours of our world had ripened and reflections in the blue green water were startlingly vivid.

Dinant comes from the Celtic meaning Divine Valley and was also settled by the Romans. It's situated in a steep sided valley, overlooked by a towering rocky eminence twenty kilometres from the border with France. It prospered from the fertile land above the town, the trading opportunities provided by the river and was famous for its brassware. The limestone cliffs supported a quarrying industry including black marble and bluestone. However, its location made it a popular target and it suffered much unwanted attention from the early Middle Ages right through to modern times. It was devasted in August 1914 during the Battle of Dinant between French and German forces, in which Lieutenant Charles de Gaulle was wounded. Germans summarily executed 674 inhabitants as reprisals for civilian snipers, the biggest massacre committed by Germans in

1914, although another five thousand Belgian and French civilians were massacred within the following month.

Charles de Gaulle was one of the most controversial characters to come out of World War II. He was born 1890 and attended the military academy at Saint-Cyr from 1909 to 1910. At the time potential cadets had to serve in the ranks and his company commander, who delayed his promotion to sergeant, was one of the early ones to comment on his ego. He felt *'nothing less than Constable of France would be good enough for him'*. He turned out to be an average student but, did improved to be 13th in his class. He rejoiced under the nick-name *'the great asparagus,'* because of his height of 196 cm. As a young officer he espoused the popular line that the spirit of the army had declined in the 19th century because of stressing the importance of firepower rather than élan and, championed the effectiveness of bayonet charges, that had worked well for the Japanese in the Russo-Japanese War. This fixation with élan and attack at all cost were exactly what decimated the French army in the upcoming war.

He fought with the 33rd Regiment as a platoon commanded in fierce fighting at Dinant, and was wounded, partly because the French battle tactics stressed bugles and bayonet charges. The casualties were heavy, and in his writing at the time he seemed to have reviewed his opinions and, criticised the 'over rapid' offensive, and the inadequacy of the French generals and, the 'slowness of the English troops'. In January 1915 he was awarded the Croix de Guerre for crawling into no man's land and obtaining valuable intelligence by 'eaves dropping' on the conversations of German soldiers! Hmm. He was wounded again as a company commander during the battle of Verdun, where he passed out from gas poisoning. He was one of the few survivors of his company and claims he was pulled from a shell crater by German soldiers and taken prisoner. Anti-Gaullists later claim he just surrendered. He spent thirty-two months as a prisoner, during which time he claimed he made five unsuccessful escape attempts.

After the war de Gaulle fought with the Polish army against Russia during the 1919-1921 war and received their highest military decoration, the *Virtuti Militari*. Later at Staff College, where he graduated with a grade signifying 'good enough' he was criticised for his arrogance, his excessive self-confidence, and having an attitude of *'a king in exile'*. He later worked as a ghost writer for Marshall Petain, who was a great hero of World War I and commander of the French armies in World War II but, was reviled by many when he surrendered to the Germans and governed 'Vichy France.'

Although fighting on would have been a useless and tremendous loss of life. De Gaulle said of him, *'Marshall Petain was a great man. He died in 1925, but he did not know it'*, despite having received considerable patronage and advancement from him. The general opinion amongst de Gaulle's contemporaries was that his *'his ego…glowed from far off'*. In 1929 there was apparently a threat of mass resignation at the Ecole de Guerre if he was posted there. In 1934 de Gaulle published a book on military tactics in which he wrote that *'a master has to make his appearance…whose orders cannot be challenged…a man upheld by public opinion'*. A not so oblique reference to himself. Seven hundred copies were sold. He was passed over for promotion to colonel in 1936 because his service record was not good enough. But with political help, which he was expert at obtaining, was promoted the following year, and led a parade of 80 tanks into the Place d'Armes at Metz in his command tank named 'Austerlitz'. By October 1938 Petain thought his once protégé *'an ambitious man, and very ill-bred'*.

At the outbreak of World War II de Gaulle was commander of the 4th Armoured Division formed on 12 May 1940. When the Germans broke through at Sedan on 15 May de Gaulle counterattacked with a hastily organised force on 17 and 19 May. His forces were devastated but did momentarily delay the Germans and, amongst the general disaster this was counted as some sort of success. The French armies retreated and on 23 May he was promoted (temporary) Brigadier-General. On 28-29 May he commanded an attacked on a German bridgehead south of the Somme at Abbeville.

Despite objections, on 5 June he was appointed as Under-Secretary of State for National Defence and War, particularly responsible for liaison with the British. On 9 June he flew to England and met Winston Churchill for the first time. He returned to Paris and on the 10 and 11 of June the government fled to Tours. There were meetings of the Anglo-French Supreme War Council— including de Gaulle—on 11 and 13 June, and a mood for an armistice developed among the French. Churchill said he understood French desires but did not agree with them and, murmured to de Gaulle that perhaps he was the *'man of destiny'*. On 16 June Petain became Prime Minister with a remit of seeking an armistice with Germany. De Gaulle, having now been dismissed from the ministry, escaped to London leaving an estimated 1,800,000 of his erstwhile comrades in arms to fend for themselves in German prisoner of war camps.

Later he told of the mental anguish about his break with the French Army and with the recognised government, that his escape to England had caused him, and which would inevitably be seen as treason by many. His temporary rank was stripped from him, but he continued to style himself as 'general'. He denied the legitimacy of Petain's government and attempted to get the French army in North Africa to continue fighting. When the armistice was signed on 21 June de Gaulle denounced it, as did the British who announced plans to establish a French national committee in exile. On 28 June, despite widespread British and French concern, de Gaulle was recognised as leader of the free French. He was sentenced to death by the Vichy government.

His relationship with the USA and Britain were always strained. Clementine Churchill advised him.

'General, you must not hate your friends more than your enemies.'

He replied, *'No nation has friends, only interests.'*

Churchill tried to get the war cabinet to remove him as leader of the French resistance.

Roosevelt saw de Gaulle as an, *'impudent representative of minority interest'* and excluded him from the Yalta conference and thought he was an *'apprentice dictator'*. De Gaulle blamed the allies for an attempted assassination, and at one time Churchill accused him of treason and demanded he be flown back to Algiers *'in chains if necessary'*. But on 20 August 1944, the officer who had sat out most of the World Wars entered Paris posing as the Great Liberator. He then tried to reclaim the old French colonies in Africa and Asia that started vicious new wars and hundreds of thousands more deaths. His dislike of the British and Americans never wavered, and he later vetoed Britain joining the EU and insisted on a French nuclear capacity outside of NATO.

***

Past Dinant the river continued to narrow, the valley still decorated with timbered hills and plenty of very nice chateaus— perhaps not quite royal mistress standard, but not bad at all. But as we neared the French border, we started to feel a little apprehensive about our welcome. Despite all the propaganda of free travel within the EU, which because of Ro's Irish citizenship should have applied to us, the rules about that and who is allowed to skipper a boat are very complicated. Every country has different rules, not at all like car licenses, where everyone can drive everywhere. In the Netherlands no license is required to skipper a boat under fifteen metres long, and I hold an internationally recognised offshore license, so we were perfectly legal there. But France is a different story. All the official literature says that you must have a French license, it can only be obtained in France and the test must be conducted in French. And I had spent hours and hours searching the internet and there was no way around this that I could find. Of course, if you hired a French boat you needed nothing. You need never have stepped on a boat in your life, not known your left from right or one word of French. So, we were rocking up hoping that my international offshore license would get us in, or the fact that it was a Dutch boat would do the trick, or in the worst scenario, perhaps I could sit the exam at the first port of call, which was the rapidly approaching town of Givet.

It was nearing midday when we arrived before the first French lock, lock 59. We were amazed the staff were not taking a lunch break, the lock gates opened, we entered and were politely asked to come to the office and complete the formalities. We grabbed every bit of official looking paper on the boat, our credit cards, fixed humble smiles on our faces and set off to do battle. But it was all too easy. Their only real interest was selling us a season ticket for a thousand euros. Once that was done, they noted *Linna's* name and engine number, took the number of my license and gave us an automatic lock opener. No one understood a word the other party spoke during the whole proceedings, and we were waved cheerily off. For the rest of the year I was worried that someone who could speak English would interrogate us, but I was assured by an old hand that no one in France ever asks to see anything. Despite that, I continued to try and find a place where I could get a license, but I was still trying when we got to Strasbourg, months later.

The village of Givet was just around the next bend, and we tied up ready to welcome Phil and Carmel Thomson from Tasmania, who had been cycling further south, to arrive. Leaving Belgium was probably a bit like leaving North Korea and we found Givet a very enjoyable place—the food was great, the women dressed with some style and quite a lot of people actually smiled. I went to the Hotel de Ville to see about a boat license and although they were very polite, they had never heard of one. I got the impression I was more likely to find the man who invented red wine, than the man who issues boat licenses.

In due course a very fit looking Phil and Carmel arrived and, we prepared for our sortie deep into French territory. We had been moored next to a charming Dutch couple who were returning north and, we had been able to get some good advice on what lay ahead. Our main worry was the height clearance in tunnels and locks. Our book told us that for the rest of our time on the Meuse river/canal the clearance would be 3.5. or 3.6 metres and as *Linna's* official height was 3.5 metres with the dodger and bimini up, there was obviously not a lot to spare. How meticulous were the French with their measurements, we wondered? Particularly with our first tunnel, which was just around the next bend. Did we need to take our windscreen down also? We took down the dodger and bimini, left the windscreen up and headed off. One of the old gods immediately spied that we had no roof and sent a heavy shower of rain, that tenaciously followed us south. The next lock was manned and, we got a green light through and then a green light to enter the 564 metre tunnel. I cannot say I enjoyed the next five minutes or so, or that I ever got to enjoy tunnels at all. It was narrow, dark, the sides and ceiling were roughly cut stone and, we were always within centimetres of raking our hull against the jagged rocks. But, with plenty of shouting we got through unharmed, sailed on to the village of Ham-sur-Meuse where we tied up to a grassy bank and raised the dodger and bimini. It stopped raining.

It turns out that the French canal system is a bit more systematic than you would expect, with the 'devil-may-care attitude' that most Frenchmen like to clothe themselves in. This is largely due to the work of Charles-Louis Freycinet, nephew to the intrepid explorer Louis de Freycinet, with whose shade we shared an anchorage in Wine Glass Bay in southern Tasmania, in Volume I. Charles-Louis was an engineer and politician who between 1879 and 1913 tried to standardise the somewhat chaotic system he inherited. In 1,519 kilometres of canals, the lock sizes were standardised to take a common Flemish barge with dimensions of 38.5 x 5.06 x 1.80 metres. This leaves a lot of canals of different sizes, and a lot with locks with a height clearance of only 3.6 metres and some really tormenting ones of exactly *Linna*'s height of 3.5metres—which nearly captured our dodger a number of times.

We were about to come to grips with our first automatically operated locks! Cooperating with a lockkeeper could be quite frustrating. What, we wondered, would it be like trying to cooperate with a machine, a French machine. The principle was easy. We had been given a hand-held remote. When approaching within a couple of hundred metres or so of a lock, we would encounter a white pole with a sign saying '*ici*' and an amber light on top. When adjacent to the sign, the button on your handheld is pressed. The amber light flashes to indicate contact has been made. Moving towards the lock, the lock gates may already be open and, a green light would advise you to enter. Or the gates may be shut and, a red light would order you to stop.

The level of water in the lock, and whether the gate is open or shut, depended on whether the last user was going upstream or down. It coming downstream the level of the water in the lock would naturally be the level of the downstream river and the gate would be open. If the last user was going upstream the water level would be the same as the upstream level, and the gate would be closed. This would seem to make it a fifty/fifty chance that the water level in the lock would be the same as yours. Not so. Of the fifty-nine locks to the top of the river, probably fifty-five were shut when we arrived. Your luck depended entirely on the numbers of boats coming down or going up. Perhaps not luck, just an indication of who was heading into France for their holidays, and the few unfortunates headed to Belgium for some reason they could not avoid. So, in our case the gates were generally shut, and the red light said to stop. Sometimes, but not always, they would remain shut until an upriver boat entered the lock and was lowered to our level. The gates would open, the lights changed to green/red—meaning prepare to enter. Then green/green, and we would motor in and secure the boat, pull a vertical rod which triggered the filling of the lock to the level of the river above. The lock fills and opens automatically. The exit lights change to green/green. We motor out.

What could possibly go wrong! Well, quite a lot actually. The *'ici'* signs had been in place for a few years and the tangled greenery along the canal bank made some almost invisible. It was easy to drive past and have to back up in search. It was often difficult to ascertain whose fault this was, but I generally got the blame. Sometimes a boat coming the other direction could slow things down a lot and then it would have to squeeze past as it left the lock. A second boat or even a third, going in the same direction as us could compromise the entering, filling and leaving sequence. More than one boat at a time in a lock could make 'tying-on' more difficult than it was in any case and, may put you uncomfortably close to the torrent filling the lock. Logs occasionally jammed in the gates, preventing closing. At times 'gremlins' could get into the system, and the lock could keep filling and emptying without opening the gates. Going upstream, particularly if the canal walls were over, say, three metres high, it could be very hard to get a line over a bollard.

All that said, we mostly had a painless time going up to the top of the Meuse, and later we opined that the automatic system was much easier than having a Frenchman in charge, though probably not as good as having a Frenchwoman on the job!

Every few miles we came to small villages spread along the twisting banks of the river. Montigny-sur-Meuse, Fumay, Revin and Montherme were all picturesque, but on close inspection they were suffering from the hard times and the drain of their citizens, particularly the young, to the cities. Upstairs windows were often bordered up, it was easier to get a pizza than a provincial dish, the churches sombre, damp and deserted. But the countryside was breathtaking—the forests and mountains pressing all around. It was becoming increasingly common for bends and shallow stretches of the river to be by passed by canals that were just wide enough for two boats to pass. Often an old tow path had been put into service as a bicycle path, while the other shore was a dense green forest with overhanging branches spilling well out over the water. Here and there, sometimes in a small clearing on the forest side, or sometimes encamped beside the path, fishermen would contemplate the serenity while keeping an alert eye on their bobbing floats. At bends in the canal and where the forest opened out, high steep ridgelines lined a close horizon. There were few craft on the water, and ahead of us it was often a perfect mirror, capturing the greens of the surrounds and, the grey, whites and blues of the calm sky. Thirteen locks took us to Charlieville-Mezieres.

Carmel and Phil were leaving us here to spend a couple of weeks working on their French at a language school. As always when friends left the boat, we felt very much alone and, were very sad as their train headed off towards Paris. Ah well, at least it was a grand place to drown sorrow. The large town square was surrounded by the very regal buildings of the Ducal palace, which in its day would have been fit for any number of royal mistresses. There were quite a few young women who, in times past may well have been candidates for such a post but, seemed happy enough to be just enticing the young Frenchmen lounging around the cafes and restaurants. At first glance I was all for investing in one of the fine apartments overlooking everything but looking closer, there were a few boarded-up windows and perhaps a hint or two of terminal decay. Still, we enjoyed the atmosphere and a bit of fairly genuine French cuisine.

The city was founded by the 8th Duke of Mantua in 1606 and it is an interesting place to wander around. We were moored on the far bank of the river on the edge of town, where there was a noble 'river-gate' sitting astride the left branch of the river. At water level it had two arched tunnels with narrow quays that had once controlled the passage of craft up and down the river, where goods would have been loaded and unloaded and taxes calculated and charged. Above the quays there was a warehouse level and three residential floors surmounted by a steeply gabled tile roof. In the last minutes before a calm and clear sunset the reflections of the intricate brickwork were spellbinding. Arresting enough to cause us to stop and contemplate the beauty, despite our urgent need to claim our table in the city square and enjoy the cool and much needed refreshments that awaited us.

It took us the best part of a week to bestir ourselves and press on. The canal had narrowed with trees overhanging from both banks and in places patches of reeds pushing out towards the centre. There was no wind, the sky was a flat silvery grey from horizon to horizon. By late morning the flatness of the sky was broken by patches of fluffy black cloud floating away to the east.

...few craft on the water, and ahead of us it was often a perfect mirror, capturing the greens of the surrounds and the grey, whites and blues of the calm sky...

As we grew closer to Sedan the shore was sprinkled with old brick houses that would once have been elegant homes but were now only half-shuttered reminders of a once prosperous past. Approaching the lock at the edge of town we had great trouble finding the *'ici'* pole to activate the lock. We backed up and down three times with no sign of it, and it was only after we appealed to some pedestrians walking along the old tow path that it was discovered.

Eventually we found a not very attractive quay overlooked by some derelict buildings on the edge of town and decided to keep going. But it does have some history that is worth looking at. In 1870, during the Franco-Prussian War the French Emperor Napoleon III and 100,000 of his soldiers were taken prisoner at the First Battle of Sedan, the war was won by the Germans. The progress of the amalgamation of a motley collection of German states, who had been pretty easy to boss around, into a world super-power was complete. There were now four super-powers: Germany, Russia,

Britain and the just defeated France. The Austrian-Hungarian Empire had faded out of the top echelon, and the greats of the past, Spain and the Netherlands were just playing junior league.

During World War I it was occupied by the Germans for four years before being restored to France. Then on the 12th May 1940 the German army captured the city and the nearby bridges, enabling it to cross the Meuse and drive westward through the Ardennes and onward to the English Channel. By the 20th May they had encircled the strongest French armies and the British Expeditionary Force.

Another hour or so, making it six locks for the day, took us to where the actual river formed a small backwater, and the way forward was canalised behind a lock. There was a quiet and secluded jetty waiting for us and, a nice walk into a small village a couple of kilometres away. Once again, the countryside was a beautiful stroll, but the village a bit down at heel. What once was a grand chateau was now a recently abandoned hotel, and there was also an empty unfashionable hotel on the riverbank not far from us. Drinks and dinner on the aft deck and nine the next morning we were waiting for the nearby lock to come online. The automatic locks have strict operating times, just like Frenchmen. The canal was raised above the actual river valley with enough width for two boats to pass easily enough. We waved good day to a cheery young Dutch couple with a small boy, who we had shared a few stops with. They were in a long narrow barge with only a small sleeping cabin and did their cooking outdoors. They had decided to take the summer off and do a loop through France then home through the canals close to the coast.

Two locks took us to a comfortable birth in the quay at Mouzon and we had a nice stroll around the town. There was a grand church and abbey, set in extensive gardens, with the old nun's quarters converted to quite a posh retirement home. Although it looked as if it would be chilly in winter. An inspection of the town square discovered nothing exciting for dinner, and we ended up with pizza again—French cuisine was definitely losing the war to Italian and Indian in these parts and sadly many boulangeries had closed. In some places there was only coin-operated machines, which heated a not too bad baguette, on demand.

Onward, the calm river lined with overhanging trees, winding its way through fertile plains, the sky light blue almost faded to grey. Three locks to the quay at Stenay, which was quite full, with a couple of boats doubled up. It was not apparent why it was so popular, although on a walk around the town there were a number of attractive buildings and a large brewery open to the public and we had a couple of fine meals in a small family-owned restaurant with a pleasant garden. There was also a thriving travelling market, as there was in most of the towns we visited, depending on which day we happened to be there. There was a small café on the quay close by, which we had avoided as it was mostly full of loud drunks. On our second night at bedtime, I poked my head up into the aft deck to pull our door shut and lock it, just as a drunk leapt from the shore onto our back ladder. He got a shock on seeing me, although I cannot imagine why he thought his noisy arrival would go unnoticed. He saved himself from falling in, mumbled something in French, made sorry signs, and lurched back to the quay. I didn't even have time to grab the baseball bat I carry to ward off unwelcome drunks. But please don't think we discriminate against merry drinkers, if we did, we would have few friends.

As we approached what was the bloody battlefield of Verdun, the western shore opened into expansive fields, dotted with golden and white wildflowers. In the distance a heavily wooded ridgeline enfolded an imperial looking stone monastery, surmounted with a soaring tower and spire. To our left there were occasional reminders of the bloody conflict: fields of crosses, mangled countryside, some old cement 'pill-boxes'. The sky was once again a washed-out grey.

Verdun was another of the great atrocities of World War I. It was fought from 21 February to 18 December 1916 in the hills a few miles north of the city of Verdun. It was the longest battle of the war, the Germans suffered around 336,000 casualties and, and the French 379,000. There have been countless books written about the causes of the war, and probably as many about the aftermath and the connection with World War II. But the more I read, the more I wonder how both sides could continue to throw away so many of their young men's lives for so long. What insanity possessed the leaderships to continue to murder their young in this way. By this stage of the war the Germans had at least worked out that artillery, machine guns, trenches, minefields, communications and logistics all favoured the defending side. The allies had not, or didn't care the cost, which is why while Verdun was being fought the British embarked on the Battle of the Somme, even after all the bloody losses suffered during their attacks earlier in the war. And why by the end of the war they had suffered around ten percent more casualties then the Germans.

However, the Germans had learnt the cost of offensive actions, and their battle plan for Verdun was to force the French into an offensive action that would bleed them to death. They chose Verdun as the battlefield because the French fortifications were in such a strategically vital position that the French could not afford to lose them and, Verdun was symbolically important to both sides. It was an ancient city and had been one of the last cities to fall to the Germans in the 1870-71 Franco-Prussian War and had become a symbol of the creation of a German state after the 1843 Treaty of Verdun.

Despite massive German preparations the French were somehow caught unawares. The Germans captured the French Fort Douaumont, the largest and highest fort of the two concentric ring of forts and the keystone to the defence, by surprise without firing a shot. By gaining access through an undefended tunnel, a Pioneer-Sergeant Kunze entered the fort unopposed. Even though his men had refused to follow him in, fearing it was a trap, he entered alone, armed only with a rifle and explored the fort until he found the artillery team, which he captured and locked up. At this stage more troops under Lieutenant Radtke arrived and secured the fort. Not a shot fired. Credit for this act of daring was claimed by a later arrival, a Captain Brandis, who was much celebrated as a hero and feted by the Emperor. The two real heroes were not recognised until the 1930's when a revue of the capture was carried out by historians. It was not so easy for the French to get it back. The recapture is said to have cost them 100,000 lives and was not achieved until 26 October.

In the end the Germans did not quite realise their aim of bleeding the French to death, but it was a near thing and without the bloody British disaster at the Somme, it could well have. The seemingly endless slaughter almost destroyed the morale of the French and resulted in mutinies by men who had just seen and experience too much senseless horror. The sacrifices of the battle are remembered with the utmost reverence. One particular memory is of the 'sacred road', the lifeline to the front, along which countless casualties were suffered bringing supplies and reinforcement to the battle. It was a under constant artillery bombardment. In one week alone 3,000 military and civilian trucks struggled through the deep churned mud and craters to bring 25,000 tons of munitions, food and supplies while 190,000 French troops struggled through on foot. Artillery shells falling around them all the way. By the end the city of Verdun was almost completely destroyed, and eight nearby towns were completely annihilated and never rebuilt.

After coming through the thirty-ninth lock since crossing the French border and as Verdun came into view, signs of the destruction had disappeared, replaced by an elegant cityscape and hallowed memorials. There had been a few spots to tie up on the way in, and as usual we agonised between grabbing what was available or taking a gamble on something better. We were lucky, there was a spot at the *port d'plaissance* in the city centre, with a fine view along the river, the grand buildings and memorials and adjacent to some interesting restaurants, and close to the market. We had a very enjoyable time, a couple of happy hours with some Aussies and Kiwis who were passing through, stayed too long but could have easily stayed longer.

Three more locks took us to Saint-Mihiel. The countryside, if possible, looked even more beautiful. It was summer, with rolls of hay in the recently-cut fields, but the forests and verges still held the green freshness of spring. A cerulean sky with only a few of the usual fluffy white clouds hanging around. The warm sun brought out the colours of the trees and reed-lined banks reflected in the water. In places the canal again ran quite high above the plain, its bank carrying a bicycle track and a line of tall trees. In the distance more memories of the war. We tied up at a jetty not far from town, and later on a traditional old Dutch barge moored alongside. Because of their length barges find it harder to find a spot, so doubling up where the canal is wide enough, is common. The crews were always friendly and entertaining and full of valuable information about everything. We had been pottering along at a very gentle pace and, although the canal had been closed in the late summer the previous year, we were now aghast to be informed that it might close earlier again this year. If we didn't get over the highest point near Troussey, a little further on, we might be trapped here with the only possible escape being back to Belgium. Perhaps. Good God, we best get a move on.

There had been some excellent restaurants in Sedan, although they all seemed to close on Sunday and Monday, which had annoyed the cook. So, we set off with high hopes for the village above. To our delight there was a restaurant with an enticing menu, and we were ushered to a table enjoying a nice outlook and a cool breeze. Perfect. We relaxed and waited for the wine list. A waiter, who we later realised must have been trained in Paris, came out and polished the table next to us, shined a few glasses, refused to catch my eye and returned inside. A few minutes later the proprietor, I think, came to the restaurant door and surveyed us and our fellow diners on the terrace with a somewhat disdainful air, and turned back inside. A second waiter came out, napkin across his forearm. Ah, I thought. Action at last. Ro will be the first to tell you that I can get a bit titchy if the wine service is slow, and it was about fifteen minutes since we had been seated. But, alas, this chap turned away from us without a glance, presented a bill to our neighbour and haughtily strode away without a backward look. Our neighbour left, the first waiter came back and cleared the table, returned to polish it and the new glasses. We were apparently still invisible. The proprietor came back to the door with the superior mien of Adolf Hitler surveying a procession of Jews straggling towards Auschwitz, shrugged and turned back. The second waiter came out and seated another couple. We were still invisible, despite Ro who was thinking I might soon assault someone, making frantic gestures.

It had been twenty-five minutes, that was enough. We stood and marched off. The proprietor came to the door, both waiters stood with dropped jaws, all wearing expressions a mixture of hurt and bewilderment.

Around the corner we found a friendly Italian restaurant with a cheerful proprietor who could have been French, probably second generation Turkish. He ushered us to a table in a back courtyard and nicely chilled white wine came within seconds, followed by a tasty Italian meal. We had almost finished the wine before we worked out his innovative business plan. On one street he had Italian, on a parallel street he had a traditional provincial French restaurant. They were joined by the courtyard at the rear of each, and one kitchen produced both the French and Italian—fortunately none of the staff had been trained in Paris and the service was good and cheerful. We enjoyed the meal enough to risk spending another day at Saint-Mihiel and came back for the French the next night.

There were four locks to our next stop at the village of Commercy where we moored directly behind a large supermarket. Very convenient for provisioning, but aesthetically very industrial. The old town, with a surprisingly elegant square was about fifteen minutes away and when we arrived was in the middle of hosting a musical festival—with everything from Chopin to Country and Western, lots of restaurants and food stands. All good. But it was while I was hobbling around, that I had to confront the truth that my old knee, which I had broken so many years ago in Papua New Guinea, was finally giving up the ghost. Not even a bottle of red wine dulled the pain, and I had to admit that it was not caused by the wrong shoes, or eating too many tomatoes, or a change in the weather. I had gone through this with my other knee a few years before when we were still sailing *Sea Dreams* and, it had not impacted too much on the actual sailing, although I did always vote for the closest restaurant. But on the canals, there was a lot more leg work going through the locks and mooring.

We had five more locks to reach the top of the Meuse, where it joined the Canal de la Marne au Rhine which basically connects Paris to Strasbourg. We were planning to turn east and onwards to Strasbourg.

Since Verdun the canal had become increasingly shallow and weedy and we had needed to change the filter of the engine water cooling system every couple of hours. Once past Commercy it was worse, and on occasions I was sure I would have to go overboard to unfoul the propeller. The bottom was soft mud and we could feel it holding our hull as we slithered through; it seemed as if we would be stuck at any second. Between the last two locks there was a giant cement factory, looking like a prop for a horror movie and, we quailed at the thought of *Linna* being trapped here until next spring. A great sigh of relief as we struggled by. Then through the top lock, lock number one, the fifty-ninth since the border. The last few days had been quite difficult, but we had grown to love the mighty Meuse, its beauty and its history, and we took with us many memories we will cherish forever.

***

We were very pleased when Pagny-sur-Meuse_came into sight,

with a few vacant mooring spots along the jetty. Ro went for a stroll around town, I disappeared into the engine room to clean the filter and do the normal checks to make sure all systems were good for the next day, which looked like being a harrowing one. We left about 8a.m which we hoped would get us to a tunnel 867 metres long at opening time. This was our longest tunnel to date, and all went okay. We got a quick green light, and with only moderate shouting, disgorged into a large basin at the far end where we were confronted with the first of twelve downward locks for the day. We were signalled to enter and, handed back our handheld remote lock control that we had used thus far and, had a quick brief from the lock operators. The new system was, they told us, that the locks would sense our approach and signal us to enter at the appropriate time. Seemed too good to be true, but all went like clockwork. Although it took us a while to get our teamwork sorted out. The last downward lock had been somewhere back in the distant Netherlands. Long before we had entered the Meuse.

Going down, you drive into a full lock. Someone jumps off the boat and takes two lines around two bollards, then pulls a switch to command the release of water from the lock and climbs quickly back on board. Keeping the lines taught so that the boat is kept in place, the water in the lock is released until it is the same level as downstream. The lock gates open and you motor out. If one of the crew has a newly-replaced hip and the other needs a new knee, we found that all the jumping on and off was bloody painful. After a few locks we worked out a much better routine. Ro lassoed the back bollard as we edged very slowly past and gave the line to me as we crept forward a few more metres. She would then lasso the forward bollard. Then, one of us could mostly reach the lever to release the water without getting off the boat. We only had one anxious moment. Approaching the last lock, we were keeping an eye on the cooling water coming out of the exhaust, the sound of the engine and its temperature, and realised we needed to change the filter immediately, even if the lock was commanding us to enter. Worried a delay might put the automatic system out of synchronisation, we rushed through the job in record time and managed to drive into the lock without confusing it. Sighs of relief as the marina at Toul came into view.

The marina was nearly full, and it took a superhuman effort, and much complaint from my knee, to squeeze *Linna* into a space that was so narrow our fenders were compressed to half their normal size. There was no chance that our neighbour, who was between us and the shore would ever be able to get out before us. But the boat looked as if no one had been onboard for some time, and hopefully there would be no problem. The weed had been bad all the way down from the top of the mountain and, was so thick in the marina that it looked more like a grassy park. Our water filter would need cleaning after we had gone a hundred metres. But we were safely over the mountain and Toul was on a railway line and a good spot to pick up Hubie, who had been visiting old schoolfriends in Annecy.

Near the headwaters of the Moselle river, Toul was on ancient trade routes. In Roman times it was the capital of the Leuci tribe and according to records, it became the seat of the bishops of Toul from either 338 or 365. Either date is illuminating, as the Edict of Milan which declared tolerance of Christianity in the Roman Empire was only issue by Constantine in 313. They would have exercised elements of government in the area around Toul from some time in the late 4th century. The 'bishops' became known officially as 'prince-bishops' from the 10th century onwards. On our journey up the Meuse we had already passed some cities whose histories had been dignified by the presence of 'prince-bishops'. I had not really given the matter much thought. Just titles to enhance the be-robed self-importance of some dignitaries of the Church. Utrecht in the 11th century, Liege, Verdun and nearby Trier in the 9th century, all cities within the borders of the Roman Empire, had similarly flattered their bishops.

But, as it transpires, these were not empty titles at all. But a now all but forgotten fusion of the religious and secular powers of the state, that originated in the reigns of the Byzantine Emperors Constantine the Great and Theodosius I, in the 4th century. The result was that throughout all, the over one hundred provinces of the empire, civil rule was administered jointly by the governor of the province and a bishop. Military command rested with the position of *Duc*, from which the later title of *D*uke originated or the *Magister Militum*. Provinces were grouped into *dioceses* – from which came the later church usage.

In 375 a German tribe, the Salian Franks was invited to settle within the northern reaches of the Empire, around the delta of the

Rhine/Meuse Rivers. In 481 Clovis succeeded his father as King, ruling from the town of Tournai, just north of the current French-Belgium border. Both he and his father were at times commanders in the Roman army, answering to the Magister Militum for the area known as Belgica Secunda, which included some of northern France, Belgium and Luxemburg. We had just sailed through the middle of it. By 486 when Clovis began expanding southwards the control of most of what is now central France was being contested by two other tribes, the Visigoths and the Burgundians. Only southern France was still under Roman control. In 486, with an army of only some five hundred men and fighting alongside his relative the King of Cambria at Soissons, he defeated the combined forces of the Visigoths and Burgundians

Over time Clovis unified most of Gaul and made Paris the capital of his new kingdom, which can be regarded as proto-France. After realising he couldn't rule Gaul without support of the Church, he converted to Christianity around 496, was baptised in 508 and reigned until 511.

His conversion brought him two great benefits. The first was that his rule was now endorsed by God. The second was that it enabled him to inherit the framework of Roman law and governance, that had been in place in Gaul for around five hundred years. The church had an executive, legal and spiritual presence at every level of government throughout Gaul and all over the empire. Although the Roman armies had been driven out, much of the church presence remained, with varying degrees of authority over the various tribes. This gave Clovis a powerful and widespread religious and civil bureaucracy, as well as a legal code. Perhaps it was this advantage that enabled the Franks, of all the German tribes, to establish a European empire that was only surpassed by Napoleon, a millennium or so later.

As Frankish power spread many Christian bishops controlled the administration of their cities, and some also became military commanders. In some cases, as in Toul, they were later elevated in title to prince-bishops. Bishops made secular decisions for the city and led their own troops where necessary. The first bishop of Toul was Mansuetus, who was later known as Saint Mansuy. From the late 4th century, as the Theodosian reforms spread throughout the empire, more and more civil authority was vested in the bishops.

This trend continued under the Frankish kings until full civil authority was formally ceded to the Prince-Bishop of Toul by the 10th century, until in 1807 when Napoleon enforced the separation of the power of church and state.

But the immense power this gave the Church certainly fanned the flames of the dynastic and religious wars that plagued Europe up until the 19th century. While the cities of the Netherlands were becoming 'free cities' governed by their free citizens, the cities of the old empire were becoming 'prince-bishoprics' governed by the Church and, once Charlemagne expanded the Holy Roman Empire into the Germanic states, the same occurred there.

Clovis's Merovingian line was replaced by the Carolingian dynasty around 720. Their first king, Charles Martel defeated the Muslim advance into France at the Battle if Tours in 732. His successor, Charlemagne conquered most of Europe and was crowned Holy Roman Emperor in 800. Under Charlemagne most important cities in the Empire were ruled by Prince-Bishops who continued to compete for power with the feudal Dukes.

At Toul there are lots of architectural reminders of times long past, a grand Gothic cathedral and many canonical residences, but the city's importance has waned in modern times and these days they are all more impressive from a distance. But the old town had a couple of enjoyable restaurants, and there was another in the marina only a few metres from the boat. We had a pleasant outlook over the green lawns surrounding the marina and the shady weeping willows. Hubie arrived, we caught up on all the news, and making him responsible for all the jumping off and on the boat, we set off. Firstly, to inspect the headwaters of the lovely Moselle and then on to the proud Ducal city of Nancy. After two locks we entered the Moselle. Already a noble river, it was one of the most beautiful stretches of water we had enjoyed so far. The banks were covered with dense woodlands through which we glimpsed the occasional chateau, while on the heights above a couple of villages spilled down the steep slopes.

By mid-afternoon we had gone through two immense locks, the sun was warm, the sky an unbroken dome of intense blue, and we had arrived at a small cove below the village of Liverdun. The water was still, a mirror of blues and dark greens and the occasional splash of silver sunlight. There was a small wooden jetty with room for two boats, but when in the late afternoon an Australian boat turned up, we squeezed them in.

We had drinks on board with John and Jill Harrison who were from Byron Bay and who were enjoying three months in France as part of a syndicate who owned a Linssen cruiser. In the morning we went our separate ways but met up again a couple of weeks later and sailed the last few days on the Canal de la Marne au Rhine Est together. They were going further down the Moselle and then back up the Canal de la Sarre, while we planned to spend a couple of days at Nancy before taking a train to Paris to meet Ro's brother Eugene and his wife Jenni.

The marina at Nancy was crowded, but again we managed to squeeze into a spot, against an ancient stone wall, where *Linna* would be safe enough while we were in Paris. It was a bit of a hike to the restaurants around the Place Stanislas - which is the top UNESCO World Heritage Site in France and fourth in the world - but it was worth the pain. It is breathtaking and there are plenty of good menus and places from which to contemplate the architecture. In comparison we found that Paris was like a war zone, but we enjoyed ourselves before leaving Hubie and returning with the new crew.

After a couple of night exploring Nancy, Eugene was promoted to head jumper and we headed off up the Canal de la Marne au Rhin Est.

We had climbed up through three locks from the Moselle to Nancy and there were another twenty-one to get to the top of the range. Three nights later we had gone through the last lock, the Rechicourt which with a rise of twenty-seven metres, is the highest in France and were moored on a remote grass bank surrounded by a dense forest of conifers. Our literature assured us that it was alive with deer and wild boar, and it certainly looked as if it was—even if we didn't spot any. But it did have a wild ambience as night seeped out of the tall dark trees and engulfed us. The crew left us at Hesse and we continue across the mountain plateau, through two tunnels, 475 and 2306 metres and down the d'Arzviller boat lift, by which time Ro was hoarse and our nerves were a bit frazzled.

... Phil and Carmel on board...twenty-one locks to the top...

But there was a very lovely mooring below the boat lift, and by nightfall we were well on the way to recovery.

We had another lovely 'swan' experience here. Towards dusk a large white swan flew up-river and splashed down close by. She—think—had a good look around, and then with frantically beating wings managed to get aloft and disappeared back into the gloom. In the morning, as we were leaving our first lock, a husband and wife swan, with a gaggle of flightless chicks, bustled in to get a ride up to the level we had just left. So, just to explain things. Last evening mother had flown up to check out the upstream reach of the river. She liked it, but as the chicks couldn't fly, they all had to take the lock. Now, that shows quite some planning and intelligence. How do I know it was the same bird? Good question.

...the lock at Rechincourt, at twenty-seven metres the deepest in France...

The canal from Hesse to Strasbourg is one of the most beautiful in France, including the villages of Lutzelbourg and Saverne. We had another thirty or so locks to go, and we weren't planning to rush. We met up with John and Jill Harrison at Saverne and we sailed in company for the last few days, which was very enjoyable. We had come to a stretch with a different automatic system for the locks, which required a rod hanging in the middle of the canal a couple of hundred metres from the lock, to be pulled energetically. Jill proved to be a natural 'puller', and all we had to do was follow along behind. They also took pity on our lameness and operated the 'closing' lever in the locks. That made it all very easy for us. There were a couple

271

of pleasant banks to overnight beside, with fine views from the back of the boat across recently harvested fields and, quite a posh restaurant on the night before Strasbourg.

Strasbourg grew from a Roman fortress which was established in 12 BCE. It was in a defensible situation close to the Rhine and the ancient trading routes that ran along the river and westward over the mountains into the heartland of France. It was governed by the bishops of Strasbourg from c346 and by c775 the bishops had extended their temporal authority into the fertile wine growing regions well to the south and, were soon promoted to the exalted rank of prince-bishops. In 1262 the city, fed up with the Church's rule and heavy taxes, rebelled and became a free city of the Holy Roman Empire. But as in just about every other city in Europe, nothing was constant for long. It was conquered by the French in 1681 and retaken by the Germans again from 1871 until 1918, and then the French after World War II.

An outside berth was waiting for us at the marina adjacent to the 11 ha Parc de La Citadelle on the outskirts of the city. We had a fine view across to the greenery and up and down the canal that surrounds it, and shortly after tying up the two lovely swans who ran this stretch of water sailed up to say hallo. Followed shortly afterwards by Guy, the charming Frenchman who ran the marina with an iron fist, 'good' Vincent, who was the head engineer and 'bad' Vincent, who was Guy's brother. At the office you could buy a wide selection of local wines and beers—the oldest brewery in France is close by—and unusually for a French marina, a wide selection of useful nautical gear and even charts.

There was a pleasant walk through the Parc to what at first glance was a rather intimidating enclave of public housing, with a lot of people wearing various Middle Eastern and Asian outfits. There are similar enclaves in most cities in Europe, and some are quite famous 'no go' areas, and the last one we had visited in Utrecht in the Netherlands, had made us feel most unwelcome. So, on my first stroll I by passed it by and shopped in a small French supermarket. Later Ro decided to explore and discovered a huge market stocked with almost everything in the world, including acres of local wine, and lots of restaurants representing most ethnic groups between Greece and the Pacific. So, we shopped and dined there a lot, but also had plenty of meals in the garden restaurants lining the canals of the *old town*, where there were lots serving the traditional dishes of Alsace and Lorraine.

It is one of the most beautiful and interesting cities we have visited, and sitting here, isolated by the coronavirus pandemic in Canberra, I would give a lot to be back onboard *Linna* with the city a short stroll away. It is the seat of over twenty international institutions, most famously the Council of Europe and the European Parliament. It is considered the legislative and democratic—very active at legislature but 'democratic' should probably be 'autocratic'—capital of the European Union. Brussels, of course, is the executive and administrative capital and Luxembourg the judiciary and financial. This status brings truckloads of gold from the EU which finances lots of huge modern buildings on the edge of the city and, lots of very expensive cars for the bureaucrats lucky enough to be on the gravy-train.

Wandering around the old paved streets, broad boulevards and leafy parks there are memories and memorials to most of the famous people who at some time have called the city home. Amongst them are, Johannes Gutenberg, (cC1400-1468) a German goldsmith, inventor, printer and publisher, whose fame rests on introducing printing to Europe with the mechanical, movable printing press—which was a milestone and a printing revolution which ushered in the modern age. And had a key role in the Renaissance, Reformation, the Age of Enlightenment, the scientific revolution, knowledge-based economies and the spread of learning to the masses. John Calvin (1509-1564) a Frenchman who developed the Christian theology called Calvinism, which was based on the belief that individuals do not have a choice of who obtains salvation because it is predestined. No one has the ability to change that. As opposed to Lutheranism which is founded on the belief that salvation has nothing to do with predestination but is acquired by faith. Luther probably never visited the city but his visit to not so far off Worms is quite famous. Johan Wolfgang Goethe (1749 -1832) a German writer and statesman, whose intellectual stature, according to many, is comparable to Plato, Montaigne, Napoleon and Shakespeare. He was a student at the University of Strasbourg, a free thinker who once criticised Christian theology as a 'hodgepodge of fallacy and violence.' Louis Pasteur (1822–1895) the French microbiologist, renowned for discovering the principles of vaccination and pasteurisation and Albert Scheitzer who received the 1952 Nobel Peace Prize.

The magnificent Gothic Cathedral dominates the narrow cobbled streets of the old town and the encircling canals. Strasbourg was known as Argentoratum in Roman times. It was one of the major sites established along the Rhine in preparation for Drusus' military campaign in 14-12 BCE. Others included Basel, Mainz, Bonn, Neuss, Xanten and Nijmegen. Roman navy galleys, which later included large trimarines, started to establish a presence along the Rhine during this period, along with commercial galleys and barges. Some barges were up to 35 metres in length, and under the right conditions could do the trip from Basel to the current Dutch border in around seven days. Coming upstream was much slower, around 15 kilometres a day, by rowing, towing and sail. The Rhine Valley, together with the valleys of the Rhone, Meuse and Moselle rivers had been trade route for centuries before the Romans, but the Romans, as they did all over the empire, created a network of paved roads, partly for trade, but mostly to allow the rapid deployment of the legions.

Much of the history of the countries we had sailed through is on display in the form of romantic old castles and awe-inspiring Christian cathedrals. It is easy to look at them as merely beautiful adornments of a beautiful country, and forget the religious wars, crusades and dynastic struggles that they stand testament to.

It is almost impossible to give a short and coherent description of the cost in lives of the evolution of France and her neighbours from, say, the death of Charlemagne when his empire was split into—more or less—France and Germany. It is hard to comprehend the bloody wars, which raged with hardly a pause. But the cause of most are easily explained, dynastic ambitions and religion. Here are some highlights, including the number of deaths:

- The invasion of England by William the Conqueror, who had absolutely no legal claim to the English Throne.
- The Crusades between 1,000,000-3,000,000.
- The Albigensian Crusade (1208-1229) 200,000-1,000,000.

- The Hundred Years War. (1337-1453) Which would not have happened if not for William the Bastards trip across the channel. 2,300.000-3,300,000.
- Louis XIV Dutch Wars (1643-1715) 175,000.
- Strasbourg Bishops War. (1592-1604) Between Protestants and Catholics for the control of the Bishopric of Strasbourg.
- German Peasants War. (1524 – 1525) Economic and religious wars between peasants against Protest/Catholic landowners.100,000-200,000. French Wars of Religion (1562-1598) Protestants against Catholics 2,000,000-4,000,000.
- Eighty Years' War (1568-1648) Protestants against Catholics 600,000-700,000.
- War of the Three Kingdoms (1639-1651) Anglicans against Catholics. 315,000-700,000. Thirty Years' War (1618-1648) Protestants against Catholics. 3,000,000-11,500,000.
- War of the League of Augsburg (1689 -97).
- Seven Years War (900,000-1,400,000).
- French Revolution (1789-1799) 400,000 executed or murdered and 250,000 battle deaths. Napoleonic wars (1803-1815) 3,500,000-7,000,000.
- French Invasion of Russia (1812) 540,000.
- Crimean War (1853-56) 356,000-410,000.

These are appalling numbers and an indictment of something in our human nature and the way our societies have been structured. But in fairness to Europe, they pale in comparison to deaths involved in the change of the Chinese dynasties or of the creation of the Mongol Empire.

But while we are talking about European wars, particularly bastardry between neighbours, France deserves special mention. By 1526 the Islamic threat to Europe as a Christian entity had been an existential one for nearly a thousand years, and the Muslim's star was in the ascendency. But the survival of Christianity was nothing to King Francis I of France, compared to maintaining his own magnificence. He beseeched Suleiman the Magnificent to aid him in his long and bloody struggle with the Habsburgs. Suleiman was amenable to the idea and answered in a tone suitable for a mighty lord replying to a no-account underling.

'I who am the Sultan of Sultans, the sovereign of sovereigns, the dispenser of crowns to the monarchs on the face of the earth, the shadow of the God on Earth, the Sultan and sovereign lord of the Mediterranean Sea and the Black Sea, of Rumelia and of Azerbaijan, ...etc... of Jerusalem, all of Arabia of Yemen and many other lands ... Night and day our horse is saddled and our sabre is girt'.

Francis's supplications gave encouragement to Suleiman in his ambitions to attack Hungary and conquer Europe. In that year he led the Ottomans to a decisive victory at the Battle of Mohacs and later to the almost successful siege of Vienna from 1529 to 1532. In 1534 Suleiman put his fleet at the disposal of the French king for attacks on Genoa and the Milanese and raids on the Italian coasts. In 1536 the relationship was formalised by the Franco-Ottoman Alliance, which lasted for over two hundred years. This was not just some sort of exchange of ambassadors and handshakes all around. It meant that in most of the bloody raids, sieges, battles on land and sea, and the resulting thousands upon thousands of Christians slain or sold into slavery, including the Barbarossas' victims, the French navy or army took part. There were many combined operations, year after year, all over the Mediterranean, in which not a port or city close to the coast was spared. In a joint campaign in 1537 Suleiman led an army of 300,000 to Albania that was taken by joint fleets to Italy. Castro in Apulia and Otranto were attacked and, thousands slaughtered and 10,000 sold into slavery. French ships were with the Muslim galleys which besieged the great Venetian castle at Corfu and Nice in 1537. Barbarossa wintered in Toulon with 30,000 men and the cathedral converted to a Mosque.

'Lodge the Lord Barbarossa sent to the king by the Great turk, with his Turkish Army and grand seigneurs to the number of 30,000 combatants during the winter in his town and port of Toulon ... for the accommodation of said army as well as the well-being of all his coast, it will not be suitable for the inhabitants of Toulon to remain and mingle with the Turkish nation, because of difficulties which may arise.' Instructions of Francis I.

The list goes on and on. They fought together in the Italian War of 1542-1546 against the Holy Roman Empire and raided the Spanish and Italian coasts. In 1544 a French fleet accompanied Barbarossa during attacks on the Italian coast and laid waste Porto Ercole, Giglio, Talamona, Lipari and took 6,000 slaves. The French aided the Muslims with troops and artillery in Hungary. In the Italian War of 1551-1559 there were joint fleet actions and invasion of Naples, Sicily Elba and Corsica. In 1558 Sorrento and the Balearics were sacked. The French received special trade privileges, an embassy in Galata across the Golden Horne from Istanbul and lots and lots of financial aid.

And on it goes.

France declined to help break the siege of Vienna and tried to prevent the Polish king from saving the city in 1683. In 1688 France attacked the Habsburgs and relieved the pressure on the Ottomans. In 1806 the Ottomans recognised Napoleon as Emperor and allied with France. By the mid-18th century France had *'re-emerged in its traditional role as the Ottomans' best friend in Christiandom'*

***

Enough.

All the way up the river Meuse we had been anticipating sailing through some of the great vineyards of France. I have to admit I had never Googled 'vineyards of France', I just presumed they would be pretty much everywhere. We had been able to buy local wine here and there. But here is the ugly truth. All the way up the Meuse from the border with Belgium, all the way across the Canal de la Marne to Strasbourg, we had seen miles of hop fields, acre upon acre of sun flowers and grain crops, ploughed fields and well fed animals, but we had seen not one solitary grape vine, let alone a vineyard. Something had to be done. So, in Strasbourg I checked a map— pretty easy really. Running south from Strasbourg, along the eastern slopes of the Vosges Mountains were the Vineyards of Alsace. We began to make arrangements to explore.

Just to digress for a moment.

Since Uber was first introduced into Australia, some years ago, we have been avid and loyal supporters. They come promptly and on time, they take the best route to your destination and provide a map to prove it, the cars are good, the cost much less then taxis, you do not have to fiddle with cash and both driver and passenger can report on each other. A much better system then when taxis could arrive whenever it suited them, then wander around town by the longest route to where you wanted to go with the meter ticking over at all the traffic lights. We have used Ubers, whenever they are available, all over the world. Their invention is up there with the printing press.

Although we would often stroll into the old town, if we were going for dinner, and probably when coming home, we would take an Uber. And, we were devastated to find that things worked differently in France. Ubers never came on time. A three-minute arrival time could easily be fifteen, a ten euro fare could be twenty and involve a very long route on the presumption of the stupid tourist having no idea of where was where. This has the same effect on me as being ignored by wine waiters. So, after a punctual, at the predicted cost, trip with a courteous young Indian driver, we took up his offer to take us in and out of town the next day. All good, and from then on, we used him all the time. So, when it came to exploring the wine region, we put ourselves in the hands of our friend, Sharjeel Rajput.

It is a wonderful area, with some truly enchanting villages, including Mullhouse, Colmar, Riquewihr, and Ribeauville which are as beautiful as any villages you could find anywhere, surrounded by viny visages, and full of great food and wine. Mainly Riesling, Gewürztraminer and Pinot Gris, and you certainly don't want to be driving home yourself. For those interested in Caesar's conquest of Gaul, the battle of the Vosges was fought just to the west of Mullhouse. The Romans were victorious, and the defeated Germans forced to flee over the Rhine to escape with their lives. The German king, Ariovistus managed to escape, but both his wives and a daughter were slaughtered and another captured.

When we had arrived back at Strasbourg, we had some decisions to make. The first priority on our itinerary was a much anticipated visit to Ro's sister, Viv, in Wales. After that, we had to face the fact that I needed a new knee before going anywhere further in *Linna,* but we wanted to complete a trip down the Rhine. That was easy, we booked on the MV Royal Crown sailing from Frankfurt. The following year we would go back over the mountains to the Rhone river and south to the Mediterranean. We had a great time in Wales with Viv and Tim and family on their beautiful farm, including a bit of gentle walking along some of the stunning Welch canals on the other side of their valley.

Back in Strasbourg, with Sharjeel at the wheel, we followed the line of the Roman road north. The river here is around five or six hundred metres wide, running gently through flat lands, dotted with forests and farmland. There were only two locks, the Gambshein and Iffezheim schleuses, between here and the North Sea. From the car it all looked as if it would have been very relaxing, romping along at 15 kph or so, with hardly anything at all to shout about. If we were in *Linna* we had planned our first stopover at a pleasant lake at Lauterbourg, just inside the French border. Then another easy day to the old harbour in the German city of Speyer, dominated by its marvellous cathedral dating from the 11th century. Then another day to Worms an ancient Celtic city that was captured and fortified by the Romans in 14 BCE. A Roman Catholic bishop was probably in place around the 4th century and it became an imperial free city in the 11th century. The Cathedral is one of the finest examples of Romanesque architecture in Europe. But travelling in a car we whipped along and had checked into a comfortable hotel in Frankfurt in time for drinks. Twenty-five years before Ro and I had flown in here from Australia in our search of our long-departed ancestors, which had eventually led us to an ancient villa in Pieczyce in Silesia. We didn't recognise anything of the rather depressing city of our memories, in this bustling city, full of life and fun, of modern Germany.

We boarded our cruise ship, the very elegant MS Royal Crown, in time to settle into our very comfortable cabin before pre-dinner drinks with our eighty or so fellow travellers. After a sumptuous five course meal, with very fine wines, I began to suspect Ro may have misled me about the price of the cruise. It seemed just too good to be true. It was rare to bump into anyone in the comfortable lounge with panoramic windows on all sides, or on the ship-length deck on the upper level and there was never anyone in the library.

In the early morning we passed from the Main into the Rhine and we were disembarked and strolling around Wiesbaden before lunch. A Roman fort was built here in 6 CE and it was famous for its hot spas right from the beginning. It was mentioned in Pliny the Elder's *Naturalis Historia* and by the 8th century there were royal palaces of the Frankish kingdom. By the 12th century it had become an imperial city of the Holy Roman Empire and despite plenty of hard times in wars and revolutions, the city and its famous spas was still a refuge for royalty and the rich and famous at the beginning of the 20th century. All the hobbling round had sharpened my appetite for another feast onboard—and although we always ate pretty well onboard *Linna*, this could easily spoil us for anything else. The next stop was at nearby Rudesheim which was probably a winemaking centre in Roman times, although its first documentation was not until the 11th century. It was a beautiful day, cloudless with a warm sun, the merest hint of a breeze, and we took a chairlift high over the surrounding vineyards to the lookout and memorials on the hills above the town.

We got to chatting to a Singaporean-Chinese couple off the boat, who were from Melbourne, and decided to share a table that night. Their story, and how they ended up living in Melbourne was very interesting and, reminded us very much of our neighbours at home, Sally and Boon. They had grown up in Singapore, Boon became a doctor, practised at home, went to England and specialised, worked in Scotland and New Zealand while trying to immigrate to Australia. Eventually he became head of gynaecology at Canberra hospital. Turned out they had all been at school together in Singapore and were still close friends. It is amazing how often the world does turn out to be a small place.

We had driven down the Rhine Gorge on our visit twenty-five years ago and had never forgotten the beauty. We had loitered in the small towns and driven up to a couple of the amazing castles perched high on steep crags. The importance of the river as a trade route, meant there were settlements in the Gorge, as with all the river, since prehistoric times. From Roman times wine growing and increasing trade made the region richer. With increasing wealth many castles were built, both as military strongholds and, tax extorters. The empires, the dynasties, the churches all wanted a cut and much blood has been spilt—what would it have been like if they had been able to grow red wine?

It was quite an experience going downstream in a large cruiser. In the narrower rocky sections, there is only enough room for two large boats to pass and the current can be up to seven knots. Near the northern end stands the memorial to one of the best known legends of the waters, the Lorelei. A beautiful maiden cast herself off a large rock, around which the current swirls, in despair over a faithless lover. She was transformed into a siren who lured countless sailors to their death.

A little further north the Rhine resumed its stately flow, the river broadened, and we arrived at Koblenz at it junction with the Moselle. Excavations have revealed there were early fortifications here from around 1000 BCE. The importance of the site, at the junction of two such rich rivers, was recognised very early on. In 55 BCE Caesar's legions arrived and built a bridge across the Rhine to allow Caesar to cross and try to put some fear up the German tribes. Drusus returned around 9 BCE and the remains of a Roman bridge built in 49 CE are still visible. There after it was conquered by the Franks after the fall of the western Roman Empire and sacked by the Norsemen in 882. In 925 it became part of the Holy Roman Empire and in 1018 was given to the archbishop-electors of Trier who held it until the 18th century.

A further illustration of the power of the prince-bishops, who in reality reigned in both a religious and secular sense in many of the important cities in the Holy Roman Empire, was their power in the election of the Emperor. In c1340 the electors were the Archbishop of Trier, Archbishop of Cologne, Archbishop of Mainz, Count Palatine, Duke of Saxony, Margrave of Brandenburg and the King of Bohemia. Until 1508 the Prince-Electors elected the monarch and the Pope crowned him, but after that the Pope's crowning was dispensed with. In practice after 1440, the title followed the order of succession of the House of Habsburg.

Like the Rhine Gorge, the Moselle River has that rare quality where breathtaking beauty unfolds with each bend of the river, as it winds its way between grand mountains and idyllic valleys. Where it seems that nothing could be more entrancing, until the next scene unfolds. The slopes covered in vines, mysterious castles with centuries of forgotten stories and colourful fairy-tale villages. We lolled on the foredeck, admiring it all without a care in the world, until we had to bestir ourselves to explore the village of Cochem. Then on to lovely Traben-Trarbach and Neumagen-Drohn which is one of a number of claimants to the title of Germany's oldest winemaking centre. For the Romans it was a stopover between Trier and Koblenz, and it is where the famous rock carving of a wine ship was unearthed. We were delighted to find a replica of a Roman wine ship floating around and, wondered for a moment if one would suit us. Certainly, *Linna's* cellar was on the small side.

I enjoyed chatting to the Dutch captain of the ship, who was letting his understudy and 'First Officer' do most of the work, while he looked on and gave the occasional comment. I also passed some time with the ship's engineer and could not help thinking how great it would be to have one on *Linna*, as well as someone to get it through the locks and things. But an 'engineer' would really be wonderful. One of the few drawbacks of 'swanning' around on your own yacht, for me anyway who relies on a professional to keep all the mechanicals functioning, was having to get someone new to do all the end and beginning of season work, each year. If the generator will not charge your batteries, or the engine fails to start or stops unwantedly, or a water-maker goes on strike, or pumps don't pump, and you are far from help, it is a real bugger. And that's before Ro carries out an investigation as to why her shower is not working or the computers are not charging. So, getting someone reliable to do the work, is of absolutely vital importance. Someone like Igor Gazin in Croatia, or the Turkish staff at Finike. But we have had the odd disaster—I think I mentioned the Greek marina in Volos and the Pommy mechanic at Majorca.

Well, I have to be frank—has that word some connection with Charlemagne's Franks? —that we have had problems in Europe. The motor failing a couple of hours after the very expensive work was carried out in Holland springs to mind. And this year got off to a bad start when we arrived back on *Linna* and we could not be sure that anything had been done other than putting anti-freeze in the water tanks—the water was still undrinkable. I thought for a moment that perhaps it had been bought by Gregory from the marina in Volos. The hydraulic leak in the steering, the jammed wastewater pump and tank, black oil in the generator and engine and smoky exhausts indicated nothing had been done. There was a lot to do before we left Maastricht, but we were still getting visits from the mechanic and his huge mobile workshop as we neared France. Which can all be very annoying, particularly if you think about it when you are miles from any mechanical help—which is nearly all the time.

I could see that I could easily get used to life on the *MS Royal Crown*, with captains, engineers and a posse of great chefs to take some of the weight off the lonely shoulders of the skipper of *Linna*. We continued downstream to Cologne, whose Cathedral is one of the architectural wonders of the Middle Ages. When completed it was the tallest manmade structure in the world. It was started in 1248, halted unfinished 1473, restarted in the 1840s and finally completed 1880. The site has been occupied by Christian buildings from the 4th century. The shrine of the 'Three Kings' with its golden reliquary has been one of Europe's most revered shrines for over eight hundred years. However, there is considerable scepticism shown by modern scholars and theologians that the remains are actually of the *Three Magi*.

In 1164 the archbishop of Cologne, who was a favourite of the Holy Roman Emperor Frederick Barbarossa, was gifted the relics of the *Three Magi*, which the Emperor had stolen from the Basilica of Sant'Eustororgio in Milan while he was campaigning to expand his empire in Italy. The story of how the relics came to be in Milan is an interesting one. St Helena, the mother of Constantine the Great, was given unlimited funds to search the Holy Land for religious relics and bring them back to Constantinople. This she did between 326-328, around three centuries after the crucifixion. She was spectacularly successful, discovering a number of relics, including the *'True Cross'*—John Calvin was to later point out that if all the extant fragments were put together, they would fill a large ship—the nails and rope of the crucifixion, *'The Holy Tunic'* and the remains of the *'Three Magi.'* In 344 they were transferred from Constantinople to Milan. Where eight hundred years later, despite rapacious visits by Visigoths, Huns, Goths, Lombards, Charlemagne himself and goodness knows who else, one of the greatest treasures of Christianity was there waiting for Barbarossa to claim.

Quite apart from questions of logistics, there are serious questions even about the very existence of the *Three Magi*, or *Three Wise Men* or the *Three Kings*. The story is only in the Gospel According to Matthew 2:12, written around 80-90 CE by an unknown author, and no number mentioned at all. Later it became Christian tradition that three distinguished foreigners visited the baby Jesus on the night of his birth, bearing gifts. Over the centuries the references became to 'three wise men' and then 'three kings' from three different countries. Whatever the number, there is no explanation as to how the three bodies were in one spot for St Helena to find, a few centuries after their visit.

Anyway, notwithstanding, the shrine has been an incredible commercial success and over the centuries it has been the most visited landmark in Germany. It still attracts, on average, twenty thousand a day. But it is not without competition. The old imperial capital at Aachen has many holy relics itself - the swaddling clothes of Christ, his loincloth, the decapitation cloth from John the Baptists head and the Blessed Virgin's cloak.

Cologne was devastated by allied bombing during World War II, and the Cathedral badly damaged, but still standing. Perhaps because it was an excellent map reading reference for allied pilots.

Looking back a few hundred years earlier, the cities along the Rhine had to cope with the depredations of the Vikings. Not to the extent of those places along the coasts of the Atlantic and the North Seas, but devastating, never-the-less. In 845 Paris was attacked for the first time, with 700 longships sailing up the Seine. The Parisians bought off the raiders with 7,000 lbs of silver, by the 860s the Vikings were establishing permanent basis and by 926 thirteen large bribes of Danegeld had been made by the Frankish Empire. In 862 they attacked up the Rhine for the first time and plundered Cologne. In 863 they conquered Utrecht and Nijmegen and established permanent winter camps. In 881 there were more raids higher up the Rhine and into the Moselle. In 882 Cologne paid Danegeld but was still sacked, as was Aachen, and Charlemagne's tomb desecrated. There were raids higher up the Rhine and the Moselle in 883, with Cologne still in ruins from the previous year.

Our last day on board the *MV Royal Crown* took us to the vibrant city of Dusseldorf. The old German tribes had held on in this area during Roman times and, small farming and fishing communities still existed in the 7th and 8th centuries. Its first historical record was in 1135 and it became a fortified outpost under Emperor Friedrich Barbarossa. It had its ups and downs over the centuries and was really devastated in WWII. But these days it is a very prosperous and busy place to stroll around. There was a huge antiques market and lots of sidewalk dining, to keep amused the thousands of university students and young professionals in finance and electronics.

We returned quite exhausted, but were soon revived by last night celebrations, with much good cheer, lots of wine and a great banquet. We had enjoyed it very much, there had been plenty of personal space on board, apart from being given and electronic guide, you were left alone to do whatever took your fancy on all of the onshore excursions. Which, to us, was much better then following a great crowd around and enduring interminable lectures.

In the morning we boarded a bus south that took us through quite a bit of our old 1995 route and it was quite nostalgic identifying many of the old places we had passed through, particularly a French border post that we had arrived at by mistake and with no francs to pay the toll, and no French to explain our predicament to the officious Frenchwoman, who did her best to make life as difficult as possible for us.

Anyway, back in the present, we arrived back around dusk. We had been looking forward to a visit of two friends we had met through Charlotte in Annecy a decade or so before. They were an American couple renting a small chateau with a beautiful view looking over the waters of Lake Annecy to the mountains on the far side. Even in France there are few better views. Mike was a remarkable man, a couple of decades or so older than me, but a lot of fun and as sharp as a tack. Linda was a very attractive blonde, a few years behind Ro. Mike had served in the US navy in WWII and the two girls got on well, so we always caught up when we were in Annecy and, had done a couple of short trips together. They had had an interesting life. Mike had made himself into a very wealthy developer, and at the time of the financial crisis in 2008 had close to a billion dollars of construction underway. His finance dried up and the banks came looking for him. Forced sales of the company's assets still left the banks searching for more, and they started examining Linda's personal assets, including some stunning jewellery that had been gifts from Mike. While this was going on Mike had a bad fall, injured his head, and was not in any intellectual condition to fight his corner. The banks' threats to take her much-loved jewellery, were too much for Linda. She loaded up the car with some cash and the jewellery and drove into Canada. Put the car in a jet and flew to Spain, and found their way to the chateau at Annecy, with their three pet dogs.

In due course the American authorities came looking. They were arrested and put in the local jail, while the US sought their repatriation. Mike and Linda sought amnesty from the French government and after some difficult times it was granted. To our mind, the collapse of Mike's company was not his fault, perhaps Linda's flight might have been hasty, but she was fighting for what was hers. Anyway, they are a lovely couple, and by the time they arrived in Annecy they had been through a lot. Mike was now ninety-four, and we were looking forward to catching up again. We had shared a couple of nights, but then Mike had another fall and was hospitalised for some days before he was fit to travel. Undaunted Linda packed him in the car and made the twelve-hour drive home. Ro was speaking to Linda only yesterday, and all is well, though of course they are trying to cope with the coronavirus. But Annecy is a lovely place to be self-isolating in.

After wandering much of the Pacific, Europe and Asia, largely on *Oceania*, *Sea Dreams* and *Linna,* we have been enchanted by most of what we have seen and experienced. Digging around in the past has also uncovered some wonderful things, but many, many immense tragedies, some almost beyond comprehension. Here is a summary of some characters and events that deserve special mention. Please don't go through it if you are easily depressed!

Firstly, the Habsburg dynasty, which was prominent in Europe for much of the second millennium as Kings of Spain and Portugal, Emperors of the Holy Roman Empire, Emperors of the Austro-Hungarian Empire and rulers of the New World. They were fervent Catholics and in the interest of their religious and dynastic ambitions were associated with the following tragedies and deaths. In the conquests of the New World: 24,000,000 deaths in conquering the Aztec Empire,1,460,000 in the Yucatan Empire, 8,400,000 in the Inca Empire and, 600,000 deaths in the Spanish American Wars of Independence. In the European religious and dynastic wars: 650,000 deaths in the Eighty Years War, 140,000 in the Anglo- Spanish War, 12,000,000 in the Thirty Years War. 500,000 Which is half of the deaths in the War of the Spanish Succession. And as Emperors of the Austro-Hungarian Empire, a share of the 16,000,000 who died as a result of World War I. And much, much more.

The Valois dynasty who were kings of France from 1461-1589. 3,000,000 deaths in the French Wars of Religion and 300,000 caused while fighting beside the Ottomans against Christian Europe from 1536 to 1798.

The Mongol nations evolving from Genghis Khan in their conquests in Europe and Asia 1206-1405. 40,000,000. The conquest of Timur (Tamerlane) in the Middle East between 1370-1405 13,000,000.

The Popes of the Catholic Church - in conjunction with France and Venice- for the sack of Constantinople and the consequent fall of the Christian Byzantine Empire. And the destruction of the vast intellectual and scientific advances of the Hellenistic period, their involvements in the Crusades, the European Religious Wars and the conquest of the New World.

Horror at the numbers who died during various dynastic wars in China. Including:

- Qins Wars of Unification (230-221 BCE) 2,000,000.
- Wars of the Three Kingdoms (184-280) 38,000,000.
- An Lushan Rebellion (755-763) 21,000,000.
- Ming to Qing Dynasties (1616-1683) 25,000,000.
- Taiping Rebellion (1850-1864) 40,000,000.
- Tongzhi Hui Revolt 1862 to 1877) 10,000,000
- Qing China vs Hui vs Kashgaria.
- Chinese Civil War (1927-1949) 10,000,000.
- Second Sino-Japanese War (1937-1945) 25,000,000.
- Attributable to Mao Zedong. 20-46,000,000 between 1958 and 1862.
- And, of course the twentieth century deaths in World War I 24,000,000 and World War II 85,000,000.

All very depressing. Even before getting on to deaths caused by disease, either with human or natural origins.

- The Black Death alone is estimated to have killed up to 200 million between 1331-1353.
- Smallpox 56 million in 1520.
- Spanish Flu 45 million in 1919-29.
- Plague 40 million in 541-542.
- HIV/Aids 36million 1981-
- Plague 12 million in 1855.

Particularly as we have the unresolved, at this time, Covid 19 pandemic with us. Perhaps the only conclusion we can reach, in view of all the misery of history, is that we should thank God, that someone invented red wine!

In early September Ro and I headed back to Australia. In late January we returned to Tasmania for a couple of weeks for our annual catch up with Sue and Don, Carmel and Phil, Margie and Paul, Sally and most of our old Tasmanian friends. And as we always do, talked of old times and rekindled old memories as we wandered through the beautiful countryside and the familiar streets of Hobart. And thought how lucky we had been to have settled here all those years ago.

~ TASMANIA ~

...overlooking Koonya and Norfolk Bay, from Don and Sue's top paddock. Windermere, our old farm is off camera to the right...

After our second tour in Papua New Guinea, I had a spell running survival training at the Jungle Training Centre Canungra in Queensland, and in 1975 I was posted to Army Headquarters in Canberra. But by this time, we both realised that we were ready for a change of life; we had in mind a few peaceful acres, probably in the north coast of New South Wales.

There were only two ways we could see of raising the necessary capital. Firstly, we had to complete twenty years of service and commute as much as possible of the army pension. Secondly, we would turbocharge our modest speculation in property. Over the years we had acquired three blocks of residential land, and on arriving in Canberra we were able to convert these into an attractive residence. Later we leveraged the house on a forty-acre block of land and built a long, low-line cedar bungalow near Hall, a few miles outside Canberra. We added a semi-detached wing for my sprightly seventy-two year old father John, better known to us and the girls as 'Poppy'. Ro had become one of Canberra's first female real estate agents and soon had her manager's license and was on the way to becoming a legend. She also had a career that was portable and was to be of inestimable value to us all. I had enrolled in a Diploma of Agriculture by correspondence, we started breeding a flock of angora goats and planted almond and walnut trees on our new farm. Life was good and the girls were happy at school. Many weekends we would barbecue a tender goat and old friends and their children would sing and laugh around the fire until late. We hauled our new trailer sailor yacht, *Prauwin,* to the south coast, Lake Eucumbene, Port Stevens and the Myall Lakes. Largely thanks to Gough Whitlam's inflation both properties tripled in value, and by 1980 we had enough for a reasonable farm and a small residual pension.

Meanwhile, work, basically as a uniformed bureaucrat, was okay, apart from the glacial pace at which the bureaucracy worked. Initially I was on a committee working on the implementation of the Kerr Report into services' pay, and then helping compile recommendations on a new superannuation scheme for the services. In 1977 I was posted to the Department of Defence to help review and co-ordinate the 'Conditions of Service' of the Army, Navy and Air Force. When I left for Tasmania, two years after we had started, not one regulation had gone to the printers and I had realised that it was not the communists who were the greatest danger to the country, but the public servants in the Department of Defence.

As retirement grew closer, we began to look more seriously at our options. A friend suggested we should consider Tasmania which has beautiful rural areas and some of the best sailing waters in Australia. In mid-winter 1979 we set off to explore. We hired a campervan in Launceston and drove eastward along the north coast. The country was beautiful; emerald green fields, forests of noble eucalypts, a dusting of snow on the higher mountains and a clear blue sky that belied the cool freshness of the air. Glimpses of the sea revealed expanses of glittering azure water running off to the distant horizon.

At Bridport we took a spot in the nearly deserted caravan park beside the bay and strolled around the waterfront. The sky was still light with the beautiful clarity that is a defining characteristic of the island, the water still looked enchanting. It didn't feel so cold when I put my toe in, but when I jumped in it was a different matter. I think that was my only winter dip for thirty years or so. A family of possums, their red eyes glittering in the darkness, visited our campfire for dinner and we all went to bed pleased with what we had so far seen.

The next day we pottered down to the east coast of Tasmania to Swansea where we camped on a peninsula with breathtaking views across Great Oyster Bay to the Freycinet Peninsula and, south to the peaks of Maria Island. This area was explored by Captain John Henry Cox in his ship the *Mercury* in 1789, only the year after the first fleet arrived in Australia and was settled in 1821. Later, we often came back to this area for holidays. It is a marvellous destination in a yacht with a number of anchorages in small coves with magically white beaches, where freshly caught fish and crayfish can be cooked over aromatic driftwood fires. For a while we a had a beach house in the sand dunes behind Seven Mile Beach where on a clear day we could just make out the mountains on the Tasman Peninsula, many miles to the south, and in the night hear the restless wash on the sandy shore. Night fell and we sat around our campfire cooking sausages on sticks and watching the blaze of the star filled southern sky, and the glimmer of the Aurora Australis on the black horizon.

The following night in our campervan, after a day of dramatic and unforgettable scenery we were already in love with the island. However, in those days there were no real estate offices anywhere on the whole east coast and it was well before the internet, so we were not doing so well searching for a farm. We were the only customers at the Port Arthur caravan park, where we got into trouble —to the immense embarrassment of Charlotte and Georgina—but were let off with a warning from a park ranger, for all using the same shower block.

Later, while we were having dinner at the pub in Port Arthur, Ro got to talking with some locals and discovered that there was a farm for sale a few miles away, and mid-morning the next day we drove off to inspect *Windermere*. Leaving the main road just south of Taranna we took the Koonya road up over the heavily-timbered Sympathy Point ridgeline. Just past the crest the view widened, and we found ourselves looking up an enchanted valley. Patches of lush pasture peeped around stands of tall straight timber, all framed by a noble eminence that dominated the skyline. To our right, through the trees, were the sparkling waters of Norfolk Bay.

'Gee, that looks all right!!' we said to each other simultaneously. 'I wonder if that's it?'

And it was. It was beautiful. And we were in love.

It was a sunny windless winter day and the atmospherics were perfect. A substantial brick home surrounded by an English garden, a couple of hundred sheep grazing peacefully, a happy group pruning the apple trees made a charming bucolic scene, distant water views. We checked out the local school, walked the boundaries, inspected the timber, did the maths on the orchard and thought that any property that had been nurtured by, and had supported, such a fine man as the owner, Bruce Heyward, would do us. It was almost within commuting distance to Hobart, which was important as we hoped I could work out my last year in the army and farm at the same time.

Bruce was about sixty at this stage and was putting the finishing touches to a fifty-tonne steel charter boat in which he would chase game fish in the Southern Ocean, while also making sure we didn't get into too much trouble with the farm. At eighty he would take up flying gliders and—after Marjory, his lovely wife of forty years, had sadly passed on—marry a professor of English Literature who had fallen in love with him many years before, when she was working as an apple picker in the orchard. I think she was lucky to get in before my wife.

***

Back in Canberra Roger Wainwright organised a posting to Hobart, we flogged our houses and the flock of angoras and after Christmas in Tamworth with Ro's sister, Gill and the extended family, we set off for Hobart. Ro driving our smart Lancia with the two girls. Poppy and myself were in the Holden One Ton Truck with the goat cage crammed with junk, two cats and Gatsby our much-loved Labrador dog, and towing *Prauwin* and looking like Steptoe and Sons. Passing through Albury one of the cats escaped from the cage, threw herself off the truck and was never seen again – despite many tears and much searching. We stopped off to see Ro's eldest sister, Deborah, and husband, Kevin, at Sandringham in Melbourne for a brief visit, sailed across on the ferry, and finally took possession of *Windermere*.

We had all been dreaming of this moment for years.

The farm was set well back from the bitumen road that skirted Norfolk Bay before it turned south over a range of hills to the township of Nubeena. Here were located the school, council chambers, the top and bottom shops, the RSL club and a jetty which was home to a small fishing fleet. In those days the population of the peninsula was around a thousand, and there was a town cop who on some Friday nights harassed the crowd at the RSL as they meandered an unsteady way home.

There was an apple orchard and an old hop field between our front boundary and the Nubeena Road, through which a dirt lane lined with poplars led up to *Windermere*. The lane continued past our large apple sheds, shearing sheds and the 'pickers quarters' and wound its way up a spur to the homestead, bounded on two sides by our orchard and pine trees. It overlooked a large dam and green paddocks interspersed with copses of tall eucalypts. The side boundaries were delineated by streams—rivulets in Tasmania—that fed into dams lower down, while behind us was a noble forest climbing up into the hills. Bruce and Marjory had established an English garden after the war, and now, some thirty years later it was superb. At the back was a large veggie garden, which Poppy immediately claimed as his own, and some chooks who thought the garden was actually theirs.

Windermere covered about eighty hectares. Creek flats at the bottom, on which ran a flock of a couple of hundred odd sheep, ten hectares of apple orchard straddling a gentle spur that ran to the edge of ten hectares of forested hill. We couldn't see another house, although on cold winter mornings we could see the smoke from our neighbour's fires rising above the trees.

On the day of our arrival, we were having a wine under the lovely maple tree in our front garden to celebrate our good fortune, when a battered truck chugged up the hill and pulled to a stop near the cattle grid into the garden, where our small sailing boat was parked. It was our neighbour, Donald Clark.

After a couple of wines Don went home and reported to his wife. 'Gawd Sue, I don't think they'll last long. Ro, was in a long dress and they were drinking champagne at five o'clock'.

We became, and still are the very best of friends, and we have covered many, many sea miles together. Their first attempt to introduce us into local society received a rebuff when Marg Hansen announced 'Sue, I'm not going to have my dinner party ruined by some stuffy old retired major, thank you very much'. But after her husband Paul ran into Ro somewhere or other, he realised his wife may have been right about the old major, but he would certainly be happy sharing reminiscences with his wife. They also ended up becoming lifelong friends and sailing a lot with us in Australia and the Mediterranean.

In mid-winter 1981, Sue and Don invited us to come cruising with them on their yacht, *Cascades,* which Don had finished building a couple of years previously. She was a beautiful thirty-six foot pilot-house ketch, with two bunks in the forward cabin and a convertible double bunk in the saloon. It had been built with the Clark family, Don and Sue and their children, Karina and Marcus, in mind, so it should have been a bit cramped with both families. But even in mid-winter it didn't seem so, and we had a wonderful two weeks. We were lucky with the weather, although in Tasmania it is not that uncommon to get a series of calm still days in winter, where the sun sparkles off the placid blue water.

We sailed down the D'Entrecasteaux channel between Bruny Island and the mainland and, for the first time visited some of the beautiful spots that make this stretch of water one of the most enchanting in Australia, including Great Bay, Partridge Island, Port Esperance and anchored for a magical night behind the sandbar in the eastern corner of Lighthouse Bay. Here there was nothing between us and the South Pole and, among the small rock islets around the corner, communities of seals came and went and basked in the weak winter sunshine. Over the next two decades we would come back to these places in a succession of yachts – the *Charlotte Rose,* which we bought as a hull and fitted her out as a ketch, *Reveille* a fibreglass cutter which we sailed to the Whitsundays, the *Tasman Isle,* a Huon Pine pilot house ketch and finally, *Oceania*. With Sue and Don, we sailed in company or, on each other's yachts all around the coast.

...on Oceania with Don and Sue.

The brick homestead of Windermere had only three bedrooms. Poppy occupied the master-bedroom, the girls the other two and Ro and I slept in an open veranda, which we enclosed with sliding glass doors before the onset of the first winter. This worked okay but did not give Dad much privacy. Our back forest had been used for sustainable logging for the best part of a century, and we continued the practice to get the timber for what was to be his new home—we provided a few trees to the local sawmill, they milled the timber and gave us back half. There was the derelict remains of an old one room cottage on a small knoll fifty metres from the homestead. By technically renovating but, really rebuilding, we were able to employ two local young men to create a charming two-bedroom cottage. It had a veranda with a fine view over our large reed lined dam, from which Poppy could enjoy an aperitif before joining us for dinner, and long discussions on how to save the world. About this time, we had to start rationing his port consumption, so as to be able to at least agree on one or two things. The finance for the construction was provided by the area's leading real estate agent, do I need to mention her name?

The next few years were quite idyllic and prosperous. As well as selling apples we installed an apple juice extraction facility. Our fresh juice was outselling all other juices all over the state, and our alcoholic apple cider was also being well received. The seasons had been good and, *Windermere* was heart-stoppingly beautiful. To walk in the fresh early mornings, from the house surrounded by Poppy's luxuriant garden, down past the orchard, through the green paddocks by the large dam to the Cider House, was a stroll through paradise. Returning in the dusk to the warm glow of the house on the hill, to a family dinner where three opinionated generations would laugh and hold forth, was alone worth a lifetime's labour. Twice Ro's parents visited us on their bi-annual trip from Ireland and my sister, Wendy, was a regular visitor as were other members of our extended families including my brother Richard and his family. The girls were starting boarding school in Hobart and we were able to buy a waterfront house in Hobart.

However, below the horizon, clouds were gathering. Our production line had been upgraded, at a significant cost, to handle the larger volume. As our business grew so did the cost of our stock on hand, apples and juice as well as packaging. So did the cost of our debtors, and we always had very significant amounts owing to us. We were lucky if we got payment from the supermarkets within three months and smaller shops within a couple. We were also forced to take our Hobart distributor to court to recover a substantial amount owing to us.

Meanwhile, during 1987 world stock markets had been buoyant and Australia had been experiencing a period of great economic excitement. Led by a group of highly leveraged entrepreneurs, including Alan Bond, Robert Holmes a Court and John Elliot the economy was booming. Fortunes were made, great trades done and, exciting dreams paraded before a public anxious to be part of them. Then, on Friday 6th of October, markets in Asia began to crash and the tremors started to sweep around the world. Tuesday 20th was the most traumatic day in the history of the Australian Securities Exchange. The share market opened 25 per cent down. Quality stocks traded at 75 percent of their value and there was no market for many lightweight stocks. In the following months many of the country's major financial institutions were devastated, most of the high-flying entrepreneurs were wiped out and the whole banking system shaken.

Then, a bombshell for us. The supermarkets decided they would take no apple juice product from either us or our former distributer until the court case was resolved, and on top of that, our bank demanded we reduce our borrowing. Eventually we got to court and after an horrendous few days we won the verdict we wanted: our money plus interest and costs. But despite having won the legal battle, we had well and truly lost the war. Being shut out of the supermarkets had left us without any income, and there was no longer a business and, we were in no position to rebuild it to what it once was. Our only option was to get onto the next thing. We had lost a lot of money and learned some hard lessons. But we still had the *Charlotte Rose* and enough money to buy a charming cottage in Battery Point which only required a little renovation, two lovely daughters and each other. And of course, Poppy was still with us.

***

Our seven years in Tasmania had been an extraordinary experience. On the positive side we had had a wonderful happy and exciting time, and we had made many good friends. But there was no getting away from the fact we had lost most of what we had. Charlotte was now at university and Georgie still had a couple of years at the Fahan School ahead of her. Ro was enjoying her work, now with a well-known Hobart real estate firm and my priority was to find a job for myself. L.J. Hooker were advertising for a commercial real estate salesman and, I applied for the job. Up until now I had not had any interest in commercial real estate at all, but I was soon fascinated by the new world I had stumbled into. Before long we were both doing well, our cash flow was good, and we started investing in commercial properties. In those days there were good properties for sale in Hobart that gave returns of above ten percent on rents, and plenty of rents were also well below market rates. If you could bring the rents up to market your return could be twenty percent or more. We traded the *Charlotte Rose* for *Reveille* a 44 foot fibreglass cutter which we sailed to Brisbane to celebrate Christmas 1989 with Eugene. The following year, Charlotte was now in Sydney and Georgie at the University of Tasmania, we sailed to the Whitsundays leaving Georgie and Poppy to look after themselves.

One balmy evening as the year was drawing to a close, we were sitting on *Reveille's* aft deck in beautiful Shute Harbour in the Whitsundays, looking at our options for the future. After many months of enjoying our life afloat, the cyclone season was approaching, and we had to make some decisions. We were enjoying life in Tasmania, had recently built a new home on a leafy block of land overlooking the Derwent with a flat for Poppy, Georgie was happy at the university and Charlotte was working in hospitality in Sydney. My uncle Keith was not coping too well in Sydney and we had suggested he might like to move closer to us. After a wine or two we decided to sell *Reveille,* return to Hobart and start our own real estate company, *Peterswalds.* By this stage, Ro especially had an excellent profile in the industry. So, it was back to work.

It went well from the outset and we had a very enjoyable and prosperous decade, using the cash flow to build up a sizeable portfolio of commercial property. Both the girls joined us, we had an excellent staff, and offered property management as well as residential and commercial marketing. We were involved in marketing the first of a number of large developments around Salamanca and the waterfront. We were working long hours six days a week, but we tried to spend Saturday nights on our beautiful new Huon pine ketch, *Tasman Isle,* moored in a quiet bay south of Hobart.

In 1996 a chance meeting opened the door to another fascinating world. When I was a young boy growing up in Taree, I was aware that a copy of a one-page extract from the publication *Burke's Colonial Gentry*, was stored for safe keeping between the pages of a large volume of Poppy's 1934 Webster's Dictionary. This is where my father stored our birth certificates, his marriage certificates and a few other pieces of important paper.

It began:

'The Peterswalds were originally a noble family of Silesia, where they resided in the castle of Peterswaldau, in the district of Reichenbach, governed by Arnold von Peterswald in 1322', and went on to sketch later events. A move to Germany, then to Jamaica, back to England and to Australia in 1853. How much was true, I had no idea.

It intrigued me enough to periodically make futile attempts to locate the 'castle at Peterswaldau'. My father was no help and maps of Europe available to a young boy in the 1950s were lucky to have

Paris and London marked, and there was very little detail of anything behind the 'Iron Curtain'. So, I grew up uncertain if this was part of a fairy-tale, perhaps created by my grandfather, or was real. Over the years I made other attempts, but most places where I found myself were very short on research facilities and the maps of Europe I could obtain, were mostly small scale and not in English. By the time we came to Tasmania and the Berlin Wall was falling I was no further advanced, and I generally had a lot else on my mind in any case.

Then, one day in 1996 Ro and myself were discussing the marketing of the home of an elderly couple, and as we were leaving the husband asked me about my name. I told the little I knew, and then he dropped a bombshell. In the closing months of World War II, he had been fleeing westward before the advancing Russians, and had briefly found a safe haven in a town named Peterswald, in western Poland. He promised to dig out an old atlas and send me a photocopy. This he did, and it transpired that after the war the spelling of the name it had enjoyed for around eight hundred years had been changed to Pieszyce, the more acceptable Polish form. I wrote to the nearest university, at the medieval city of Wroclaw, and arranged for some archival searches of the name. There were hundreds of references dating back to 1258, many were actual minutes of the Duchal council. I arranged for the papers to be translated through the University of Tasmania and in 1997 we set off to visit a long abandoned schloss in Poland.

It transpired that around four hundred years ago the *schloss* had belonged to our family. We eventually found it. The rain that had followed us for most of the day continued to fall from a leaden sky, saturating the ancient oaks and their wind-blown leaves. Before us a rutted carriageway led past a stone gatehouse and over a scarred stone bridge to the old *schloss* half-hidden in dark shrubbery. Once it must have been magnificent. A rich and exotic palace surrounded by acres of high-walled gardens. The Italian marble and tiles laid by Renaissance craftsmen had brought the colours of the Mediterranean, and a central tower, capped by a large dome and gleaming spire, spoke of the Eastern steppes.

But now it stood abandoned. Parts of the red tile roof were missing; soot and grime blackened the rest. At some time, the windows had been roughly bricked in and the beautiful surrounds defaced. The plasterwork of the walls was stained and peeling, uncovering crumbling red brick and grey granite. The forecourt was overrun with damp weeds and littered with the detritus of the adjoining grimy slum that now occupied part of the old gardens.

Above the entrance there was a date, 1594, and a dedication carved in Latin.

'Freely, with joy and courage, love and honour your family.'

But in its desolation, it was no noble ruin capturing something of a romantic past, but only a derelict and grim reminder of the vagaries of history. After a while we left the ruin and followed the course of the old waterway that led towards the nearby mountains. Beside the overgrown banks were some fallen stones half-buried and worn with the passage of time; perhaps the remains of an older castle that had stood here before the *schloss.*

The stream wound through the town that had once enjoyed a prosperous elegance before the Red Army became the last of many overlords. Now it was only a decaying collection of grimy brick houses lining the dirty, cobbled pavements. No doors were open, and windows were shuttered or darkened behind dull curtains. Little relieved the oppressive poverty brought by war and communist rule. Only in the well-tended graves and the potted flowers of the cold cemetery was there a memory of something else.

As we left the town behind, the grim houses soon gave way to the forested walls of a valley. The stream began to come to life, chattering over a rocky bottom held between low stone embankments. Before long the valley entrance began to open out and on the far side of the creek a thickly wooded spur climbed towards the higher peaks. Leaving the narrow, cobbled road we crossed over a rocky ford and began to climb a dirt path that wound upwards. Beneath the thick canopy of autumn tree-tops a quiet green light enveloped us. Our footsteps made no sound on the thick mat of fallen leaves and the smell of the wet earth stirred old memories of other forests I had walked in other times.

The grimness of the derelict *schloss* and the village receded, belonging to another world. It seemed as if we climbed in an ancient forest unchanged from times long past. After a sharp rise, we reached a small knoll with steep slopes falling away on three sides, while farther up the spur continued towards the mountain tops. We had reached the place we sought. The trees had been partly cleared to allow the view to be enjoyed, and fate willed the late afternoon sun to break through the mist and cloud. The panorama opened around us. Looking back over the way we had come, we saw the Silesian plain stretching into the distance: a fertile, rolling land covered with tilled fields, the new green of late crops, small copses quilted with autumn hues and scattered villages. In the sun's late glow even the village below us seemed to recapture its old charm.

To the west, mountains formed a majestic barrier, the thickly-forested slopes clothed in greens, browns, and gold. Below, once the narrow neck was passed, the valley opened into a section of rich alluvial flats divided by the clear waters of the stream. Farther up, undulating fields ran to the precipitous escarpments of the mountains.

We stood for some time, not talking, content in what surrounded us, enjoying the quiet noises of the forest: the soft call of feeding birds and the gentle rustle of a small animal fossicking for fallen nuts. Dusk was settling and little was left of the day. There was a mystic feel about this place, a connection with the distant past. Protected by the mountains, with the late sun playing on the autumn colours and tendrils of misty cloud, we could sense the passage of souls long passed, the call of ancient voices and the forgotten sounds of lovers' gentle laughter. In the rustle of the trees we could hear the jingle of armoured men, the tramp of cavalry long gone, and the clash of sword on sword. In the last of the rain we felt the soft fall of tears on the rocky ground.

We turned to study the scattered rocks and the few pieces of an ancient stone wall barely visible on the forest floor. Beyond them a slight indentation may once have been a moat. Not much remained of the stone tower that had been built here nearly a millennium ago. In these old stones, the ruins of the castle and *schloss,* we had found what we had come for: memories of the time, so long ago, when our family had lived in these troubled lands.

And in the quietness, we resolved to discover their forgotten story.

The internet had now begun to function and within a few years the reference to our name grew from a few to thousands. Together with the documents from the Wroclaw university, the story of the family began to unfold. Then in 1998 we had another fortunate meeting. A woman wondered if there was any connection between our name, and a memorial in the garden of her most favourite chateau in the whole of Europe, in Buchlovice in the Czech Republic, to the Baroness Eleonora von Peterswald. This took the story along another long-forgotten path. In 1999 we visited the chateau and an older castle with Georgie and Simon and later on with Charlotte. Over time we pieced together this story of the Peterswalds and the times they lived in.

By the end of the first millenium nearly all Europe was Christian. Christian kings sat on the thrones of Poland and Bohemia, Christian princes and dukes ruled the German states, and all swore fealty to the Holy Roman Emperor, consecrated in his court at Aachen by the Pope, God's voice on earth. In 1187 the Duchy of Silesia, uncomfortably surrounded by these great powers, was ruled by Duke Wyoski Piast from his seat in the nearby city of Breslau (now Wroclaw). From the year 1000, bishops appointed by the Pope to Breslau had spread the Lord's word from pulpits carved in fine wood and worked with silver and gold. And when force was required to convert the pagans in the nearby lands beside the Baltic, there were many good Christian knights only too ready to join new crusades. Such missions were repaid handsomely with land, wealth, and power.

In these times the calendar no longer celebrated the ancient gods but, marked only Christian observances. The long, dark night of the winter solstice now celebrated Christ's birth. His resurrection was celebrated at Easter, during the approach of the warmer months, when once an ancient festival thanked the goddess, Eostre, for the earth's renews by the sun's warmth. As Christianity had taken root in Eastern Europe, many of the ancient names for places had fallen into disuse and had been replaced with Christian names. Such had been the case with an area of forest adjoining the Owl Mountains, southwest of Breslau. It had become known as Saint Peter's Forest, and after a time, simply Peter's Forest; or Petri Silva or Peters Wald, depending on your language.

Our family's story began early in the 13th century. German settlers had already begun spreading east into the sparsely populated lands of Silesia, between Germany and Poland. They were welcomed by the Dukes of Silesia and some were granted land, which in time grew into small fiefdoms. Strongholds were built, villages and churches established under their protection. The surrounding farmlands were extended and those working them swore loyalty, promised military service and paid taxes. For many centuries, up until the end of World War II, one of these fiefdoms in the border between the independent Duchy of Silesia and the Kingdoms of Bohemia and Poland, was named Peterswalde. Today the town which was established there is called Pieszyce, which is the Polish spelling of the name. (Peterswald/Pieczyce). Our family lived there, initially as 'edlers' and later as 'ritters' the equivalent of 'knights or baronets' and later still as freiherrs or barons, until all that was theirs was destroyed during the Thirty-Year War in the 17th century.

Records still held at the University of Wroclaw show that Otto von Wilin Peterswalde was the edler of Peterswalde in 1258. He is our first recorded ancestor. The history of this part of central Europe is a bloody one. Before Roman times the Scythians and Celts fought over the area that was to become Silesia. Later the Celts were devastated by the Cimbri and Teutone who were among the Germanic tribes heading south to attack Rome, whose empire had pushed up to the Danube and Rhine rivers.

From the 5th century Slavic tribes began invading, but by the 12th century the Holy Roman Empire, the Kingdoms of Bohemia and Poland and the Duchy of Silesia were all established. However, the border areas were in an almost continual state of internecine warfare. Either between greater powers trying to extend their borders or by the cruel and competing factions within them particularly in Silesia and Poland. Time Lapse Map.

In 1241 hard and dangerous times became unimaginably worse. When the great Mongol warlord, Genghis Khan, died in 1227, he left behind the largest empire the world had seen, a mighty army and the belief of his heirs in their divine role to conquer the world. He had proclaimed '... *the joy of man lies in killing his enemies, tearing down his towns and cities so that nothing remains, taking his wealth and his children and taking his wives for his pleasure.*' (Somewhat harsher than those instructions issued by King George and Governor Phillip in regard to the indigenes of New South Wales).

Genghis practised what he preached. There are estimates that one in two hundred of the population within the borders of what was his empire are his direct descendants. Recently my daughters gave me a DNA kit and the results were largely as expected, forty-percent

303

British, twenty-eight percent central European, thirty-percent Irish. But there were two outliers. A one percent from the old Mongol heartland. Am I related to Genghis? And another strand of one percent from the area southeast of the Black Sea. This is also interesting. The Mongol warlord, Tamerlane, established an empire in this region, which was succeeded by the Ottoman Turks and later became part of Turkey. The DNA trail could have been taken back to Asia by a captured slave and then been brought back to Europe by the army of Suleiman. This leaves the door open to being related to both Tamerlane and Suleiman the Magnificent, who extended his empire to the border of Austria. I suppose there is a small chance that the relation just might have been a common soldier. Further research is needed.

By 1240 the Mongol Empire extended from the Pacific Ocean to the borders of central Europe. It included all of Russia, China, India and Arabia. Whole nations were murdered, cities so broken that only heaps of bones and scattered charred stones remained. Russia and Persia were soaked in blood and unimaginable wealth was dragged off to the palaces of the Khans. The countries were left in such devastation that they would not recover for centuries. Seventy thousand were bound and slaughtered at <u>Nisa</u>. At <u>Merv</u> over a million were butchered. At Nishapur, watched over by Genghis's daughter, every living creature was beheaded, and their sculls used to build a macabre tower, to avenge the death of her husband.

The armies of the Mongols were comprised of mounted archers organized in 'Tumans' of ten thousand men, broken into units of one thousand, one hundred and ten. The men were hardened warriors from the harsh lands of central Asia, and they rode horses as tough and resilient as themselves. They and their mounts could travel vast distances fast and live off the land on their way. Their leaders were chosen on their proven ability, ruthlessness, bravery and experience. Their main weapon was a sophisticated and powerful bow that was designed for horse-back use and made by gluing together bone, wood and horn. It fired armour piecing arrows that could kill a fully armoured knight at over two hundred metres.

But it was not just these brave, hard and well-armed warriors that made their armies great. They had sophisticated intelligence networks that gave them a clear view of what they faced – from the political situation in Europe, down to the defences of cities and the movements of armies. Spies, disguised as traders, moved years ahead of the armies and, travellers from the west were interrogated. The conquest of China had given then gunpowder, napalm and siege machinery so that no city or castle was safe. In battle they used flags, horns and drums to co-ordinate and manoeuvred their warriors far more quickly and effectively than Western armies could. Tactics and deceptions were masterful, and alone won victory after victory. In all their major engagements in the West they were able to overcome heavy numerical disadvantages.

To put the Mongol armies into perspective. It is very hard to imagine a Western army before those of the late 19th century being able to defeat them in the field, given a reasonable balance of size and terrain. The Roman legions at their peak could not defeat the Parthian armies of horse archers and would have been defeated by the mobility and firepower of the Mongols. Likewise, the armies of Wellington and Napoleon—in my opinion, Napoleon's may differ. Their horse artillery would not have been mobile enough to bring fire to bear, and whose muskets were much inferior in range, accuracy and firepower to the Mongol bow.

In 1241 the Mongols mounted a two-pronged attack aimed at conquering Europe and extending their empire to the Atlantic Ocean. The main army pushed up the valley of the Danube, through Hungary towards Vienna and the heartland of Europe. Another army of two tumans swept through Poland and to threaten the German states, so as to stop the armies of northern Europe combining against the main Mongol army.

It was this army that devastated Silesia. While the land was still frozen it galloped towards the golden spires of Krakow, fabled for its wealth, devastating everything in their way. Villages were sacked and burned, the population slaughtered or sent eastward as slaves. In March the city was besieged and stormed and given over to four days of rape and pillage. In April, as the Mongols were attacking Wroclaw and having laid waste all that lay in their path, two Christian armies were now preparing to face them. One commanded by the Duke of Silesia, the other by the King of Bohemia.

The Mongols decided to attack the Silesian army before it was joined by the Bohemians. Near the city of Legnica, a few miles north of the village of Peterswalde, some fifty thousand Christians faced the two tumans of the Mongols, something less than twenty thousand strong. The Christian army was destroyed, and the Duke's head rammed on a spike and paraded around the walls of Legnica. The ears of the twenty-five thousand slain Christians were cut off and sent to General Batu, the commander of the main Mongol army. (Battle of Legnica).

When news of the calamity reached the approaching Bohemian army, they decided that they would be better off behind the walls of Prague and retreated westward. The northern Mongol army, having achieved their aim of neutralizing the armies of the Germans, Bohemians and Silesians turned southward to re-join Batu. They were laden with booty, gold, silver and precious stones taken from the cities, churches and villages they had left in ruins. Over five hundred villages, sixteen cities and a hundred castles had been destroyed and over a hundred thousand taken as slaves, on top of the many more that had been slaughtered. (Once again you will notice a difference to the behaviour of Captain Cook and Governor Phillip and their men).

About two day's march south of the battlefield they passed through the small area that was known as Peter's Forest. Most likely there had been a village and stronghold before, but there would have been nothing more than ruins and death when they had passed by. But possibly, leaving behind the genes of some long-forgotten Mongol warriors.

In the wake of this great national calamity the country began to rebuild and, in 1258 we have the record of Otto von Peterswalde being the Edler of Peterswalde. It is possible he had been this before the invasion. But perhaps he benefited from the vast number of deaths in every strata of Silesian life, and had been promoted because he had survived, still had two ears, and had perhaps fought with enough distinction to be rewarded. Among the translated papers, it is recorded that Otto had three surviving sons; Helmbold, Otton and Gunther and that the Bishop of Wroclaw authorized the payment of one and half gold marks every year to them. (Witnessed by the Dean, Milejus the Archdeacon, and the Procurators).

By early the next century Peregrin von Peterswalde has become Sir (Ritter) Peregrin.

Between 1289 and 1292 Silesia passed into the hands of the Bohemia Kings as part of the Holy Roman Empire, and a Peterswalde coat of arms was issued. But Silesia was soon fragmenting into seventeen principalities, which seemed to be continually at war with each other, and much of the country was in a state of anarchy and lawlessness. Famine and disease were widespread.

In 1304 Heinrich von Peterswald was connected with a failed attempt to kill Konrad, the brother of Baroness Beatrix of Silesia. It was judged a political matter; he was able to settle it by paying compensation and there was no further action taken. In fact, in 1306 he became a magistrate. In 1332 Arnold von Peterswald is Governor of Richenbach and his brothers are the proprietors of the fiefdom of Peterswalde, and over the next few years more estates are granted by the Duke, including churches, villages, forests, orchards and rights of taxation.

In 1403 Heinrich Peterswald was captain of Liegnitz. Franz Peterswald is Dean of Mathius Willusch in Riechenbach and in 1422 receives permission to rebuild the destroyed castle. (Reichenbach).

Things in Silesia went from bad to worse with the outbreak of the Bohemian Wars of 1419 to 1434. Fought between the Protestant followers of the reformist priest Jan Hus (known as Hussites) and surrounding rulers supported by the Catholic Church, it resulted in another round of bloody warfare and devastation sweeping over Silesia. Some of the major encounters, which were fought with all the bloodiness usual in religious wars were fought close to the village of Peterswald, and the surrounding countryside and villages were ravaged. The fighting was followed by starvation and disease. In 1428 Heinrich Peterswald was in command of troops that defeated a force of Hussites near Reichenbach, but the next year he was captured by the Hussites and hung drawn and quartered.

The Hussites became a major military force and defeated the armies of the five crusades proclaimed against then by the Pope. They developed a number of innovative tactics based around firearms, the most successful being mounting cannon in wagons and linking them in stockades, which were devastatingly effective against armoured cavalry. (Hussite War). Even after the Catholic armies were defeated, fighting continued between the moderate and radical factions until 1434, when they agreed to recognise the authority of the King of Bohemia and were allowed to practice their variations of the religious rites.

Within a few years Silesia became a battleground again as rivals for the Bohemian Crown fought each other, and it was not until 1471 that a compromise of sorts ended the fighting. But civil wars and turmoil among the Duchies and Principalities continued to rage for the next hundred years. Times were bloody and difficult and, this contributed to a decline in economic activity and trade. In 1509 Hans Peterswald married Catherine of the House of Konigsberg and bought more estates and in 1532 his son established a brewery that was still going in 1884. Despite the wars and difficult times, the Peterswalds had steadily acquired more estates, particularly around the area of Makowice, and by the end the 16th century had become extremely wealthy. They owned tumbling, wool and weaving mills.

In a delightful 15th century Gothic Church enhanced with a Renaissance Portal, beside the village of <u>Makowice</u> we discovered a number of sarcophagus of family members, their names and details chiselled into the stone in German. Men in armour with spiked shoulder plates, with swords and maces. All with beards and long drooping mistouches, some with helmets, others bare headed. Pious women, hands in prayer with neck ruffs and padded shoulders.

In May 1578 the original castle was destroyed by fire, and work on a modern schloss commenced. A plaque was erected with the inscription: *'Freely, with joy and courage love your parents and care for them. Respect your father and mother so that they may be without the burden of worries.'*

It passed to Hans von Gellhorn through his marriage to Ursula Peterswalde and became one of the finest Schloss's in central Europe. Other estates around Pieszyce were also purchased from the family. By the middle of the 16th century much of Silesia had become Protestant and in 1609 the Protestant estates ceased paying taxes to the Holy Roman Emperor. The situation escalated into war, with the Battle of White Mountain in 1618 marking the beginning of the Thirty Years War, a religious war between the Protestant and Catholic states of Europe, which raged until 1648. Proportionally it resulted in more deaths in the German states than the total of World Wars I and II. It was an absolute disaster for Europe, but particularly for Germany and Silesia. Silesia was devastated, cities destroyed by fires and plagues and, many were forced to flee to escape the holocaust and be able to practice their religion. It was one of the longest and the most destructive conflicts in European history. At the end there were no Peterswalds surviving in Silesia.

When we visited Wroclaw University in 1997 in search of our ancestors, we were assured that the Peterswalds had been wiped out during that war. So, we were delighted to share with them the rest of

...Ro and Charlotte, our Chateau Buchlovice...

our story, some of which was saved by our great great grandfather who came to Australia in 1853. Much more information has become available since the borders were opened to Eastern Europe and the expansion of information on the internet.

The magnificent schloss somehow survived the war. In 1762 the Prussian King Fredrick Wilhelm II (probably accompanied by some of our relations) established his headquarters there and is said to have commented: *'Finally, a real castle.'*

Two members of the family are now on the historical record as surviving the war, and they may well have left the area before it was ravaged. They both appeared to be wealthy, presumably from the proceeds of the sale of the estates around 1600.

Bernard Divis von Peterswald had married the Bohemian heiress Kunhuta Zastrizly in 1622 and had become the lord of <u>Buchlov Castle</u> in eastern Bohemia in 1644. Though not in the vampire country of Vlad the Impaler, which is a bit further east, it is getting that way, and the history of this old royal castle built to safe-guard ancient trade routes, makes interesting reading. In 1581 the owner was killed in a duel and, it was handed over to his brother who was killed 'in strange circumstances'. The next owner died prematurely and, it passed to Kunhuta's brother, who converted to Catholicism and did not have children, and then to Kunhuta and Bernard.

The Peterswalds had a great run from 1644 to 1800. However, Bernard Jan Peterswald died prematurely in mysterious circumstances in 1763 and his, by then, vast estates passed to his younger sister, Marie-Therese Berchtold. Marie-Therese later died in a horse riding accident and all the Peterswald estates, including the priceless Buclovice Schloss built by Jan Dietrich Peterswald (his name is still engraved beside the entrance) and half the land between Buchlovice and Vienna, passed to her son, Leopold Frantisek Xavier Berchtold and into the Berchtold family. The last Peterswald resident was the Baroness Eleonora Peterswald, Marie-Theresa's elder sister who was allowed to reside there until her death in 1800. Her, 'Silver Room' is still a feature of the schloss.

There was enough money to put together probably the greatest art collection in central Europe—which included 6378 works from the 16th to 18th centuries including forty graphic drawings by Rembrandt, and works by Durer, Cranach, Rubens and Brueghel—to name a few of hundreds. The Berchtolds created a famous arboretum in the twenty-acre gardens surrounding the schloss, with trees from all over the world, and went on to lead lives which were productive in many fields, including the arts, science and diplomacy.

In the second decade of the 20th century, Count Leopold Berchtold was reputably one of the richest men in the Austria-Hungarian Empire—even before he married Countess Ferdinanda Karolyi the daughter of one of Hungary's richest aristocrats—and was the Minister for War of the Empire at the outbreak of World War I. By some accounts he was a good man, others have him as the prime cause of the war, in that he prepared and presented the perhaps unacceptable demands that were rejected by the Serbian government, precipitating the war. The Berchtolds kept Buchlovice until the end of World War II, when it was confiscated by the government. There are a number of books available about the family and plenty on the net. It is quite sad to look at their family tree and see that the source of their fortune is there, almost as a footnote. Marie-Therese von Peterswald, first wife of Count Prosper Berchtold—and the great great grandmother of the Duchess Sophie who was assassinated alongside her husband the Archduke Franz Ferdinand and a great grandmother of imperial foreign minister Count Leopold Berchtold.

While Bernard had headed south to Bohemia, his brother, Georg von Peterswald left Silesia for the Protestant heartlands in Germany, where despite the troubles of the times, he and his descendants continued to move in the right circles. He was amongst the one prince, five princesses, one duke, two duchesses, nine counts, five countesses, three barons and one baroness who were amongst the great great great great great grandparents of Hans Heinrich XI, Ist Duke of Pless, who was born in 1833 and was the largest landholder in Germany. The family had been near neighbours in Silesia living in the magnificent Castle Ksiaz. The succeeding four generations of Grand Parents all included Georg's progeny.

Georg's son Rudolph Maximillian von Peterswald had estates in Reckenthin and Poglitz and married Elizabeth von Kussow of the Hardt and was also amongst the forebears of the Duke of Pless. Their son, Carl Friedrich became both Chancellor, and Royal Master of the Kings Horse to George of Brunswick-Luneburg (Hanover) who in due course became George I of Great Britain.

George of Hanover cannot have been an easy man to work for. This is his mother's description of the future King. '...the most pigheaded, stubborn boy who ever lived, who has around his brains such a thick crust that I defy any man or women to ever discover what is in them.' When his wife to be, Princess Sophia Dorothea of Celle, was told of the arranged marriage she was reported to have shouted, 'I will not marry the pig snout.'

Sophia Dorothea was to discover just how stubborn and pigheaded 'the pig snout' was, and how he could hold a grudge. After she was accused of an affair with Count Philip Christoph von Konigsmark, the handsome count mysteriously vanished, never to be seen again and was almost certainly murdered. Sophia spent the remaining thirty years of her life imprisoned at the Castle of Ahiden, and was never allowed contact with her children, the later King George II of Great Britain and Princess Sophie, later Queen of Prussia. No proof of an affair was ever produced, and many attested to it being solely a platonic relationship. One can only hope that Carl Friedrich von Peterswald, with his important roles at court and intimate relationship with the king, was not also George's enforcer, and murderer of Count Philip of Konigsmark. Particularly as in 1509 Hans Peterswald had married Catherine of the House of Konigsmark.

Carl Friedrich was an immensely wealthy man and died without children. He made his heir Count Friedrich Wilhelm von Eickstedt-Peterswald (1704–1772) the eldest son of his sister, Countess Helene Juliane Eickstedt. He was to inherit all Carl's property but was to make the following provisions. An annual allowance of 2400 Riechsthalers—twice the annual salary of a high government official—to Carl's beloved other sister, Eleonore Margarethe von Flemming and a further 20,000 to various relations and retainers.

In 1755 Friedrich Wilhelm was a Prussian State Councillor and Minister of War at the beginning of the Seven Year War, and he and his brother Philip Maximillian Eickstedt-Peterswald were made hereditary Counts by King Friedrich II (the Great) of Prussia.

My great grandfather notes that his grandfather, Wilhelm von Peterswald the son of Philipp, left Germany and resettled in Exeter, England in 1770 for 'political' reasons. He gives no further explanation or why the Eickstedt was dropped. However, in a Prussia that was almost continually embroiled in war it would not be hard to get on the wrong side of an autocrat like the king—you certainly wouldn't need to sleep with his wife to get into trouble. It seems he bought some money with him, but certainly not on the scale of what remained in the family in Germany, and he was also a beneficiary in Carl Friedrich's will—of which we have a copy— and which brings across the feeling of a just and thoughtful man—possibly not a murderer after all.

Wilhelm had two English born sons, William and John who died in 1814 aged 38 years. Both emigrated to Jamaica in the early 1800s where they had enough money to purchase a sugar plantation near St. Mary's, which was already named, with some coincidence, Petersfield. There is a detailed painting of the property completed for the original owner, Henry Shirly, by John Henry Schroeter in 1800. They show a large number of slaves cutting cane in the central foreground, the bundles being collected and transported by mules and oxcart. The main buildings are clearly defined with the mill, boiling house, curing sheds and other ancillary buildings such as the overseers house, hospital, blacksmith's and cooper's shops. Further up the hill is the Great House, to the middle left is a very large slave village consisting of many huts shaded by coconut trees. The basis of the early sugar estate was to design the plantation in a circular fashion so that no great distance needed to be travelled from the huts to the fields and return to the mill.

In 1832 Jamaican Almanacs show William's properties incorporating 600 acres, and in a sorry indictment of the times, lists the number of slaves and the number of stock. 198 of the former and 107 of the latter. In today's money a slave could cost close to A$100,000 giving a cost of up to A$20 million for the slave labour alone, so the plantation represented a very sizeable investment. How much of the money was his and how much was borrowed—who knows? However, when slavery was abolished the British Government paid compensation to slave owners, and in William's case it would have been close to the market value of A$20 million in today's dollars. But probably, as in recent financial emergencies the Government would have been looking after the banks first, so there could have been debts involved.

It was a shock to discover that only four generations ago our ancestors were slave owners, who listed fellow human beings as mere chattels alongside their horses, mules and oxen. It has prompted me to cast a quick eye over the prevailing situation in the world at that time—and in defence of my ancestors they were certainly not outliers. In the USA slavery was not abolished until the civil war in 1862 to 1865. In Europe, although slavery has not existed since feudal times, the system of serfdom which was a condition not much better than slavery, continued until 1781 in the Austrian Empire, 1791 in Poland, 1807 in Prussia and 1861 in Russia. In England the Peasant revolt in 1381 led to the formal abolition in 1500. However, the system of tenant farming throughout the UK was not very pretty and the Irish Famine between 1845 and 1852 led to a million deaths and a million emigrants and, at the same time there was famine and foreclosures in Scotland.

In the Ottoman Empire, which controlled most of the land between the Balkans and the Red Sea and North Africa until late in the 18th century, female slaves were still sold openly until 1908, the forced collection from the Balkans of boys and girls for the army and the harem continued into the 18th century and hundreds of thousands of Christian slaves were taken by Barbary Pirates between the 16th and 19th Centuries. The trade of African slave's dates back to at least Roman times and was endemic once Islam had conquered the north coast of Africa, and Moslems and Africans themselves were complicit in the American trade.

After joining as a lieutenant, William became the colonel of the St. Mary's Regiment, and when looking into this I was amazed at the size of the British army in Jamaica. There were seven regiments of militia—including the St. Mary's Regiment—and two regiments of regulars—one infantry and one cavalry. There were fourteen generals hanging around, goodness knows what they all did. Then of course there was the West Indies Fleet.

Why so many? Two main reasons. They were sitting on a powder keg and sugar was known as 'white gold' and accounted for twenty percent of the value of all imports into Europe. It has been suggested that Britain lost America because it was more interested in holding onto all the 'white gold' in Jamaica. And given that George III was the grandson of the 'most pigheaded and stubborn boy who ever lived', as well as being mad, it could be true.

William married a Scottish lady, Jean Gray, who was much younger than himself. They returned to England after the abolition of slavery. William died in 1848. Writing in Adelaide in 1887, the Reverend Edward Dewhirst, a well know South Australian minister of religion and educationalist, had the following recollections of William.

'He was the owner of a large and valuable sugar plantation in St. Mary's Jamaica; and was at the time, and I daresay long after wards, Colonel of the Militia Regiment of the Parish, being about 800 men. I can scarcely say that he would have occupied that position if he had not been possessed of good ability and considerable influence in Jamaican society. So far as I remember him, he was gentlemanly in deportment and genial in disposition. He had good conversational ability, but spoke with a slight foreign accent, German in all probability as his name would suggest.'

The 'Dictionary of African Christian Biography' mentions a Louisa Peterswald, 'a free woman of colour' who was teaching in Jamaica in 1840 and later was a prominent missionary in Africa. Perhaps this fine woman has some connection with William marrying late in life. The good reverend obviously had no problem with slave owners, but probably knew nothing of Louisa.

His one son, my great grandfather, William John Peterswald, was born in Jamaica in 1828. After returning to Britain with his parents he had an extensive education, including attending the Military Academy in Edinburgh and St. Peter's College, Guernsey. He travelled on the continent with a tutor and for a while lived in Paris Reverend Edward Dewhirst, he says later he was expelled for political reasons (seems to have been a family tradition). There is no record of him looking up his relations, the Eickstedt-Peterswalds, who had continued to prosper in Germany. Friedrich William Eickstedt-Peterswald (1703-1772) was made a count in 1753 and was a member of the Royal Prussian Secret Council of State and Minister of War. Also, he was Grand Maître de la Cloakroom, Knight of the Order of St. John, Hereditary Chamberlain in the Prussian part of Western Pomerania, as well as being the owner of castles at Koblentz, Gellin, Lebbehn and Grambow.

William's great-aunt, Philippine Juliane Eickstedt-Peterswald, the daughter and heiress of Friedrich William Eickstedt-Peterswald, had married Captain Ernst Friedrich von Bismarck, and had begun the so called Schonhausen branch of the Bismarck family. The most famous scion being Prince Otto von Bismarck, the 'Iron Duke' who is credited with the creation of the German Empire and is still regarded as one of history's most influential statesmen. The last Count of the Eickstedt-Peterswald line died in Monaco, France in the 1990s.

In 1852 William was a captain of the militia on the island of Jersey, and at the age of 23, married Emily Mary de Sainte Croix the daughter of the chief magistrate of the island. Probably her father would have been unimpressed with the idea that his young daughter was being taken on a dangerous voyage to the other side of the world, although he did have fourteen children. The reasons for emigrating are undisclosed, other than Australia was a land of opportunity. William, his mother, Jean, and Emily, embarked on the ship, 'Charlotte Jane', and arrived in Adelaide in 1853, carrying letters of introduction to the Governor-in-Chief, Sir Henry Young. There must have still been some money left after the sale of the plantation and the British Government's slavery compensation package some twenty years before. But unfortunately, it was not going to last for long.

The following is an edited extract from his obituary published shortly after his death in 1886. *'Widespread regret will be felt at the death of Mr. William Peterswald, the Commissioner of Police. There are few names that are better known in South Australia than his. During the many years he presided over the Police Department he served the state faithfully and well and became one of the most popular officials in the Civil Service, respected for his uniform courtesy and the fairness and impartiality which characterized all his dealings with the large body of men under his control. Mr. Peterswald possessed a remarkable memory, which served him in good stead in connection with the apprehension or prosecution of criminals and it is said that he could remember the smallest details of cases heard years ago. He took a special interest in the Criminal Investigation Department and was very proud of members of that branch. He was truly father of the force, and any member of it who had a grievance knew when making his statement to the Commissioner he would be treated with courtesy and justly dealt with. Only but last week the annual departmental report was published, and no-one but his family and a few of his more immediate friends were aware of the serious character of the author's illness....*

In 1852, attracted by the fame of the gold discoveries, he and his wife left Jersey ... and arrived in Adelaide in May 1853. For the first seven years he was engaged in 'farming and losing money' in the Munno Para East district. Whilst in that part of the colony he enrolled, drilled and commanded a volunteer company of 100 men selected from the district settlers, and the records of the time show that this company was one of the smartest colonial troops of the period. While residing in Jersey he had commanded the first rifle company attached to the Channel Islands Militia, and his military tastes were at all times pronounced. For dairy farming, however, he had not the required experience. As he once remarked to the writer – 'I had no intention of remaining in Adelaide. My first idea was to go on to Melbourne, but I was persuaded to remain in South Australia, and on the advice of a man who I thought was honestly my friend, I embarked my money in dairy farming on a large scale, and leased some land ... from my adviser, paying a high rental. Knowing nothing of farming ... I was ruined in seven years'.

He then removed to Adelaide and was soon afterwards appointed assistant-clerk to the House of Assembly. In 1862 Mr. Pettiuger, Inspector of the Metropolitan Police was murdered at a sale at Government House by a discharged constable, and Mr. Peterswald applied for and obtained the vacant post under Major Warburton. After four years' service he was obliged to resign owing to pecuniary difficulties arising out of his dairy farming operations.

Two years later he was appointed warden of the gold fields. In 1873, in the consequence of the disorganized state of police force, he was advised to apply for his old position. In 1876 he was made superintendent and in 1881 Commissioner.

Since that time his career has been public property, and few public men have been so deservedly popular at once with the general public and his own subordinates'.

If only all public officials could be so praised! An honourable man. Pity he lost the last of the family fortune. He was survived by Emily who passed on a few years later and; William Ernest who married Jane Spicer (no children), Arthur Charles Turner (married a widow with two children), John (my grandfather) and Emily Jane Mathilde (married Burtenshaw Wilkinson), Frances Dumaresque and Florence (died unmarried).

He is commemorated by the naming of 'Mount Peterswald' in the Northern Territory in 1873. The larger Mount Ayers—now Uluru— some miles to the south was named after his friend the Chief Secretary of South Australia. The two ended up being interred in adjoining crypts in the North Adelaide cemetery. A few years ago, we extended the lease on his plot for another fifty years to ensure he could continue to lie in peace with Emily and his daughter Frances.

My grandfather was also a policeman. The edited extract from the Goulburn Evening Post of 22 October 1922 gives a good account of his life.

Retires after 35 years. Adventures and Impressions.

Faithful service and meticulous attention to duty are the principal features which stand out in the record of John Peterswald, superintendent of police in the Goulburn district, who has now embarked on extended leave of absence before retiring next year. He has been in the force of upwards of 25 years, during which his promotion was steady and from a brief survey of his career well deserved in every instance.

Mr. Peterswald was born in Adelaide in 1863 and continued his father's association with the police force.

In connection with his ancestors he has an interesting document. It is the appointment of his father, over a century ago, to the St. Mary's Regiment in Jamaica. The paper is signed by the Duke of Manchester and is dated 21 March 1808. He later became colonel of the regiment.

During the Great War two sons enlisted one seeing three years' service in France, where he was wounded.

Mr. Peterswald was reared in a police barracks but when he was old enough to go to work, he did not follow in his father's footsteps immediately. He loved an outdoor life and was fortunate as a youth to secure employment with the Beltana Pastoral Company, who at that time owned a string of stations in SA. They were the first to bring camels to the state. One of his first jobs was to take some camels to Cordillo Downs near the Queensland border. While he was with the company, he gained considerable experience with horses and cattle.

When the Kimberly Diggings broke in NW Australia, he left the company and set out for the scene of the historical goldrush. He joined the escort there and was sworn in as a trooper. Two troopers and an aborigine used to take the gold halfway to Derby—a distance of some 300 miles. During one of the trips he visited McDonald station on the Fitzroy—one of the finest stations in Australia. Mrs. McDonald of Goulburn is the owner of the station and he had known the family before heading to the gold fields. In 1885 the McDonald brothers had driven a mob of cattle through the Northern Territory to Kimberly. At this time the whole country around Kimberly was overrun by wild blacks, who were always on the lookout to spear stray whites. Very many whites met their death at the hands of murderous natives.

He describes the NW of Australia as being wonderful country where Mitchell grass grows higher than a man seated on his horse. In the days of which he speaks there were only three or four settlers between Kimberly and Derby. During the trips to and from the gold fields he had numerous adventures with blacks.

In 1887 Mr. Peterswald left the wild north west and came to NSW where he joined the police force. Adaminiby was his first station and he was later transferred to Delegate, where he met his present wife who was a Miss Keith. The young constable saw service in Goulburn and Crookwell, and he was promoted to take charge of Collector.

He was there for six years, being promoted to first class constable and later to senior constable and then sergeant and sent to Wyalong. This was when the town had caught gold fever and had a population of 12,000. The country around there in those days consisted for the most part of dense mallee scrub. It was purely an agriculture district, but a large amount of gold was won from stone averaging 40 ounces to the ton. Gold was yielded from stone where not a speck of colour was visible. From Wyalong he was sent to Cootamundra where he spent several years.

After serving as a sergeant at Penrith, Kiama and Nowra he was uprooted to Walgett as a sub-inspector in 1911. While at this outback township he had to travel long distances as the police stations were 50 to 60 miles apart. At this stage of his career he found how useful his lifetime associated with horses was. He was later transferred to Dubbo as an inspector, remaining there for six years, after which he was appointed acting superintendent in the Grafton district. In 1919 he was made Superintendent in Goulburn, the place where he practically began his career as a probationary constable.

I have never had anything to do with bushrangers as none of them ever crossed my path. My work brought me into contact with criminals of a tamer kind and I have had my share of big cases, though. I've arraigned men for horse, cattle and sheep stealing, housebreaking, murder and countless crimes. On no occasion however has an offender given me the slightest trouble while being arrested and I have never had to draw my revolver, although I have had a few scrapes without firearms. But any policeman must expect that in a long career.

After he retired, he moved to Manly and when Jemima died, he moved in with his daughter, Grace Smithers, in Balgowlah. Unfortunately, I only met him twice when I was ten and he was a frail ninety and confined to bed. On my second visit he presented me with his father's sabre, embossed with the insignia of the South Australian Mounted Rifles, which is a very treasured memento of two remarkable men. My father John (Poppy) had been born in 1903 and had finished his secondary schooling in Sydney before joining the Bank of New South Wales and later marrying my mother Hazell Daphne Earngey. My mother passed away in 1974 and, Poppy while visiting Richard in Goulburn in 1996 after spending twenty very happy years with us, which enriched all our lives. He had developed a very special relationship with Cha and Georgie. He was predeceased by Keith, who had come to spend his last years with us and, had passed away in the Whittle Palliative Care Ward in Hobart. They are buried side by side, along with Winsome and Hazel, overlooking the Derwent River, where no doubt their vigorous discussions about just about anything, still continue.

***

Meanwhile, by the end of the decade, our real estate business continued to flourish, and we had opened two fashion boutiques and a gallery of Tasmanian art and crafted furniture. Charlotte had married Stephen Auld, a Hobart builder, and Georgina had married her long-time boy-friend Simon Merchant who had crewed on *Reveille* when we sailed to Brisbane a decade before and who had since joined us in the business. We enjoyed living in a large penthouse that overlooked the Hobart docks.

In 2000 we had bought a beautiful 52ft fibreglass ketch, *Oceania*, in Mooloolaba and with Stephen and Simon were sailing her south when we decided we would just keep sailing and follow our dreams. Our businesses were sold to the staff, Charlotte took over the property management and has since created very successful businesses in North and East Sydney as well as Hobart. Georgie and Simon wanted a change of climate and have their own very well-regarded business in Cairns.

That settled, we sailed *Oceania* to Port Davey to begin our voyage following in the wake of the great navigators who first sailed the coasts of Australia—which I cover in Volume 1 of this series—and then on to the waters of Europe. It has been a decision which has greatly enriched our lives and has given both Ro, myself, and our family and friends who have joined us onboard, many, many memories to cherish. Thank you for coming on our journey.

...Cha and family in Greece   *...Georgie and family in Turkey*

~ ACKNOWLEDGEMENTS ~

Once again very special thanks to our family who shared so many good times with us on the back of yachts, particularly our daughters and families. Charlotte and Stephen, Hubert, Rufus and Ferdinand, and Georgina and Simon, Joseph and Eleanor. To John (Poppy) and Hazel Peterswald, Wendy Peterswald, Richard and Francis Peterswald, Owen and Toni Esmonde, Eugene and Jenni Esmonde, Deborah and Kevin Scott, Gill and Colin Rosewarne, Viv and Tim Creswell.

To our friends who have shared back decks. Particularly Don and Sue Clark, Lenny and Helen Griffin, David and Jill Henry, Mark and Remy Towers, Eric and Eileen Tang, Margie and Paul Hansen, Sally Cerny, Phil and Carmel Thomson, Roger and Tina Wainwright, Max and Viv Doerner, Margie Murray, Vince and Megan Thompson, Mike and Diana Battle, Peter Langford, Peter and Susie Knight.

Thank you very much, Annie Seaton, for your advice and help in editing both volumes.

...serenity from the back of a boat...thanks and good wishes to everyone who has been aboard, in body or spirit...

Lightning Source UK Ltd.
Milton Keynes UK
UKHW052311090920
369545UK00003B/48